Leadership
Psychology

Leadership Psychology

How the *BEST* leaders inspire their people

Alan Cutler

KoganPage

LONDON PHILADELPHIA NEW DELHI

First published in Great Britain and the United States in 2014 by Kogan Page Limited

2nd Floor, 45 Gee Street	1518 Walnut Street, Suite 1100	4737/23 Ansari Road
London EC1V 3RS	Philadelphia PA 19102	Daryaganj
United Kingdom	USA	New Delhi 110002
www.koganpage.com		India

© Alan Cutler, 2014

The right of Alan Cutler to be identified as the author of this work has been asserted by him in accordance with the Copyright, Designs and Patents Act 1988.

ISBN   978 0 7494 7081 4
E-ISBN 978 0 7494 7082 1

British Library Cataloguing-in-Publication Data

A CIP record for this book is available from the British Library.

Library of Congress Cataloging-in-Publication Data

Cutler, Alan (Leadership specialist)
    Leadership psychology : how the best leaders inspire their people / Alan Cutler.
    pages cm
    ISBN 978-0-7494-7081-4 (paperback) – ISBN 978-0-7494-7082-1 (ebk)   1. Leadership.
2. Leadership–Psychological aspects.   3. Employee motivation.   I. Title.
    HD57.7.C88 2014
    658.4'092–dc23
                                                                                        2014023625

Typeset by Graphicraft Limited, Hong Kong
Print production managed by Jellyfish
Printed and bound by CPI Group (UK) Ltd, Croydon, CR0 4YY

To my wonderful grandchildren, Molly, Toby, Florence and Matilda. May they take example from their parents and grow up to be fine adults.

Also to my father, Deryck, the senior member of a loving family, who passed away whilst this book was being prepared for publication.

CONTENTS

FOREWORD

Everyone has been led, whether by teachers, parents or bosses. Many of us have also had, at one time or another, experience of poor leadership, which can be detrimental to followers' well-being, performance and commitment to their task. Good leadership, on the other hand, inspires people to achieve the highest levels of performance.

Whilst a lot of books on leadership have discussed relevant theories, this book is unique on two counts. First, it is based on case studies and interviews with exemplar leaders who span various industry sectors, including public and private organizations. The book also covers new ground by exploring, from a psychological perspective, the relationships between leaders and followers.

The content provides practical guidance for operational and strategic leaders considering the challenges of the future, such as global leadership and extreme leadership, whilst also taking into account relevant academic theory. This book should be on every leader's – or prospective leader's – shelf in order to provide them with guidance on how to lead effectively in an ever-competitive global marketplace.

Dr Gail Steptoe-Warren
Principal Lecturer
Psychology & Behavioural Sciences
Coventry University

ACKNOWLEDGEMENTS

I must acknowledge and record the contribution I have received from those who have supported me in writing this book. First and foremost, the inspirational leaders who afforded me the time to interview them and then allowed me to use their words that have, I hope, added so much value to the content. I should also mention their PAs, unsung heroes all of them, who liaised with me before and after the interviews.

I have tried to support the issues discussed within the work by including relevant previous research and, in this respect, I am hugely indebted to the researchers of the Chartered Management Institute who provide such a valuable service to institute members like myself. They are Michelle Jenkins, Robert Orton, Sarah Childs and Catherine Baker.

Colleagues within the Psychology Department of Coventry University have assisted me in the project, notably Dr Gail Steptoe-Warren and Dr Christine Grant, as well as Sophie Bratt, who transcribed several of the leaders' interview recordings.

My friends Ann Redding and Ann Smith typed my words and without their help I would probably still be prodding my two fingers at the keyboard to this day.

I hope that the case studies and examples of leadership *BEST* practice have provided useful and interesting supporting material and I must thank Peter Bluckert for providing information on his 'Courage and Spark' leadership development programme. The inspirational story of Captain Simon Cupples offered a unique insight into extreme combat leadership and I am most grateful to him for telling me his story. I must also thank Major Rachel Brunt and Captain Lydia Cugudda for facilitating the army's approval of the case study, and to Major General Skeates for allowing me to attend the Royal Military Academy Sandhurst to meet Captain Cupples.

I hope that this list includes all those who have helped me in this project. If I have missed anyone out, please accept both my apology and heartfelt thanks.

Introduction

To me, leadership is fundamentally a basic human capability – how to inspire others to share and contribute to your vision. After all, writers for hundreds of years, such as the wonderfully astute philosopher Lao Tzu in his book *Tao Te Ching*, written in the 5th century BC, have understood and expounded the principles of leadership. He wrote: 'Good leadership consists of motivating people to their highest levels by offering them opportunities, not obligations.'

Yet these straightforward principles appear to be unknown to, or at least not practised by, so many people holding leadership positions across the world. As Ann Francke, chief executive of the UK's Chartered Management Institute (CMI) said to me, 'Everybody knows what good looks like, but nobody does it!' She went on to explain the results of CMI research that measured job satisfaction levels of 28 per cent amongst staff working within bureaucratic, autocratic, directive management cultures, compared with 69 per cent in engaging, trusting and collaborative cultures.

My argument is that a need continues to exist for managers to enhance their leadership skills, even though there is a plethora of written advice out there, readily accessible. Moreover, I contend that the need could be met, at least in part, by an approach that focuses on the psychological relationship between leaders and followers. In 2013, when I was undertaking a psychology course with Open University, I had something of a 'light bulb' moment. Having been writing, speaking and delivering training on the subject of leadership for many years it suddenly occurred to me that, if psychology could be defined in its simplest terms as 'understanding the mind and how it affects behaviour', that is exactly what leaders seek to do. Their prime objective is to influence followers' actions – and the only way to do so effectively is to understand their minds and how their thinking affects their behaviours. Psychology is, of course, an age-old social science but, surprisingly, there has been very little work linking its theory and principles to the application of leadership. Yet this link provides an exciting opportunity for leaders to enhance their skills for the benefit of their people and their organizations.

There are a limited number of books connecting the two disciplines but they have been largely academic in nature. In this book I have attempted to include a balance of theoretical and practical content, thus offering an applied approach that will appeal to, and more importantly assist, both practising managers and those studying for qualifications in either management or psychology. The psychological theories included here are supported by showcasing how real-life leaders in a range of roles understand the psychological needs of their people, and how they use that knowledge to effect behaviour and enhance performance. Personal interviews with selected leaders reveal the application of inspirational leadership, underpinned by sound principles of occupational psychology.

It would have been easy to identify leaders who were widely promoted in the media as being 'inspirational', but I wanted to learn from those who had been recognized by their own people through detailed and independent research. Every year since 2001, *The Sunday Times* has published its 'Best Companies to Work For' reports, which are researched and compiled by Best Companies Ltd. The reports are derived from the opinions of around 250,000 employees from over 1,000 UK businesses and are the result of their answers to 70 insightful questions on their workplace experience. These questions relate to eight workplace factors, one of which is 'leadership'. Winning organizations are recognized in one of four categories: Best Small Companies, Best Companies, Best Big Companies and Best Not For Profit Organizations. I interviewed selected leaders from all four categories (their photographs and details accompany each of their *BEST* leadership quotes), ranging from the chief people officer at McDonald's (Europe), a managing partner at one of London's most high-profile law firms and a chief executive of a social housing organization. In addition, the managing director of Best Companies Ltd, along with the chief executive of the CMI, also spoke to me about their findings and views on the practice of leadership. Finally, as one of the book's chapters offers a unique analysis of leadership under extreme conditions, a polar explorer, a senior commander of the Fire and Rescue Services and a decorated army officer were also interviewed. The interviewees' words and examples of *BEST* practice are included throughout the book.

The book starts with a review of leadership theory, from the great man theory prevalent in the 19th century to the contemporary approach of shared social identity, where leaders create an 'in-group' as a means of winning the hearts and minds of their followers and, hence, harnessing their emotions and energies. Looking forward, the main leadership challenges of the 21st century – innovation, talent management, globalization and communications, especially social media – are then identified and discussed in Chapter 2.

It is a well-established fact that highly motivated staff perform better, so in Chapter 3 I consider motivational theory, from that proposed by American psychologists in the 1950s, to more modern approaches, including the concept of positive psychology. The chapter also includes my own findings that suggest that one of the earlier motivational theories is as valid today as it was when first created. Emotional intelligence is a relatively new psychological concept, where leaders learn to identify and understand their own emotions, along with those of their followers, as a means of creating powerful and mutually beneficial relationships. Chapter 4 explores how it can be measured and, most importantly, applied in a business context.

Chapter 5 is entitled 'Leader Development', and whilst this might sound rather an unusual term, it focuses mainly on the enhancement of intrapersonal skills, described in the included 'leadership *BEST* practice' case study as 'developing the *inner* leader in order to become a great *outer* leader'. The book continues with an exploration of the unwritten needs and expectations of both employer and employee – a new concept entitled the psychological contract. Particular attention is given to the employment expectations of different generations at work, especially Generation Y, also known as millennials. After all, they form a significant proportion of the workforce already and, in time, they will rule the world so we had better understand their approach to employment relationships!

Following the psychological considerations surrounding the role of strategic leaders, the penultimate chapter, entitled 'Extreme Leadership', covers an aspect of leadership about which very little has previously been written. Subtitled 'Leading when life is threatened', it considers the roles of leaders operating in survival conditions, international conflicts, emergency response situations and in combat. The latter section contains a *BEST* practice military leadership case study offering exclusive, primary source material. Continuing the applied approach of the book, the chapter explains how the lessons learnt from leading in extreme conditions can be translated to a business environment – with some surprising conclusions.

Finally, Chapter 9 looks to the future, proposing two psychological leadership approaches that the 21st-century leader would be well advised to consider, as well as three that are more philosophical in nature: servant leadership, ethical leadership and authentic leadership.

I hope readers will find this approach to the subject both challenging and enlightening. Leadership is founded upon the relationship between leader and follower, which at its very essence is a psychological relationship, because without both parties understanding each other there can be no meeting of minds and, therefore, sharing of the leader's vision. For leaders it is more about what they say and how they say it, rather than what they do. Let us, therefore, allow Lao Tzu the final word: 'Good leadership consists of doing less and being more. Of the good leader, when the task is done, the people will say "we did it ourselves".'

Leadership theory

– past and present

*Great men theory to
relationship theory → Page 12
because*

In order to forecast how successful leaders will flourish in an increasingly uncertain future, it is necessary to understand how the theory and application of leadership has developed since the concept was first seriously considered around the end of the 19th century. I therefore begin this book by reviewing how leadership theory has developed over the past 100 years or so into approaches designed to meet the challenges facing leaders in this culturally diverse, communication-driven age, where change is a constant and only those organizations that are able to adapt and innovate will succeed.

That is not to say that academics and, in particular, philosophers long before our modern age did not have an appreciation of how wise leaders get the best out of their followers. As I mention in the Introduction, Lao Tzu, for example, in his book *Tao Te Ching*, written for Chinese political leaders in the 5th century BC, emphasized the importance of leader–follower relationships. However, recent decades have seen an exponential increase in the study of leadership.

Before we review past leadership theories let us understand what we mean by the term leadership. In 1966 the Smith Richardson Foundation commissioned Ralph M Stogdill to undertake a systematic analysis and review of the literature on leadership, which culminated in him publishing the book *Handbook on Leadership* in 1974. In it, he sought to group the various definitions of leadership into 11 classifications, namely:

- a focus of group process;
- personality and its effects;
- the art of inducing compliance;
- the exercise of influence;
- act or behaviour;
- a form of persuasion;

- a power relation;
- an instrument of goal achievement;
- an effect of interaction;
- a differentiated role;
- the initiation of structure.

Whilst there are many different definitions of leadership, it is generally agreed that the act of leading people involves influencing them to undertake a course of action that contributes to an objective defined by the leader: his or her vision. The word 'lead' derives from the Anglo-Saxon for a journey, a road, a way. Thus, leading is concerned with moving from one place to another; from one situation to another. It therefore involves change and it is, indeed, in periods of great change that exceptional leaders emerge. Perhaps one of the best definitions of leadership is from Charles Handy (1992): 'A leader shapes and shares a vision which gives point to the work of others.'

We will now consider the following theories, which encapsulate the progression of leadership thinking up to the modern day:

- great man theory;
- trait theory;
- behavioural theory;
- situational leadership;
- functional leadership;
- relationship theory.

Great man theory

It was only in the 19th century that historians and philosophers began to consider the concept of leadership and those who displayed it, mainly in a military and political context. Indeed, it was entirely through consideration of recognized, historical heroes that the first leadership theory was conceived. The great man theory proposes that at times of need leaders will rise, almost mystically, to control events and lead people to safety or success. Hence, history can be explained to a large extent by the emergence of these highly influential men – the great man theory does not mention women – of their times.

It was the Scottish historian Thomas Carlyle in the 1840s who developed the great man theory, saying: 'The history of the world is but the biography of great men', using the example of figures such as Muhammad, Luther and Napoleon to make his case. Moreover, he proposed that by studying such heroes one could not help but develop one's own potential heroic nature.

Implicit to Carlyle's theory is that these great men are born to lead: they have inbred qualities that come to the fore when their leadership destiny unfolds. Of course, his examples were largely political, religious or military men from the aristocracy and upper classes, hence the theory dismisses the potential of those of lower social status (and the entire female gender!) to rise to positions of leadership. Great leaders were *born*, not made.

Trait theory

The trait theory followed from the great man theory as a means of categorizing the qualities displayed by successful leaders. By identifying these traits it was believed that people having them could be identified, recruited and placed in positions of authority. This practice was applied in particular for officer selection within military organizations and, indeed, still is to some extent.

Table 1.1 sets out the main leadership traits (genetically determined characteristics) and skills identified by Stogdill (1974). More recent authors have proposed different sets of qualities required by leaders, as shown in Table 1.2.

It is interesting to note how the required leadership qualities change through time, according to the challenges that leaders face. Bennis (1998),

TABLE 1.1   Stogdill's leadership traits and skills

Traits	Skills
Adaptable to situations	Clever (intelligent)
Alert to social environment	Conceptually skilled
Ambitious and achievement-orientated	Creative
Assertive	Diplomatic and tactful
Co-operative	Fluent in speaking
Decisive	Knowledgeable about group task
Dependable	Organized (administrative ability)
Dominant (desire to influence others)	Persuasive
Energetic (high activity level)	Socially skilled
Persistent	
Self-confident	
Tolerant of stress	
Willing to assume responsibility	

TABLE 1.2   Various authors' proposed leadership qualities

Authors	Leadership Qualities
Lord, De-Vader and Alliger (1986)	Dominance, masculinity, conservativeness
Kirkpatrick and Locke (1991)	Drive (achievement, ambition, energy, tenacity and initiative); leadership motivation (personalized or socialized); honesty/integrity (trusting relationship between leaders and followers); self-confidence (emotional stability); cognitive ability (able to process large amounts of information and develop strategies); knowledge of business (to enable well-informed decisions to be made and understand consequences).
Bennis (1998)	Building teamwork (committed to organizational goals); understands the business; conceptual thinking (select innovative strategies); customer-driven (create value for the customer); focused drive (goal-focused); drives profitability (cost-effective and efficient operations); systems thinking (connects processes, events and structures); global perspective (addresses cultural and geographic differences); emotional intelligence (understands own emotions).
Daft (1999)	Alertness, originality, creativity, personal integrity and self-confidence.
Adair (2009)	Enthusiasm, integrity, toughness, fairness, warmth, humility.

for example, proposes that leaders should be customer-driven and have a global perspective, reflecting the service-driven, international nature of business in the 21st century.

Note also that the earlier review by Lord, De-Vader and Alliger identified masculinity as a trait. This is due to the relatively recent involvement of women in prominent roles (Collinson and Hearn, 2003) and the adoption of leadership styles by women that tend to promote more interactions with employees, information-sharing, and employee participation in decision-making (Meyerson and Fletcher, 2000). However, research by Welte (2004) found that women hold 51 per cent of management and professional positions and therefore traditional stereotypes should be challenged. Any beneficial gender-specific traits do not, however, appear to be readily translated in more senior positions, as female participation still tends to be more prevalent in junior management posts.

BEST leadership quote

'Lots of women enter the workforce:
69 per cent of junior managers are women.
But by the time it's middle management the
number is 40 per cent; by the time it's
director level it's 25 per cent; and for CEOs
it's single digits.'

Ann Francke
Chief Executive
Chartered Management Institute

Whilst it is generally accepted that leaders, male or female, require a certain set of traits if they are to be effective, there is no consensus as to a definitive list of those required. Surely, each situation faced by the leader will call for a different combination of qualities, as will the environment within which the leader operates – military, business or charity, for example. Yet even within one sector, opinions are divided as to the most desirable leadership qualities.

A further limitation of the trait theory is that it assumes that leadership qualities are inherent, stable characteristics that leaders are born with. Zaccaro, Kemp and Bader (2004) define them as 'stable and coherent integrations of personal characteristics that foster a consistent pattern of leadership performance across a variety of group and organizational situations'. That being so, leaders will be selected according to the qualities they possess, set against those required of the position they are being considered for. Such an approach implies that the required qualities cannot be developed by means of training or the benefit of experience. Yet it is difficult to imagine a personal characteristic that cannot at least be enhanced as a leader becomes more experienced or knowledgeable.

Hence, whilst the trait theory adds to the question of what makes a great leader, it cannot be the complete answer, as was generally accepted during the first half of the 20th century. Stogdill (1975) quoted Carter (1953) and Startle (1956) in maintaining that the trait theory had reached a dead end, and suggested that attention be directed towards the behaviour of the leader.

Behavioural theory

Behavioural theories emerged in response to the criticisms of the trait approach, in particular the lack of consensus as to the necessary, measured qualities required by leaders and also the assumption that they are inborn. Hence, the focus of leadership thinking turned towards the behaviour of leaders and how it related to their followers. The view now was that leaders are made not born, with the behaviour of leaders (what they do) being more important than their physical, emotional or mental traits. Moreover, effective leadership, it was now believed, could be developed through the teaching of relevant skills and the observation of others.

Early work on the concept of leaders' behaviour was undertaken by the German-American psychologist Kurt Lewin and colleagues (1939) who identified three different leadership styles that were applied, in particular, when making decisions, namely:

- *Autocratic:* here the leader takes decisions without any consultation with other team members. This style is considered most appropriate when speedy decisions are required and there is no need for team input or agreement, for example in a crisis situation where safety considerations are paramount. In Lewin *et al*'s experiments, however, it was found that the application of the autocratic style caused the greatest level of discontent amongst team members.

- *Democratic:* democratic leaders sought team input, to a greater or lesser extent, in the decision-making process. This style is important when team consensus is required, and will be appreciated by members who value their views being sought. It can, however, be difficult to manage when there is a wide range of opinions.

- *Laissez-faire:* the laissez-faire style requires leaders to take a back step and allow people a high degree of decision-making. It does, though, necessitate both capable and motivated team members, and no requirement for central co-ordination of resources, for example. Adoption of the laissez-faire approach is a conscious decision by the leader, rather than an excuse from one who is lazy or otherwise occupied.

Lewin, Lippit and White (1939) discovered that the democratic style was most effective in producing effective decision-making. Conversely, excessive autocratic styles tended to lead to revolution, whilst some team members – those less able and capable of self-regulation – responded less well to the laissez-faire approach than when they were being actively led.

Although Lewin *et al*'s research may now be seen as limited, it was highly influential for its time and was a precursor for further thinking about the impact of a leader's behaviour. For example, a study was undertaken at Michigan University, aimed to determine the methods and principles of leadership that lead to higher levels of satisfaction and productivity in staff. Two general leadership behaviours were identified: an employee-orientation and a product-orientation. The former represents leaders showing concern for members of the organization, whilst product-orientation leaders focus primarily on the task to be completed. The study found that productivity was increased most by the application of the employee-orientation style of leadership.

FIGURE 1.1   The Blake Mouton Managerial Grid

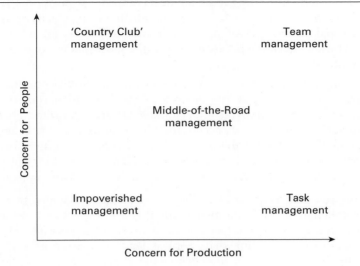

This concept of leaders adopting a greater concern for their people or for levels of productivity was expanded by Blake and Mouton (1964) who devised their Managerial Grid (see Figure 1.1), based upon two behavioural approaches: i) *concern for people*: the degree to which a leader considers the team members' needs, interests and personal development when planning the achievement of a task; ii) *concern for production*: the extent to which a leader sets objectives, and defines efficiency and production targets when planning a task.

The grid has two axes: concern for people and concern for production, and identifies five styles of management:

- *Country club – high people / low production*: here, leaders try to ensure that their people feel secure and comfortable in their roles, assuming that as long as they are happy they will work harder. This results in a relaxed and fun work environment, but one where production suffers due to lack of direction.

- *Task management – high production / low people*: similar to Kurt Lewin *et al*'s (1939) autocratic leadership style, such leaders believe that employees are only a means by which tasks are completed. Their needs are always secondary to the requirement for efficient production. The leaders use rules, procedures and punishment to pressurize their people to achieve goals.

- *Impoverished – low people / low production*: these leaders are largely ineffective as their main concern is to avoid being held responsible for any problems that occur. Yet problems will occur in an environment where disorganization, dissatisfaction and disharmony prevail.

- *Middle-of-the-road – medium people / medium production:* whilst at first sight appearing to be an ideal compromise position, the reality is that neither the people's potential nor that of productivity are realized. Leaders adopting this style are ready to accept average performance, in the belief that this is the most that anyone can reasonably expect.

- *Team management – high people / high production:* according to Blake and Mouton (1964) this is the style that leaders should aspire to and adopt. Employees understand what the organization is trying to achieve and willingly accept their importance in meeting agreed goals. When all contributors strive towards organizational success, both people and production needs coincide. The resulting culture is one of trust and respect, which results in high-performing teams.

We have seen that the great man theory of leadership assumed that leaders had an inherent set of traits that made them 'born leaders'. Behavioural theories, on the other hand, focus on the actions of leaders rather than their inborn qualities, and assume that people in leadership positions can learn to adapt their behaviour through teaching and experiential observation. This leads us to consider the extent to which either inherent qualities or learnt behaviour contributes most to effective leadership: are leaders born or made?

In 2005, Richard Arvey, professor of human resources and industrial relations at the University of Minnesota, and colleagues conducted a study of 325 selected pairs of identical and fraternal male twins who were born between 1961 and 1964 and were raised together. Previous studies of twins who were reared apart had proved that similarities in terms of personality, interests and attitudes were due to genes rather than environmental influences: the environment makes them different, whilst their genes make them similar. As identical twins share 100 per cent of their genes, with fraternal twins only about 50 per cent, Arvey *et al*'s study sought to quantify the contribution of genetics and environmental factors in leadership.

To do so, participants were asked a series of questions centred on the wish to influence others; a desire to be the centre of attention; the ability to persist when others give up; being comfortable in other people's company. The assumption was that, as those questions have a genetic component, if the respondents answered positively they were probably 'genetically wired' for leadership. The study then took an inventory of the leadership roles that the twins had held throughout their lives, including as supervisors, directors, vice-presidents or presidents. Arvey explained: 'A great deal of personality is genetic-based. If your personality is such that you aspire to, and have held, these positions, then the roles also suggest a genetic link.'

What they found was that approximately 30 per cent of leadership is based on genetics, whilst the remaining 70 per cent is dependent upon environmental factors. They concluded: 'While environmental influences determine many of our leadership behaviours and the roles we obtain, our genes still exert a sizeable influence over whether we will become leaders. Although

At the highest level its about
Leadership Theory – Past and Present 13
$\mathcal{I}\, ^{o}\!/_{o}$

30 per cent may not seem like a high number, statistically it is strong. Leaders aren't just made!'

It should be stated, however, that the study merely considered those who became leaders, and why. It did not take into consideration leadership effectiveness. Nonetheless, the research does shed light on the 'are leaders born or made?' conundrum, suggesting that neither extreme position tells the complete story. It appears that leadership is both inherited and acquired. When examining the differences between individuals with regard to whether they took up leadership roles, over one-quarter of the differences were explained by genetics. The remaining almost three-quarters were accounted for by external influences such as training, job experiences and education, as well as other forms of environmental exposure.

Returning to the behavioural theory of leadership, whilst it is undoubtedly helpful to understand the impact on people and performance of a leader's actions, it could be said that it gives insufficient attention to the differing situations that a leader will face. The behaviour, or actions, adopted are seen to have an impact on people and productivity regardless of the environment in which the leadership is operating at the time. Yet situations change and will call for leaders to adapt their style according to the challenges they face at that time.

Situational leadership

Also known as the contingency model, the situational approach to leadership requires leaders to adapt their style according to the situation they face: there is no one optimal style, rather leaders should be able to be flexible and adaptable. This approach has generated a number of models, the most significant of which are detailed below.

The least preferred co-worker model

An early proponent of situational leadership theory was Fielder (1967) who encouraged users to consider someone they least like working with, in any situation, and then score this person on a table that included extremes such as unfriendly/friendly; tense/relaxed; hostile/supportive; insincere/sincere, etc. The model works on the principle that task-oriented leaders tend to view their co-workers more negatively, resulting in a low score, whilst relationship-oriented leaders tend to score them more highly.

Task-oriented leaders were seen to be very effective at task organization and completion but only considered their relationship with followers when they were satisfied that the task was under way satisfactorily. On the other hand, relationship-oriented leaders would prioritize relationships, even ahead of the task, and were particularly proficient at connecting with people and avoiding and managing conflict.

The next stage in Fielder's approach was to determine the 'situational favourableness' of the leader's situation, according to three factors:

- leader–member relations: the level of trust and confidence between leader and followers;
- task structure: the type of task being faced – clear and structured or vague and unstructured;
- leader's position – the extent to which the leader has to direct followers and provide reward or punishment.

Fielder concluded that task-oriented leaders operate best when the situation is either extremely favourable, that is, when:

- there is a great deal of trust, respect and confidence;
- the task is very clear;
- followers accept their leader's position of authority without question.

Or when the situation is extremely unfavourable, when:

- there is no mutual trust and respect;
- the challenge facing the group is vague or undefined;
- the culture within the group is anarchic, even rebellious – perhaps during a crisis or change situation.

Conversely, Fielder found that relationship-oriented leaders function best in less extreme situations: those that are neither favourable nor unfavourable.

Although the least preferred co-worker model was one of the first to link a leader's style to the situation faced, it was subsequently criticized on the following grounds:

- Fielder believed, as was a common conception at that time, that a person's personality was fixed and could not be changed. His theory was based upon matching a leader (according to his or her personality) to a particular situation. Hence, it does not allow for the potential for leaders to adapt their approach to different circumstances.
- It offers no guidance to leaders as to how they can improve their performance through training and development interventions.
- The approach is an insufficiently flexible model for leadership within the modern, constantly changing work environment.
- It infers that leaders should be replaced if their style does not match the situation they face – which obviously poses many employment difficulties.
- Finally, if your least preferred co-worker is a genuinely confused or unpleasant individual, then under Fielder's theory you may be classified as task-oriented when, in reality, you may be very much a people person!

The path–goal model

A further situation leadership theory, following on from Fielder's least preferred co-worker model, was first developed by psychologist Robert House in 1971 and republished in 1997. It seeks to address one of the limitations of the least preferred co-worker model in that it asserts that leaders can, and should, adapt their behaviour according to the challenges and opportunities of each situation. It is called the path–goal theory because House suggested that the main role of leaders is to motivate their followers by: i) increasing or clarifying followers' personal benefits by striving for and achieving the group's *goal*; ii) clarifying and clearing a *path* for the achievement of the group goals. The model proposes that leadership styles should be influenced by the characteristics of both the followers and their workplace.

Follower characteristics include:

- How confident and experienced they are.
- How much control the group members feel they have with which to execute and achieve their goals.
- What attitude they have towards authority and those that wield it. Do they want to be directed or left to their own devices? What do they think of their leader?

Workplace characteristics include:

- The kind of task to be completed: repetitive, uninteresting, structured – or the reverse.
- Whether the leader's authority is defined and understood.
- Is there a sense of team spirit within the group?

House used these two sets of characteristics and suggested four leadership behavioural styles, as detailed in Table 1.3.

Whilst the path–goal theory does match leadership styles to four different situations (combinations of workplace and follower characteristics) it fails to give weight to any emotional bonds that may occur between leader and follower and the subsequent influence those may have on behaviour. For example, if you have a respectful and trusting relationship with your leader you are likely to go above and beyond the minimum effort required to achieve organizational goals.

Hersey and Blanchard's model

This model explores the relationship between leader and follower and was first published in 1969 by Dr Paul Hersey and Ken Blanchard (of *The One Minute Manager* fame). They posited that the competence, confidence and developmental levels of specific followers should play the greatest influence on determining the most appropriate leadership style (Hersey and Blanchard, 1977). Moreover, the model requires leaders to adapt their approach according

TABLE 1.3 Path–goal leadership styles

Leadership Style	Workplace Characteristics	Follower Characteristics
Directive – clarifies the goal, gives clear direction and expects followers to follow instructions	• Unstructured, interesting tasks • Clear, formal authority • Good team-working	• Inexperienced team members • A belief they lack power • Desire to be directed
Supportive – demonstrates concern for followers' welfare and seeks to provide a supportive working environment	• Simple, predictable tasks • Unclear or weak authority • Poor team-working	• Experienced, confident team members • A belief they have power • Rejection of close control
Participative – consults with followers before taking any decisions involving goal-setting	• Unstructured, complex tasks • Authority could be clear or unclear • Team-working could be good or poor	• Experienced, confident team members • A belief they have power • Preference to have control over their work
Achievement-oriented – sets challenging goals and has confidence in followers achieving them	• Unstructured, complex or unpredictable tasks • Clear, formal authority • Team-working could be good or poor	• Experienced, confident team members • A belief that they have insufficient power • Acceptance and respect for the leader in setting the goals

to the progression of the followers' development (or 'maturity' as they call it). For example, as a follower moves into a high-maturity state, less interaction and feedback would be required from the leader. Hence, the leader should first assess the maturity level of the employee (experience, skill level, confidence, commitment, etc) in relation to the task and then adapt their leadership style accordingly.

The theory suggests four leadership styles: telling, selling, participating and delegating – to be adopted according to the level of maturity of the employee (as listed in Table 1.4).

TABLE 1.4   Hersey–Blanchard leadership model

Maturity Level of Follower	Leadership Style
Low maturity – lacks experience, skills and confidence to achieve task. May also be unwilling to do so	*Telling* – leader gives firm instructions and deadlines. Closely monitors progress
Medium maturity / limited skills – lacks ability but is enthusiastic to achieve task	*Selling* – leader explains task and how / why it should be achieved. Remains available to offer support
Medium maturity / adequate skills – is capable of achieving task but lacks confidence or commitment to do so	*Participating* – leader works with follower, seeks input and encourages commitment
High maturity – is capable, confident and committed to task completion	*Delegating* – leader gives responsibility for goal-setting and achievement

One criticism of both the path–goal and Hersey–Blanchard approaches is that they suggest that a leader should adopt a style according to the defined characteristics of the workplace or their followers: once the situation is defined and understood, then use the recommended style.

Tannenbaum and Schmidt leadership continuum

In the belief that situations change continually and, hence, leaders should also be able to change their approach, contingency theorists Tannenbaum and Schmidt (1958) proposed that leadership behaviour varies along a continuum from the autocratic extreme to one where followers are heavily involved in decision-making (see Table 1.5).

TABLE 1.5   Tannenbaum and Schmidt leadership continuum

Leadership Style	Application
Autocratic	Makes decisions without input from followers and tells them what actions to take / the autocratic leader does not expect to be questioned by subordinates
Persuasive	Still makes decisions without group input but seeks to persuade followers to buy into the decision by selling it as a good one

TABLE 1.5 *continued*

Leadership Style	Application
Consultative	Followers are asked to contribute to the decision-making process, although the decision remains the responsibility of the leader
Democratic	The leader presents the problem to the group and encourages a discussion about any possible solutions. The leader facilitates the discussion, that leads to a group decision

Functional leadership

One of the most long-standing leadership models is John Adair's Action-Centred Leadership (ACL). First conceived in 1973, the model is still used across the world, as well as extensively in the UK, where Adair has worked with the NHS to introduce the model in several of its regions. It is a functional approach to leadership in that it is concerned with what actions a leader takes to accomplish a task. It is based upon the principle that a leader achieves a task through individuals working together in a team. Hence, in order to be effective, a leader must meet the needs of the task, the team and the individual. The model is represented by three overlapping circles (as shown in Figure 1.2).

FIGURE 1.2   Adair's Action-Centred Leadership model

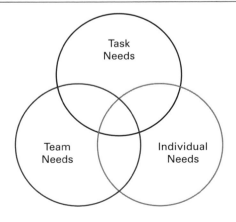

The circles overlap to represent the fact that if a leader fails to meet the needs of either the task, team or individual it will impact on the other two circles. The ACL concept can most succinctly be described as the leader 'taking actions to fulfil functions to meet the needs of the team, task and individual'. Moreover, Adair proposes that leadership functions differ according to the level the leader operates at, specifically:

- Team leadership: leaders of a team of up to, say, 20 people with clearly defined tasks to achieve.
- Operational leadership: leaders of one of the main parts of the organization, with responsibility for more than one team leader.
- Strategic leadership: leaders of a whole organization, with a number of operational leaders reporting to them.

The roles and functions of the three levels of leadership are set out in Table 1.6. ACL is, therefore, a model that offers the opportunity to introduce a co-ordinated leadership approach throughout an organization, understood and applied by all levels of leadership within it.

Another functional leadership model, more prescriptive than Adair's and targeted mainly at strategic leaders, is Kouzes and Posner's Five Practices of Exemplary Leadership. James Kouzes and Barry Posner contributed to research into the trait theory of leadership during 1983–87 by surveying 630 managers and conducting 42 in-depth interviews, from which they identified 10 key leadership traits:

- honest;
- forward-looking;
- inspirational;
- competent;
- fair-minded;
- supportive;
- broad-minded;
- intelligent;
- straightforward;
- dependable.

It is, however, important to note that their research differed from previous work on the subject as they sought opinions as to the most important traits the interviewees looked for in their ideal leader, as opposed to the actual traits displayed by real-life, successful leaders.

Kouzes and Posner continued and extended their research over the following 20 years by conducting hundreds of interviews, reviewing thousands of case studies and analysing very many questionnaires. The work culminated in their best-selling book *The Leadership Challenge*, which introduced their

TABLE 1.6   Adair's leaders' roles and functions

Leadership Level	Role	Functions
Team leaders	• Achieve the task • Develop the individual • Build and maintain the team	• Defining the task • Planning • Briefing • Controlling • Supporting • Motivating • Evaluating • Setting an example
Operational leaders	• Achieving the departmental task • Providing opportunities for development • Building and maintaining the departmental culture	As above, plus: • Influencing • Informing • Interpreting • Implementing • Networking • Succession planning
Strategic leaders	• Delivering the strategic vision • Ensuring opportunities for development of all • Building and maintaining organizational culture	As above, plus: • Providing direction • Strategic thinking and planning • Making it happen • Relating the parts to the whole • Building key partnerships • Releasing the corporate spirit • Choosing and developing today's and tomorrow's leaders

functional leadership model that they called the Five Practices of Exemplary Leadership, which is summarized as follows:

1 *Model the way*: set an example by demonstrating shared values. Achieve small successes that build confidence, commitment and consistent progress.

2 *Inspire a shared vision:* communicate an exciting, motivational and meaningful future. Encourage others to share that vision by appealing to their values, interests and aspirations.

3 *Challenge the process:* seek challenging opportunities to change, grow, innovate and develop. Be prepared to experiment and take calculated risks and learn from any mistakes and failures.

4 *Enable others to act:* encourage collaboration by promoting shared goals and building trust. Use delegation and empowerment to develop increased competence, whilst offering visible support.

5 *Encourage the heart:* recognize and reward individual contributions to group goals. Celebrate team achievements regularly.

Kouzes and Posner (2008) conclude that 'good leadership is an understandable and universal process' and one that comprises a set of observable behaviours that, with training and experience, can be applied by those in senior leadership positions to great effect. For them, leadership is a learnt skill, not an inherent quality available only to a select few. Leaders are *made* not *born*.

Relationship theory

Relationship leadership theory describes leaders who are primarily motivated by, and concerned with, the interaction they have with their followers. They work hard to understand and communicate with their people and seek to find ways to make the work experience enjoyable and rewarding through creating a positive and enriching working environment. Such leaders recognize that the key to organizational success lies with the people who work within it.

This approach argues that leaders should find ways to motivate their people, rather than passively applying leadership styles to followers or situations. They can achieve high levels of motivation by transforming followers' attitude and commitment through communicating a meaningful and appealing vision and facilitating a collective and collaborative culture whereby it can be realized. Two very different models of relationship theory are considered below, namely transformational and leader–member exchange.

Transformational leadership

James Burns (1978) in his book *Leadership* was the first to put forward the concept of 'transforming leadership', describing it as occurring 'when one or more persons engage with others in such a way that leaders and followers raise one another to higher levels of motivation and morality'. Bass (1985) subsequently developed Burns's concept of transforming leadership into 'transformational leadership' where the influence is imposed only by leader to follower, unlike Bass who conceived it as a potentially two-way process.

The transformational model assumes that people will follow a person who creates an attractive vision and is able to inspire them through his or her enthusiasm and energy. It contrasts with transactional leadership, which assumes people are motivated by reward and punishment and that their prime purpose is to undertake tasks, as directed by their manager.

Bass, with colleague Avolio (1994), developed the concept to categorize five transformational styles applied by leaders:

- *Idealized influence:* express their beliefs and values and have a strong sense of purpose.

- *Inspirational motivation:* communicate their optimism regarding the future; have a compelling vision of the future; talk enthusiastically about what needs to be achieved; and express confidence in ability to achieve.

- *Intellectual stimulation:* seek different perspectives to problem-solving; encourage creative thinking; question ideas that have not been questioned before.

- *Individualized consideration:* spend time teaching and coaching individuals; consider individuals' needs, abilities and strengths; listen to people.

- *Idealized attributes:* build respect; have power and competence; make sacrifices for others; and instil pride in others.

Hooper and Potter (1997) alternatively proposed seven key competencies required of transformational leaders:

- setting direction;
- setting an example;
- communications;
- alignment;
- bringing out the best in people;
- the leader as a change agent;
- providing clear decisions in a crisis and in ambiguous situations.

Much has been written about the need for transformational leaders to be charismatic. Certainly, we would describe many leaders who have been instrumental in achieving change on the world stage as being charismatic: Mahatma Gandhi, Winston Churchill, Martin Luther King, even Adolf Hitler, being notable examples. In a business context, company leaders such as Steve Jobs (Apple), Richard Branson (Virgin) and 'Jack' Welch (General Electric) are often cited for their charisma. They certainly all demonstrate exceptional communication skills, applied on a very powerful emotional level. Charismatic leaders focus heavily on developing group identity: creating a sense of elitism that separates it from other groups. Such group identity will be inextricably linked at an emotional level to the leader, thus creating a potentially powerful force for change. But do transformational leaders have to be charismatic? I consider this question in more depth in Chapter 8.

In Jim Collins's book *Good to Great* (2001) he describes the results of five years spent researching American companies that made the leap from achieving good results to great results, and sustained them for at least 15 years. He also compared those to a control group of companies that either failed to make the leap or, if they did, failed to sustain it. The overall objective of the research was to discover what essential factors distinguished both groups. The good-to-great companies included well-known names such as Gillette, Kimberly-Clark and Wells Fargo. What Collins found was that the leaders of all these companies were, in fact, self-effacing individuals who did not seek the spotlight in any respect or at any time. They could in no way be described as charismatic; rather, modest and humble. That is not to say that they were found to have no ego or self-interest: they were, in fact, incredibly ambitious – but their ambition was, first and foremost, for their institution, rather than themselves. They channelled the needs of their ego away from themselves and into the larger goal of building a great company. They were truly inspirational leaders, motivating their people to create great companies – but not by having a charismatic personality.

Leader–member exchange theory (LMX)

Unlike relationship leadership, which encourages leaders to work hard to build mutually supportive and rewarding working environments for all members of the organization, LMX theory seeks to explain relationships that leaders can have with individual followers. It is inevitable that leaders relate differently with different team members and this theory assumes that the senior person in the relationship develops an exchange with each subordinate member; and that the quality of these leader–member exchanges influences the degree of mutual respect, trust, loyalty, support and commitment. Psychological research associated with LMX theory has added knowledge to the understanding of group relationships and processes, in particular the tendency for groups to develop subgroups – some of which are regarded as in-groups and others as out-groups.

Members of the in-group, often forming an inner circle of advisors, are favoured by the leader, receiving more attention and support, whilst those from the out-group receive less. Due to the favoured attention received by the in-group members they tend to be more motivated, with higher levels of performance. Not surprisingly, therefore, they are less likely to leave their job, and tend to benefit from enhanced promotion and remuneration opportunities.

These positive relationships tend to form soon after the subordinate joins the larger group and usually follow three stages:

1 *Role-taking:* the leader quickly assesses the new arrival's skills and qualities and may offer him or her opportunities to demonstrate his or her capability.

2 *Role-making:* in this stage both parties undergo informal and unstructured negotiations to create a role for the member with vague promises of benefit in return for loyalty and commitment to the leader. A demonstration of trust is important at this stage, with any suggestion of betrayal by either party resulting in the member being relegated to the out-group. Members who have similar interests and profile (including gender) to the leader have a greater chance of gaining entry to the in-group as they will have been assessed as being more likely to demonstrate the required loyalty.

3 *Routinization:* here, social exchanges between leader and follower become established as the latter works hard to retain his or her in-group membership through building and sustaining trust and respect.

In-group members are more likely to receive and enjoy more rewarding work, be offered additional responsibility, and be invited to contribute to the leader's decision-making. Not surprisingly, out-group members display less job satisfaction as a result of the apparent favouritism shown by their leader to in-group colleagues. It is, therefore, incumbent on the leader to recognize his or her tendency to favour certain team members and the implications of doing so on organizational efficiency. The extent of group differentiation may be significant in some organizations, but much less so in others. However, research by Liden, Sparrowe and Wayne (2006) found that some differentiation is healthy within an organization, as members of the out-group recognize that they must perform better to gain their leader's favour.

Whilst LMX, as a theory, is helpful in understanding and rationalizing relationships between leaders and individual subordinates, it is less useful in describing leadership behaviours that promote high-quality, supportive relationships with followers. At best, it generalizes the need for leaders to demonstrate trust, respect and openness. At worst, it may appear to justify the leader apportioning special attention to those viewed as being valid members of the in-group.

Shared social identity

Haslam, Reicher and Platow (2011), in their book *The New Psychology of Leadership: Identity, Influence and Power*, propose a new way of considering leadership: not simply about getting people to do things, rather getting them to *want* to do things. It is, they suggest, about achieving influence, not securing compliance – winning the hearts and minds of others and harnessing their energies and passions. Leadership is not about raw power or incentivization, as these are indicators and consequences of the failure of leadership. The authors recognize that the application of force can be used to affect the behaviour of others: threatening the dire consequence of disobedience is, indeed, likely to result in obedience. The same outcome may occur if a great inducement was offered, but neither approach is likely to result in people considering that they have ownership of what the leader is trying to achieve. More likely, they will reject the objective, as it has been forced upon them – either by carrot or stick. In contrast, if the leader can inspire them to take a desired course of action, they are likely to continue the journey, even if the leader is absent.

The authors argue that, if effective leadership depends upon influence as opposed to coercion or incentive, a leader needs to focus on the mental states and processes that encourage followers to listen to leaders and to buy in to their vision. Such psychological processes always depend on the social content: good psychology indicates what to look for in our social world, as opposed to merely looking only in the head. More specifically, the social factors include the culture of the group being led; the nature of the institutions within which the leadership is being applied; and the gender of the leaders themselves. These factors influence the 'mental glue' that binds leaders and followers together in sharing a common vision – what drives them to push together in a desired direction, and what encourages them to keep pushing.

The book seeks to offer an alternative approach to the traditional psychology of leadership, which the authors suggest has previously concentrated on the traits, character and qualities of recognized leaders. They characterize this approach as treating leadership as an 'I thing': quoting Drucker (1992):

> The leaders who work most effectively, it seems to me, never say 'I'.
> And that's because they have trained themselves not to say 'I'. They don't think 'I'. They think 'team'. They understand their job to be to make the team function... there is an identification (very often quite unconsciously) with task and with the group.

The authors propose that effective leadership is never about 'I': it is about how leaders and followers come to see each other as part of a common group – as members of the same in-group. Leadership is very much a 'we thing'. This concept requires a greater understanding of what it involves, where it comes from, and how it works – the answers to which centre on issues of social identity, a shared group membership that encourages members to engage with each other as fellow representatives of a common in-group. Members stop thinking of what divides them as individuals, rather focusing on what unites them as in-group members. The psychology behind this approach is founded in terms of four principles, as set out below.

1. The leader must be seen as 'one of us'

Leaders will be more effective if they are perceived as representing a social identity that other 'in-group' members share; one that distinguishes them from other 'out-groups'. The leader needs to be seen as an 'in-group prototype' – one who stands for the group representing it, as opposed to standing apart from it.

2. The leader must be seen to 'do it for us'

Their actions must been seen to be directed towards the interests of the in-group, which will encourage followers to devote their energies towards achieving their leader's vision. The leaders must stand up for the shared social identity, rather than his or her personal interests or, even worse, the interests of an out-group.

3. The leader must 'craft a sense of us'

Leaders do not simply work within pre-existing constraints; they actively advance a sense of 'who we are'. They seek to craft an identity that they, and their vision, are prototypical of the group. Representing the group, and their norms, values and priorities, are powerful influences in shaping the understanding of 'who we are'. A powerful example here is Nelson Mandela wearing the Springbok rugby shirt whilst celebrating, with the team, their World Cup Final win in 1995.

4. The leader must 'make us matter'

Successful leaders are 'identity impresarios' who initiate identity-embedding structures, for example goals, practices and activities. This ensures that the rhetoric of 'us' is translated into a world in which the group's values are realized and its potential fulfilled.

'We'll never call you employees; we'll never treat you like employees. We'll never call you staff; we'll never treat you like staff. You're family and we'll treat you like family. The only thing we ask in return is that you treat each other with the same respect – like family.'

Karen Forrester
Chief Executive
TGI Friday's

Chapter summary

The understanding that wise leaders are more effective in influencing the behaviour of those that follow them has been acknowledged for very many centuries, although serious study of the 'science' of leadership has happened much more recently. If this book is to propose approaches that leaders should take to meet the challenges of the 21st century, it is necessary to understand how leadership theory has developed to the present day.

Initial thinking in the 19th century was that, in times of need, leaders will emerge to guide their people to safety or success. These 'great men' were born to lead as a result of the inherent qualities they were born with. This understanding led to attempts to identify the qualities, or traits, they were equipped with. Several authors proposed sets of traits they believed were necessary for effective leadership.

However, due to the impossibility of agreeing a definitive set of necessary leadership qualities, research turned towards the behaviour of proven successful leaders and how others can learn and develop those skills. This led to many theories proposing appropriate leadership styles necessary to impact positively on followers' performance. Yet these behavioural theories tended not to consider the challenges faced by leaders that are due to the environment in which they operate.

Hence, the situational, or contingency, approach was conceived, requiring leaders to adapt their style to the situation they face. Again, a number of theories were conceived, largely considering situations in terms of variations of task, followers' characteristics, and operational environments. Functional leadership took a similar approach in that it focused on what a leader must do to achieve the required task through people working together in teams.

The imperative of leaders to understand the critical importance of followers achieving their objectives led to relationship theory. Here, leaders are encouraged to find ways to inspire and motivate their people to achieve a shared vision, rather than applying a specific leadership style. Seeking similar relational outcomes, contemporary psychologists have proposed a leadership approach based upon an understanding of the social context surrounding group formation, whereby leaders and followers come to see each other as members of the same group, with leaders becoming the 'in-group prototype' that stands for, and represents, fellow group members. All communications with, and behaviour towards, their people should be designed to cement that feeling of common purpose – a shared identity.

Thus, the understanding and application of leadership has developed from the great man theory, based upon the assumption that 'leaders are born', to current thinking that recognizes that it is no longer realistic to assume that people will blindly follower a leader, whatever situation they face. In my view, and those of the leaders interviewed for this book, 21st-century leaders must work hard to build relationships with their people in the understanding that, without their support, they will be isolated and ultimately unsuccessful in whatever situation they face or environment they operate in.

Future challenges
– the 21st-century leader

02

In Chapter 1 we have seen how leadership theory and practice has changed over the past century or so, but how will successful leaders adapt to the challenges facing them in the future? During these early years of the third millennium we have seen the internet give us access to information, as well as enhanced communication through social media, never before imagined. The world of work has changed and leaders have had to capitalize on opportunities offered by the huge advances in technology, as well as facing the equally huge challenges of economic crises on a global scale. Moreover, customer expectations of the products and services they receive have escalated and are continuing to grow, thus organizations are having to become more customer-focused through the development of their front-line staff.

From employees' perspective in the Western world, the old days when they automatically respected, or at least showed respect for, their leaders are over. Employees are more inclined to question company policy affecting their work and personal lives if they feel it is inappropriate or unjust. An acceptable work–life balance is an expectation held by most employees in the 21st century, as are opportunities for personal development. Talented members of an organization expect their skills to be recognized and if that fails to occur they will more readily take their talent to another organization that will value it more.

Hence, moving forward to the future, leaders face a number of challenges, the most significant of which are:

- innovation;
- talent management;
- communications, including social media;
- globalization.

Innovation

Innovation is not about introducing new processes within a company that its competitors have been doing for some time, nor is it conceiving and delivering a new concept that adds little, or no, value to the company's stakeholders, especially its customers. Innovation involves the introduction of something new that adds value to either business efficiency, leading to increased profitability; human resource management for the benefit of staff motivation, productivity and retention; or to the customer experience, driving up sales. The challenge for leaders is to create an innovative and entrepreneurial culture that reaps achievable benefits in all of these aspects and, by doing so, steals a march on their competitors. Such a culture encourages and embraces people who are constantly looking for improvement by seeking new and innovative ideas, in the knowledge that they will be rewarded, financially or otherwise, for doing so.

BEST leadership quote

'Businesses miss a huge number of beneficial comments because they do not allow their people to make them. How valuable is it for me to have someone say "Why do we do it this way? If we did it that way it would be better." We have had so much positive change because someone has suggested a better way to do things. It's enormous, because you know what happens next? People suddenly start saying "Hey, I've got an idea too." That's the environment you want.'

William Rogers
Chief Executive
UKRD

The companies that succeed and flourish in the future will be those that are able to compete best within their own sector in their home country as well as on a global stage, especially in the rapidly emerging economic countries such as Brazil, India and China. Moreover, the previously clear boundaries of industry sectors are becoming less well-defined as cross-sector competition increases. UK companies such as BT, Sky and Virgin are broadening their services across telecommunications, media and entertainment sectors; whilst supermarkets now offer a wide range of financial products on their shelves. Customers have become used to shopping around for the best deals within and across traditional sectors. For business leaders the message is clear: unless their companies find new ways of meeting customer needs they will be overtaken by competitors that have. Unless they lead companies where innovation is embedded within their business philosophy they will be seen by their previous customer base as being tired and outdated.

But where are these innovative ideas to emerge from? Senior managers may have some themselves but the more astute will ensure that employees' ideas are continually sought, valued and seriously considered. Ricardo Semler (1999), in his inspirational book *Maverick*, describes how he inherited his father's company that he described as a 'traditional company in every respect, with a pyramidal structure and a rule for every contingency'. Through his belief in the potential of his staff he transformed the company to one with an inclusive culture where upward communication was not merely encouraged, it was expected. There follows an excerpt from a booklet given to each new Semco employee:

> Our philosophy is built on participation and involvement. Don't settle down. Give opinions, seek opportunities and advancement, always say what you think. Don't be just one more person in the company. Your opinion is always interesting, even if no one asked you for it. Get in touch with factory committees, and participate in elections. Make your voice count.

In order to realize the potential for creative ideas from amongst an organization's people, leaders must have a clear vision of where the company is going and, most importantly, make the future seem bright, achievable and beneficial to its entire staff. Staff must be encouraged to contribute to what Garry Hogan, managing director of Flight Centre (UK), quoted in Cutler (2004), described as a 'brightness of future'.

Yet truly innovative leaders seek contributions from all stakeholders involved in the business: staff, customers, suppliers and other strategic allies. Customers, in particular, can be a fertile source of innovative ideas. As founder and CEO of Dell Computers, Michael Dell says: 'I am sure that there are a lot of things that I can't imagine, but our customers can. A company of this size is not going to be about a couple of people coming up with ideas. It's going to be about millions of people, and harnessing the power of those ideas' (Leavy, 2012).

Michael Dell's belief in the power of customer feedback was confirmed in 2005 when Jeff Jarvis launched an internet blog entitled 'Dell Hell' as a result of the lack of response he believed he'd had from the company to problems with a new laptop he had purchased. As a result, Dell launched a Direct2Dell blog and subsequently followed it up with its innovative IdeaStorm website designed to encourage customer involvement.

Research by Vaccaro *et al* (2012) considered both the impact that transformational and transactional leaders can have on management innovation, as well as the moderating role that organizational size can have on the leader's success in the process. They found that, whilst driving through innovation, *transformational* leaders:

- enable organizations to change management practices, processes or structures by inspiring team success and developing mutually respectful relationships based on common goals;
- consider staff individually and generate greater predisposition to experiment with changing tasks, functions and procedures;
- may even promote staff to rethink existing structures and task specializations and reconsider new ways of 'getting things done';
- may be able to make sense of otherwise ambiguous aspects of innovation where goals and outcomes may not be too clear.

BEST leadership quote

'To capitalize on the best ideas you have to create an environment of continual change. Don't be frightened of it. You would not be frightened in your personal life if you bought a new television – you would be excited by it, as you know you want something that feeds your life and environment. Yet in work, we often talk about change being an unsettling, scary process, when it should be engaging and energy-giving.'

Phil Loach
Chief Fire Officer
West Midlands Fire Service

On the other hand, Vaccaro *et al* (2012) found that *transactional* leaders:

- contribute to lowering potential barriers to innovation;
- may be helpful in the implementation phase of innovation schemes;
- may be able to induct organizational members to meet innovation targets through reward initiatives.

As regards the moderating factor of the size of the organization, the research found that:

- Organizational size decreases the effectiveness of both transformational and transactional leadership approaches.

- Transformational leadership, however, becomes more important for innovation in larger organizations as it may mitigate the negative impact of larger hierarchies and greater bureaucracy. It could complement these factors by maintaining a sense of meaningfulness in staff, which in turn is more conducive to innovation.

- Transactional leadership is more effective when smaller organizations are seeking to be more innovative, as leaders' and followers' expectations may be more easily established and monitored through face-to-face interaction. Under transactional leadership, staff find more flexibility to introduce innovative change.

- Whilst organizations are small there is a greater need to achieve short-term goals – which are more conducive to the application of transactional rewards for doing so. However, as the organization increases in size, leaders may become more transformational in order to instil a sense of urgency for members to deliver.

The research concluded that both leadership styles are relevant for management innovation – but smaller, less complex organizations benefit more from the transactional approach. On the other hand, larger organizations should adopt a more transformational style to compensate for their complexity and to encourage greater innovation at all levels.

Talent management

The term 'talent management' was first introduced by McKinsey and Company in 1997, and further discussed in their book *The War for Talent* (Michaels *et al*, 2001). It is defined by the Chartered Institute for Personnel Development (CIPD) as:

> The systematic attraction, identification, development, engagement, retention and deployment of those individuals who are of particular value to an organization, either in view of their 'high potential' for the future or because they are fulfilling business/operational-critical roles.

Note that the definition does not only cover the need to attract talented individuals but also to develop, manage and retain them. The concept should also encompass not only the identification of external talent but also the nurturing of that which already exists within an organization.

Michaels, Handfield-Jones and Axelrod (2001) expand McKinsey's 1997 research and make the point that in the modern competitive, knowledge-based world a company's success is increasingly determined by the calibre of its talent. Yet, attracting and retaining great talent is increasingly difficult as demand for people equipped for the changing business landscape outstrips supply. As they say, 'the war for talent is a business reality'. The current and future business reality is one of increasingly competitive global markets; skill shortages across many sectors; demographic trends within and across countries; greater expectations of corporate governance; and the need for more flexible and innovative business strategies. Leaders must integrate a talent management strategy that:

- is aligned with the corporate strategy so that HR managers can identify and provide the skills necessary to meet the business needs of the organization;

- gives attention to the talent development needs of the company as a whole, as well as those of particular core groups and individuals – both an inclusive and exclusive approach;

- encompasses all those involved in the strategy, namely: selected participants who will benefit from it; directors and senior managers to support and guide it; line managers who accept their responsibility to identify and develop talent within their department; HR managers to take a lead in the design and support of the strategy.

BEST leadership quote

'The statistics of hiring leaders from the outside are pretty poor. I would much rather bring someone talented in and let them spend a number of years in the organization to learn how it works and what its culture is. Developing people up from within offers much more management certainty and stability, which is important to the future of the organization.'

Henry Engelhardt
Chief Executive
Admiral Group

The Institute of Leadership and Management (ILM) 'Creating Future Leaders 2010' report set out to identify what employees want from their future leaders by interviewing 50 senior HR professionals from commercial organizations, the majority employing over 1,000 people. It found that the most important feature was a set of personal characteristics associated with interpersonal relationships. The HR managers looked for visionary, ambitious, inspirational people who were trustworthy and naturally good communicators. However, the most important personal qualities were the ability to motivate (36 per cent) and emotional intelligence (34 per cent). Moreover, future leaders need to demonstrate a broad mix of all these characteristics if they are to reach the most senior positions: strengths in some does not compensate for weakness in others.

The report further identified the need for a range of skills and knowledge to support their personal qualities, in particular:

- technical and professional skills in relevant areas such as law, accounting or engineering – cited by 56 per cent of respondents;
- commercial and financial skills to ensure that future leaders understand the world of business – 54 per cent of respondents;
- soft skills including people management (26 per cent), communication (24 per cent), coaching and feedback (20 per cent), and team management skills (20 per cent).

A broad range of experience was also seen as crucial, especially across different sectors and industries. Appropriate experience will equip leaders to cope with the pressures and stress of the modern business world.

Two years later, in 2012, the ILM published a further report, 'The Leadership and Management Talent Pipeline', which assessed the UK's readiness to produce the steady stream of talent necessary to meet the challenges faced by 21st-century leaders. It commissioned independent research with 750 public and private organizations to identify the challenges they face in recruiting and developing the necessary talent. Its key findings were:

- *Pipeline deficiencies:* whilst 93 per cent of respondents expressed concern that low levels of management skills were having a direct impact on them achieving their business goals, the report found that most organizations lacked a functional talent management strategy, with many having no plan at all.
- *Reliance on external recruitment:* driven in large part by shortcomings in internal talent development strategies, most UK firms rely heavily on external recruitment to fill senior positions. Only half of senior manager appointments come from within the organization.
- *Recruiting the wrong skills:* employers recruiting first-line managers on the basis of technical skills and knowledge are likely to end up with senior managers lacking the necessary strategic and financial skills. Poor leadership skills at lower managerial levels result in 'expert novices' who are ill-equipped to progress to senior positions.
- *Poor talent planning:* despite the lack of managers who have the necessary skill sets, especially in terms of emotional intelligence, motivational ability and innovation, only 57 per cent of employees have a plan to ensure they have the talent to fill future vacancies. Having a talent management plan to match skills development with business needs was the report's main recommendation – a talent pipeline.

McKinsey (2001) argued for a new way of thinking about talent management: one best able to provide the leadership required to meet the challenges of the 21st century, as shown in Table 2.1.

TABLE 2.1 Thinking about talent management
(from *The War for Talent,* by Michaels *et al*, 2001)

	The Old Way	The New Way
1. Talent Mindset	**1.1** Having good people is one of many important performance levers	**1.1** Having the right talent throughout the organization is a critical source of competitive advantage
	1.2 HR is responsible for people management, including recruiting, compensation, performance reviews, and succession planning	**1.2** Every manager, starting with the CEO, is responsible for attracting, developing, exciting, and retaining talented people; indeed every manager is explicitly accountable for the strength of the talent pool he/she builds
2. Employee Value Proposition	**2.1** We expect people to pay their dues and work their way up the line before they get the top jobs and big bucks	**2.1** We think of our people as volunteers and know we have to try to deliver on their dreams now if we are to keep them
	2.2 We have a strong value proposition that attracts customers	**2.2** We also have a distinctive value proposition that attracts and retains talented people
3. Recruiting	**3.1** Recruiting is like purchasing: it's about picking the best from a long line of candidates	**3.1** Recruiting is more like marketing and selling: it's a key responsibility of all managers
	3.2 We hire at entry levels only – primarily from the same six or seven schools	**3.2** We hire at all levels – entry, mid, and top – and look for talent in every conceivable field
4. Growing Leaders	**4.1** Development is training	**4.1** Development happens through a series of challenging job experiences and candid, helpful coaching
	4.2 Development happens when you are fortunate enough to get a really good boss	**4.2** Development is crucial to performance and retention... and it can be institutionalized

TABLE 2.1 *continued*

	The Old Way	The New Way
5. Differentiation	**5.1** Differentiation undermines team work	**5.1** We shower our top performers with opportunities and recognition. We develop and nurture mid-performers. We help our lower performers raise their game or we move them out or aside

Leadership *BEST* practice

McDonald's recognize that the challenge with talent management is to understand the important disciplines that it encompasses, such as recruitment, succession planning and performance management, in other words having clear links to the business strategy, especially in terms of learning and development, rather viewing it as the organization's X Factor!

David Fairhurst, chief people officer for McDonald's (Europe), explains that it is about ensuring they have leadership talent to drive business success today – having high-performing, committed leaders in key positions – and in the future. Creating tomorrow's leaders involves the business strategy teams identifying future leadership talent requirements; mapping existing talent against those requirements; and then planning to build, buy or borrow (from elsewhere in the company) that talent in a timely manner.

Social media

The 21st century has seen the emergence of a 'knowledge economy' that has far-reaching implications for leaders, both in terms of the people and the organizations they lead. With employees increasingly using social media sites as their primary means of non-verbal communication, organizations are seeking new ways of using such technology to engage with and develop their people. This is particularly the case with the rising number of knowledge workers who are less likely to have permanent bases and who often have a responsibility to make digital networks for both personal and business purposes.

Customers also are increasingly using mobile and interactive devices to decide where and what to buy: becoming instant experts on the benefits of products and services as well as communicating their evaluation and experiences with other potential customers via social networks. Hence, forward-looking business leaders are seeking new ways of harnessing these information technologies to innovate, differentiate and develop more effective customer interaction and collaboration. Customer loyalty becomes more critical to an organization's future, whilst customers' bad experiences can be spread through social media sites and pose a frightening potential for organizations and those that lead them. Yet a survey by software security firm Clearswift in 2012 found that only one in four companies were planning to invest more in social media that year. Moreover, those that are confining investment merely to their sales or marketing activities will soon be at a disadvantage to those that incorporate social media throughout their organizations – from top down and bottom up.

Within organizations, leaders also need to increasingly meet employees' expectations for more transparency, trust and clarity by taking a close, hard look at existing communication tools and structures within their organizations. Srikanth Iyengar (2013), head of UK and global head of sales at Infosys, suggests:

> I don't think leaders have a choice but to use social networks. People want to talk to you: they want to get a response. If your leaders sit outside this stuff it sends the wrong message. You've got to be there, you've got to respond. But you've got to trust leaders to use their judgement on what's appropriate to say and what's not.

Whilst some companies use existing social media sites such as Facebook and Twitter to communicate with their staff, others have designed bespoke internal platforms for that purpose. The UK's Big Lottery Fund, for example, developed an interface called the Big Connect, described by Perry Timms, head of talent, as a hybrid of Facebook, Twitter, LinkedIn and Yammer. One example of its use is to maintain a current skills audit, as the company asks its employees to record their personal skills and experiences on it. Whether using internal or external platforms, the extent to which they provide benefits for organizations depends upon whether all parties embrace them and are prepared to input their personal and company data.

The main danger for companies and their leaders is if they fail to recognize the power that social media platforms offer disgruntled staff and, in particular, customers. Those companies that are aware of the destructive power of the public's dissatisfaction, voiced through social media, ensure that they are serious about listening to customer complaints and are open and honest in their responses to them. Individual complaints can go viral via Facebook and Twitter: when an angry mother created a Facebook page to accuse Pampers nappies of causing a rash on her baby, the story found its way onto ABC news.

BEST leadership quote

'My God, Twitter is just an explosion because if someone makes a complaint about your brand it goes out there and you think, "How can you cope with all of them?" So, for me, the biggest challenge for leaders in the 21st century is to stay real, to stay close to your people because technology makes it far too easy to be more remote.'

Karen Forrester
Chief Executive
TGI Friday's

Perhaps the most famous mishandling of a complaint aired via Facebook involved the world's largest food company, Nestlé, in 2010. Its problem began when Greenpeace raised an online protest, alleging that Nestlé's palm oil supplier in Indonesia was illegally deforesting that country's rainforests and, hence, posing a threat to the orang-utans that inhabited them. The protest included calling on its supporters to speak out against Nestlé via social media sites, as well as encouraging them to wear a Kit Kat 'killer' logo on their clothes. In reaction, Nestlé censored its critics for using an altered version of one of its brand logos, whilst the company moderator entered in an exchange of posts with protestors that became increasingly sarcastic and vitriolic.

By the time the company realized its mistake the damage was already done. What had initially started as a reasonable question about its product-sourcing quickly became, as a result of the company's perceived rude and overbearing response, a major publicity own-goal. If Nestlé had had a considered social media strategy to respond to posts with a listening ear and empathetic tone, the critics' views may have been quickly dissipated, without major impact on the company's reputation. Sites such as Facebook allow all voices to be heard and emotions shared. As a result, companies must learn to respond to those voices and emotions without appearing to threaten the values upon which they are based. It is impossible for any company to predict what messages will appear on social media sites; what it can do, though, is to ensure that a strategy exists to ensure that criticism is handled appropriately, in the full knowledge of its potential to explode and create real reputational damage.

It is the leader's responsibility to manage new-age digital communications to ensure positive and productive interchange between staff, customers and the public in general. Openness, transparency and collaborative working are the new expectations from all stakeholders. In the past, companies have sought to create a brand image, supported by tight controls to ensure that its reputation remains untarnished in the eyes of the market. However, in the new communication age, controls are becoming increasingly difficult to impose and the culture of secrecy behind them breeds mistrust. Consumers are more likely to purchase according to other users' recommendations, on Trip Advisor for example, rather than the company's brand message. The new modus operandi must be based upon a culture of openness, collaboration and transparency, where mistakes and shortcomings are recognized and acted upon speedily. In an environment where the likes of Wikileaks probe and publish, companies can no longer expect to sit on bad news and hope to bury it. Better to raise your hands, admit your mistakes, address them and hope to move on.

The same applies to staff: if leaders hope to engage with their staff on every level they must be seen as transparent and trustworthy. Increasingly, employees expect to be informed of aspects of the (their) business that would previously have been kept under wraps at head office. The leader's role is to create a culture based upon respect, openness and collaboration. Leena Nair, SVP Leadership and Organizational Development at Unilever, suggests that:

> It's interesting to see what the power of social networking can do to engage and unlock the future of the organization. But I'd also like to underline authenticity. People know when leaders have written a blog themselves and when someone else has written it.

Unfortunately, however, not all leaders are responding adequately to the demands posed by the digital age, in particular those associated with social media – even in companies that are actively using social technologies. The Social Media Survey (2012), conducted by Notter and Grant in companies that actively use social media tools, found that nearly half (44 per cent) of respondents were concerned about the lack of involvement by their leaders in using and promoting such new communication tools, yet 84 per cent felt that leadership involvement potentially creates a competitive edge.

Leadership *BEST* practice

Henry Engelhardt, chief executive of the Admiral Group, holds regular online chats, to which 700–800 regularly log in, with staff asking him any questions they want – from 'Why do we trade in France' to 'Which baseball team is going to win?' – which he will answer straight away. There is also an 'Ask Henry' facility on the internet, which allows staff to raise questions at any time.

New Charter Housing has a social media feed for the company to facilitate two-way communications, and Ian Munro, the CEO, also writes a regular blog covering work and other issues from a purely personal perspective.

TABLE 2.2   McKinsey's six skills of the social-media-literate leader

Personal Level

Producer	• Develop creative competence (authenticity, storytelling, artistic vision)
	• Hone technical skills (especially video production)
Distributor	• Understand cross-platform dynamics and what causes messages to go viral
	• Build and sustain a body of social followers
Recipient	• Create resonance via selective replies/linking
	• Make sense of noise through intelligent thinking

Strategic Level

Advisor	• Enable and support a 360-degree environment in social media usage
	• Co-ordinate and channel activities within span of control
Architect	• Balance vertical accountability and horizontal collaboration
	• Leverage social media for key business functions
Analyst	• Monitor dynamics of social media industry
	• Understand cultural and behavioural impact

McKinsey Quarterly for the first quarter of 2013 suggested six skills that leaders need in order to become social-media-literate at a personal and strategic level (as shown in Table 2.2).

Globalization

In a global business world, organizations and their leaders must appreciate how leadership is applied, defined and understood in different countries and cultures. Even in businesses that do not have multinational operations, few have a workforce that is entirely indigenous. International mobility of labour means that most organizations will have a proportion of employees originating from overseas. A large London hotel, for example, may well have staff of over 40 different nationalities. Far-seeing leaders recognize the benefits of having a diverse staff team. Bob McDonald, president and CEO of Procter & Gamble, when speaking on a US university tour during 2008–09 (see case study in Chapter 9) cited one of his personal beliefs to be: 'Diverse groups of people are more innovative than homogenous groups', explaining:

Diversity is a necessity at P&G to reflect consumers we serve and to drive innovation, one of our five core strengths. The role of a leader is to create the environment for connections and collaboration to occur. Leaders of the most effective diverse teams follow the 'Platinum Rule' – treat others as they want to be treated. The leader should know the people he or she works with well enough to know how they want to be treated.

That said, cross-cultural staff teams can pose significant challenges for leaders over a range of issues from interpersonal communications to the application of health and safety regulations. The host nation's understanding of management and leadership principles and practice differs widely across different cultures. Hence, leaders increasingly need to be aware of how their messages and actions could be interpreted by different staff, who may originate from a country that adopts very different leadership styles.

BEST leadership quote

'In this office we have many cultures. It is important to recognize that diversity is something we have to understand and embrace. Different cultures have different needs and requirements. It doesn't matter if you are from the same culture, you still cannot treat everyone in the same way.'

Will Schofield
Partner
PwC

Generally speaking, British people believe in equal opportunities in a work environment. Increasingly, strict hierarchical management structures are being deconstructed, resulting in:

- more flexibility in work roles;
- less command and control by senior levels of management;
- staff empowered to make decisions and take calculated risks;
- upward communication being encouraged, even to the extent of challenging authority;
- gender equality.

In some other countries, however, little progress in such matters has been made and hierarchical levels of management still exist, where employees:

- expect clear instructions from their managers;
- like clearly defined roles and responsibilities;

- automatically respect, or at least show respect for, those in authority;
- will not challenge decisions;
- would be uncomfortable to have their opinions sought;
- accept gender inequality.

Hence, a member of the management team of, for example, a London hotel employing staff from 40 different countries will need an appreciation of how the expectations of each of them differs. It may well be reasonable to expect those from some Western cultures to relish the opportunity for a degree of self-control and to have their views sought and welcomed. Yet those with experience of more autocratic leadership regimes may be confused, even fearful and insecure, when faced with a more egalitarian leadership style.

Moreover, as hierarchical cultures expect to be controlled, even dominated, by their leaders, those with a more empowering, consultative approach may be seen as weak and ineffective: 'why are they asking my opinion?'; 'do they not know their job?'; 'it's not my role to make such decisions'. Equally, most UK staff now have certain expectations within their workplace that may not be met by managers from a culture where they expect to be obeyed without question.

Indeed, the method and style of communication between managers and staff best exemplifies potential cultural divides. Some cultures, those from Germany, the United States and Scandinavian countries, for example, tend to adopt a direct style where:

- the truth is told, regardless of sentiment;
- difficult issues are confronted face-on;
- what is said is more important than how it is said;
- things are not left to interpretation;
- non-verbal clues, including body language, are not used, intentionally or non-intentionally, to convey the message.

Staff from less direct cultures, especially Arabian, Indian and even British, could find this direct style to be rude, inconsiderate and sometimes embarrassing. Leaders from, or communicating with, such cultures should be conscious of the need to:

- be aware not only of what is said but how it is said;
- avoid confrontational exchanges;
- use diplomacy and tact;
- assume that the recipient may interpret a different meaning to the message.

Communication considerations such as these have implications for a range of leadership roles such as: informal feedback and formal appraisals; gaining staff support for the leader's vision; staff motivation; the application of discipline, formal and informal; recruitment; and creating multicultural teams.

Leadership *BEST* practice

Haven Holidays, part of the Bourne Leisure Group, employ a large number of Eastern European workers on a seasonal basis, along with other European staff who have been with the company for a number of years. Rather than expecting the immediate manager to coach and train a new employee from a different culture, they encourage and support one of the more experienced non-British supervisors to act as a mentor and confidant, using his or her own experience to ease the new starter into his or her position. The mentors receive training in the role, which acts as a career development opportunity for them.

In a report entitled 'Global Leadership: Developing Tomorrow's Leaders Around the World' (2012), *Forbes* magazine analysed 30,576 leadership assessments from around the world to identify characteristics by country. It concluded that leaders from emerging markets, especially India and China, have a strong focus on operational execution; hands-on management; operational process; and managing individual performance. Benelux and Nordic countries, on the other hand, focus on planning strategy, communications and being 'change ambassadors'. The United States and the United Kingdom tend to have more hybrid leadership models: the United States, for example, sets great store on the application of change management – focusing on individual accountability for execution of defined projects.

So what qualities and skills does the global leader need in order to operate effectively in a multicultural environment, either within one country or internationally? House *et al* (2004) in Phase II of the Global Leadership and Organizational Behavior Effectiveness Research Program (GLOBE) used some 170 investigators from over 60 cultures to identify universally endorsed leader attributes, as well as those that are universally recognized as impediments to outstanding leadership. The research found that 'one size does not fit all' – executives must develop leadership skills tailored to the unique culture in which they operate. Nair (2013) again:

> Recently, I talked to young people from Indonesia, Brazil and China. I asked them what they expected from the leader of the future and their answers amazed me. The qualities that came up were humanity and compassion. They also wanted leaders who had the ability to put staff at the centre of what they do. They want leaders who aren't so charismatic – they want people who are humble enough to admit they don't know all the answers.

Focusing on the transformational leadership style (see Chapter 1), House's research found that different cultural groups varied in their evaluation of what were the most important characteristics of that approach. In some cultures, leaders are expected to take strong, decisive action in order to motivate followers to go beyond their self-interest to achieve the organization's objectives; whilst in others, such an aim may be more effectively achieved by a more consultative, democratic approach.

BEST leadership quote

'In a business covering 38 markets across a region with 7,427 restaurants from Morocco in the south and west, to Russia in the north and east – and where almost 75 per cent of our restaurants are owned and operated by franchises – it's clear that a "command and control" style of leadership would be wholly inappropriate. The key word for me is "influencing".'

David Fairhurst
Chief People Officer, Europe
McDonald's Restaurants

The research identified 22 specific leadership attributes and behaviours that were universally viewed as contributing to leadership effectiveness across cultures, namely:

- trustworthy;
- just;
- honest;
- foresight;
- plans ahead;
- encouraging;
- positive;
- dynamic;
- motive arouser;
- confidence builder;
- motivational;
- dependable;
- intelligent;
- decisive;
- effective bargainer;

- win-win problem solver;
- administratively skilled;
- communicative;
- informed;
- co-ordinator;
- team builder;
- excellence-orientated.

Eight leader attributes were universally negative:

- loner;
- asocial;
- non co-operative;
- irritable;
- non-explicit;
- ruthless;
- dictatorial;
- egocentric.

Interestingly, the research found 35 attributes that were culturally contingent, that is, contributors in some cultures and impediments in others. The numbers after the attributes represent worldwide minimum and maximum values on a seven-point scale ranging from 1 (substantially impedes) to 7 (substantially facilitates) effective leadership:

- able to anticipate (3.84–6.51)
- ambitious (2.85–6.73)
- autonomous (1.63–5.17)
- cautious (2.17–5.78)
- class conscious (2.53–6.09)
- compassionate (2.69–5.56)
- cunning (1.26–6.38)
- domineering (1.60–5.14)
- elitist (1.61–5.00)
- enthusiastic (3.72–6.44)
- evasive (1.52–5.67)
- formal (2.12–5.43)
- habitual (1.93–5.38)
- independent (1.67–5.32)
- indirect (2.16–4.86)
- individualistic (1.67–5.10)
- intragroup competitor (3.00–6.49)
- intragroup conflict avoider (1.84–5.69)
- intuitive (3.72–6.47)
- logical (3.89–6.58)
- micro-manager (1.60–6.58)
- orderly (3.81–6.34)
- procedural (3.03–6.10)
- provocateur (1.38–6.00)
- risk taker (2.14–5.96)
- ruler (1.66–5.20)
- self-effacing (1.85–5.23)
- self-sacrificial (3.00–5.96)
- sensitive (1.96–6.35)
- sincere (3.99–6.55)

- status-conscious (1.92–5.77)
- subdued (1.32–6.18)
- unique (3.47–6.06)

- wilful (3.06–6.48)
- worldly (3.48–6.18)

Although perhaps not defined as a leadership attribute, an awareness of cultural sensitivities is essential when conducting international business if embarrassing and costly mistakes are not to occur, such as:

- ☹ A US telephone company tried to market its products and services to Latinos by showing a commercial in which a Latino wife tells her husband to call a friend, informing her they would be late for dinner. The commercial bombed since Latin American women do not order their husbands around and their use of time would not require a call about lateness.

- ☹ A cologne for men pictured a pastoral scene with a man and his dog. It failed in Islamic countries as dogs are considered unclean.

- ☹ Procter & Gamble used a television commercial in Japan that was popular in Europe. The advertisement showed a woman bathing, her husband entering the bathroom and touching her. The Japanese considered this an invasion of privacy, inappropriate behaviour and in very poor taste.

- ☹ A Japanese manager in an American company was told to give critical feedback to a subordinate during a performance evaluation. Japanese use high-context language and are uncomfortable giving direct feedback. It took the manager five tries before he could be direct enough to discuss the poor performance so that the American understood.

SOURCE: http://www.kwintessential.co.uk/cross-cultural/cross-cultural-awareness.html

On a more significant scale, Rupert Murdoch's original business strategy for News Corporation's new satellite TV network, Star, was to use it to introduce its English-language programming library across Asia, as many of the target demographic were English-speaking. Shortly after purchasing Star, Murdoch described satellite TV as 'an unambiguous threat to totalitarian regimes everywhere'. However, this Westernized straight-talking approach was not appreciated by the Chinese government, which reacted by banning satellite TV dishes – a business catastrophe for News Corporation.

The message is clear: a major challenge for 21st-century leaders is to put in place measures within their organizations so as to operate effectively across the global business community – either within their own multicultural teams or when trading across international boundaries. Yet a 2008 study conducted jointly by Ashridge Business School and the UN Global Compact Principles for Responsible Management Education, entitled 'Developing the Global Leader of Tomorrow', found that whilst 76 per cent of senior executives believe that their organizations need to develop global leadership capabilities, only 7 per cent think they are doing so effectively.

BEST leadership quote

'With so many leaders in our hotels we need to create something that works in the context and culture that they live and work in. What we suggest might work in China, but not in the United States or India, so there has to be that gap where they can say "We understand what you are trying to achieve and here is how we need to execute it here, or this is the nuance we need to put on it." The better leaders learn how to craft what they say and how authentically they speak, which tends to work across cultures better than trying to be too prescriptive.'

Gregor Thain
VP Global Leadership Development
InterContinental Hotels

Thomas *et al* (2012) quote R Gopalakrishnan, executive director of India's Tata Group, as describing competing in the global marketplace as 'creative tensions', and proposed three attributes necessary to enhance the performance of global teams and their companies:

1 Global teams need clear operating procedures as a means of maintaining focus and enhancing their ability to speak with one voice. Simply encouraging a leadership team to 'think and act globally' fails to recognize the impact that cultural differences can have on business success. The research suggests that global teams must be very clear about their unique roles and responsibilities. Such an understanding can reduce the frustration and duplication of effort that can build up in diverse and dispersed workforce due to issues such as communication blockages, linguistic barriers, or different cultural perspectives.

   Clear operating procedures, often condensed to a few simple rules, can also alleviate tensions caused by operating across diverse markets. A CEO of a Chinese global IT company is quoted in the survey as explaining: 'Normally, someone can know whether or not they need to go elsewhere for a decision. But in China, everything is slightly different than we are used to – and we need to know how to navigate those differences, including when to make decisions and who should take them.' Critically, having laid-down procedures are likely to make it more likely that a decision will actually be made!

2 Effective global teams need to be agile and flexible – adjusting who makes decisions, and how, according to different business contingencies. A willingness to empower others to make decisions when situations require it was also seen as crucial to effective global leadership. Traditional structures may not be appropriate for decision-making on the international stage. Kingfisher, the home improvement retailer with brands across Western and Eastern Europe, Turkey and China, has forsaken the traditional hierarchical management structure for a global network of company specialists, such as supply-chain managers or internet development specialists. Ian Cheshire, group chief executive, explained that: 'We are going to work as a collective and intelligent network. Networks are the vehicle through which we can create common range.'

3 Global teams must be able to change policies and practices ahead of the rest of the organization so as to lead others into an uncertain future. They do this by:

- confronting challenging ideas and people as a means of identifying future scenarios;
- finding ways of analysing the mass output of enterprise IT systems in order to discern possible future trends and outcomes;
- the CEO and executive team taking personal responsibility for developing future global leaders within their organizations.

Perhaps the ultimate paradox for global leadership is that, whilst faster communications and easy accessibility of knowledge shrink the international business landscape, individual cultures will never homogenize to a fully global community. The most successful businesses will be those that understand and make provision for the nuances of different cultures. The most successful leaders will be those that adjust their style according to the characteristics of the situation at an international level, the nature of the task, and the cultural sensitivities and expectations of the people they deal with, both internally within their own organizations and externally across countries and continents.

As John Adair, professor of leadership studies at the United Nations, advised me:

> There is an emerging global body of knowledge that leaders of diverse groups should have a much clearer understanding of their generic role: that is, to appreciate that people from varied cultural backgrounds will have some common or human expectations of those that lead them as well as some specific ones that arise from their own distinctive history and way of life.

Chapter summary

Changes in the world of work, including increasing expectations of both employees and service users, are imposing new challenges on leaders, the most significant of which are:

- *Innovation:* the challenge here is to create an innovative and entrepreneurial culture that meets ever-increasing customer needs and, as a result, ensures the organization competes effectively within its primary sector of operation, either nationally or internationally.

    Development ideas should be encouraged and sought from all stakeholders: staff, service users, suppliers and all other strategic partners. Research has indicated that transformational and transactional leaders can have differing positive influences on management innovation in organizations, although transactional leadership can be more effective in smaller operations, whilst the transformational approach was found to offset the complexity of larger organizations and to encourage innovation across all levels.

- *Talent management:* this involves not only attracting exceptional individuals, but also developing and retaining them. Whilst in the modern competitive, knowledge-based business environment a company's success is increasingly determined by the calibre of its people, attracting and retaining talented individuals is an increasing challenge.

    It is the responsibility of senior leaders to create an effective talent management strategy, yet reports by the Institute of Leadership and Management suggest that, whilst HR managers are clear about the skills required of future leaders, mainly associated with interpersonal relations, significant blockages exist in creating a talent pipeline. A new way of thinking about talent management is proposed by McKinsey in Table 2.1.

- *Communications:* the 21st-century knowledge economy poses both threats and opportunities for leaders. Service users are increasingly using technology to influence their purchasing decisions, whilst also using it to share their experiences with other potential users. Hence, companies must harness the communication opportunities of the internet, and social media in particular, in order to innovate, differentiate and encourage positive customer interaction.

    Equally, companies must meet the expectations of their staff for transparency and information-sharing. Leaders who recognize this imperative take a personal involvement in creating a culture based upon mutual trust and shared values. It is incumbent, therefore, on leaders to develop the necessary skills to make best use of digital communications at a personal and strategic level.

- *Globalization:* in an expanding business world, organizations and their leaders have to appreciate the challenges it poses – both in terms of multicultural teams working in one location, and across international borders. Cultural norms can impact on leader–follower relations due to the behaviour and expectations of both parties.

The chapter listed a number of attributes that can contribute to, or hinder, leadership effectiveness across cultures. The most effective leaders will have the ability to adjust their style according to the cultural sensitivities of the people they deal with internally and externally.

Motivation
– the enduring principles

03

In this chapter we explore the concept of motivation, from seminal work undertaken by US psychologists, one theory of which my own personal experience continues to endorse, to a contemporary and rapidly growing branch of psychology that focuses on employees' well-being as a means of enhancing motivation at work, entitled positive psychology.

The word 'motivation' derives from the Latin verb *movere*, to move. Hence, having a motive is to have a stimulus to take action. The stimulus is an inner need – conscious, semi-conscious, or even unconscious – that leads to action in some form or other. In general terms, George Miller, one of the founders of cognitive psychology, described motivation as 'all those pushes and prods – biological, social and psychological – that defeat our laziness and move us, either eagerly or reluctantly, to action'. Within a work environment, Jones and George (2004) defined motivation as 'psychological forces that direct a person's behaviour in an organization, a person's level of effort, and a person's level of persistence in the face of obstacles'. It is obviously a fundamental requirement for leaders to understand and apply appropriate motivational stimuli at individual and group levels.

Such behaviour, effort and persistence may be generated from within a person, intrinsically, or from external, extrinsic sources. Intrinsic motivation is driven by an interest or enjoyment in the task itself: it exists within the individual, rather than being driven by external influences, such as a desire for reward or fear of punishment. Intrinsic motivation is derived from the nature of the job, in so far as the work satisfies personal needs or goals. We shall see that it is affected strongly by factors such as recognition, achievement, responsibility and empowerment.

Extrinsic motivation, on the other hand, refers to actions done to, and on behalf of, people for the purpose of motivating them. Examples are rewards (financial or otherwise), employee benefits, status or promotion. Competition can also be a powerful extrinsic motivator as it can encourage employees to outperform others, rather than simply enjoy the intrinsic rewards of the activity. In addition to the encouraging 'carrots' of positive extrinsic incentives there are also the enforcing 'sticks' associated with the negative consequences of poor performance that can be used, counter-intuitively perhaps, to motivate people.

The 1950s and 1960s saw a surge in research into the causes and effect of human motivation, notably in the United States. Three of the most notable resulting models were:

- Maslow's hierarchy of needs;
- McGregor's X–Y theory;
- Herzberg's hygiene and motivation factors.

Maslow's hierarchy of needs

One of the first to consider what motivates us into action, Sigmund Freud (1856–1939) argued that a person's make-up is determined by drives, impulses and desires that are not accessible to one's conscious awareness. Outward personality, what a person appears to be, is therefore just the tip of an iceberg, the remainder of which, the unconscious, lies hidden deep below. This psychoanalytical approach to understanding behaviour is, by its very nature, therefore, based upon a subjective assessment of what is going on in a person's mind.

Subsequent psychologists, notably B F Skinner (1904–90), sought ways of using objective, observable data to measure and understand a person's behaviour. Behaviourists such as Skinner explored how animals' actions could be influenced by external stimuli, such as obtaining food by turning a latch or negotiating a maze – a change of behaviour that became known as classical conditioning.

Abraham Maslow was a professor in psychology at Brandeis University from 1951 to 1969. He considered himself to be a psychological pioneer and in 1954 published a volume of papers under the title *Motivation and Personality*, which explained the model he entitled the hierarchy of needs. He described it as 'the third force', after psychoanalysis and behaviourism. It considered the whole person – his internal needs and potential for self-fulfilment – and was to be the forerunner of the humanistic psychology movement, which in turn paved the way for the positive psychology theory that is gaining favour in the 21st century. He proposed that a person is motivated not by extrinsic influences such as rewards or punishment, but by an intrinsic set of five needs, as portrayed in his hierarchy of needs (see Figure 3.1).

Maslow argued that all people are driven by needs, which he saw as being in a dynamic, interdependent relationship. We must satisfy each need in turn, starting with the first upon which our very survival depends. Once a lower need is satisfied it loses its power to motivate and we concentrate on achieving the next higher level, moving up the hierarchy until we satisfy

FIGURE 3.1   Maslow's hierarchy of needs

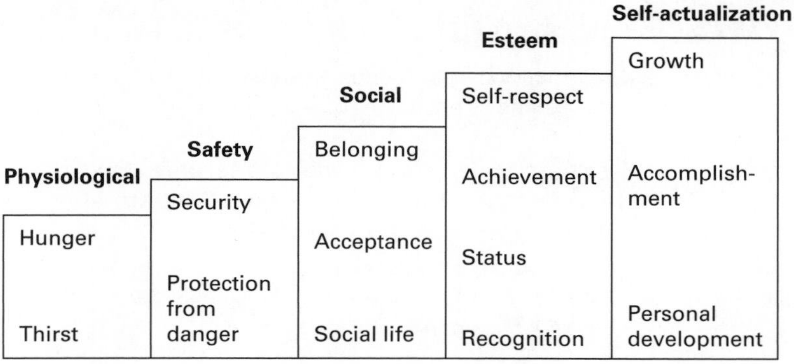

the need for self-actualization. However, the lower the need is in the hierarchy, the stronger and more basic it is. Hence, if a lower need is threatened we will turn our attention back to it in order to ensure that it is fulfilled. For example, if the team we belong to (social need) faces external threat we will defend it, even if our self-esteem could be compromised. Conversely, an individual will not work effectively in a team (social) if his or her job is at risk (safety).

Whilst Maslow's theory was well received at the time, and continues to be referenced to this date, it is difficult to see how it can be strictly applied by a leader within a working environment. The concept of a person travelling along the heightening steps, dispensing with each need once met, to then concentrate solely on the achievement of the next step appears overly formulaic. Moreover, individual employees will have a unique set of needs and values, which may well include those from Maslow's five groups – but not necessarily in that priority order. Take, for example, a creative person who is so intent on producing beautiful artwork (self-actualization) that she ignores her own personal physiological well-being; or a mountaineer who, in pursuit of the summit of his achievement, is prepared to put his life at risk. Maslow believed that the final, self-actualization of the need – what he described as 'everything one is capable of becoming' – could only be achieved by a small proportion of the population. We shall, however, see later in this chapter that self-actualization is a concept also addressed by more contemporary psychologists.

Although the strict interpretation of Maslow's model does pose several difficulties and has incurred some criticism from other social scientists, it does offer a powerful incentive for leaders to consider the needs of their employees. The best leaders ensure that the lower needs are met and then concentrate their efforts on achieving the upper needs of their people. It is therefore necessary to convert the five categories into practical benefits that leaders should ensure are provided for, such as is shown in Table 3.1.

TABLE 3.1   Practical applications of Maslow's hierarchy of needs

Need	Application in the Workplace
Physiological	Staff meals; available drinking water; flexible working arrangements; equitable rotas
Safety	Health and safety training and policies; protective workwear; job security; addressing bullying at work; employee pensions; available counselling
Social	Team development; social activities; embracing cultural diversity; promoting team success
Esteem	Recognizing and celebrating personal successes; appraisals; sharing positive customer feedback; recognizing length of service
Self-actualization	Offering training opportunities; career planning; delegation and empowerment; job rotation

McGregor's X–Y theory

Shortly after Maslow proposed his needs-based motivational theory, a fellow US social psychologist, Douglas McGregor, wrote a book entitled *The Human Side of Enterprise* (1960), in which he challenged business leaders to reconsider their assumptions about human behaviour: assumptions that are still unfortunately held by some less enlightened managers to this day. He argued that most leaders of that time believed that their people fundamentally disliked work and would, therefore, take steps to avoid it whenever they could. Workers feared taking responsibility; craved security; were relatively unambitious; and, hence, needed constant supervision. 'Most people must be coerced, controlled, directed and threatened with punishment to get them to put forth adequate effort towards the achievement of organizational objectives', was how McGregor described that belief. He termed this assumption theory X – the authoritarian management style.

He suggested, however, that there was an alternative view of employees: one that more accurately assessed their psychological make-up and formed a more effective managerial position. This alternative perspective assumed that taking an interest in their work is 'as natural as play or rest'; that creativity and ingenuity were widely held human qualities; that people usually accept, and often seek, responsibility; and commitment to objectives is a function of rewards associated with their achievement. Managers who accepted these counter-assumptions practised what McGregor termed theory Y – the participative management style.

In attempting to influence business leaders of his time, McGregor proposed that if their starting point was theory X their managerial approach would inevitably produce limited results or even fail completely. If they believed in 'the mediocrity of the masses', then their business would achieve only mediocrity. If, however, they wished to make the most of the potential of their workers and, in turn, reap the resulting rewards, they should adopt the assumptions of theory Y managers, who could be characterized as:

- authentic and true to their beliefs;
- willing to use delegation as an aid to develop team members;
- clear about acceptable standards of behaviour;
- able and willing to trust others and to receive trust in return;
- determined to support their team;
- receptive to people's hopes, fears and dignity;
- able to face facts honestly and squarely;
- encouraging of personal and team development;
- aware of their role in ensuring a happy and rewarding working environment.

It can be seen from the premise behind a theory Y manager's assumptions and resulting managerial style that McGregor drew heavily on the work of Maslow, published a mere six years previously. Theory Y managers recognize the higher-level hierarchical needs, notably those of esteem and self-actualization, and use their authority to ensure that policies and practices are in place to give employees every opportunity to realize them. What McGregor did, however, was to relate the concept of motivational needs to the workplace – converting them into a language that practising managers could understand and apply.

Like Maslow, who wrote largely for the general public rather than the academic community, McGregor was a pioneer of psychological thinking whose work was based upon limited empirical research. His basic assumption was that all people, not just the privileged few, possess the ability to exercise a high degree of imagination, ingenuity and creativity. Although more modern leadership theory would certainly not disregard such a position, at that time it was much more of an unproven hypothesis. Fortunately, at about the same time, the third psychologist in the contemporary trinity of motivational theorists, Frederick Herzberg, was conducting detailed research that suggested that both Maslow's and McGregor's hypotheses were, indeed, based upon sound psychological principles.

I will explore Herzberg's theory in some detail because my own personal experience in the field of leadership development continues to prove that his proposition in relation to motivational factors is as relevant today as it was when he first published it. It is, indeed, an enduring principle, and one that today's leaders should know and apply. My work with junior and middle managers repeatedly proves that what motivated employees in the middle of the last century are still powerful factors now, and will, I am convinced, continue to be so in the foreseeable future.

Herzberg's hygiene and motivation factors

> There are few problems of more basic importance to our culture than an understanding of the motivation to work. As with all problems of psychology, there is an abundance of opinion on this subject, most of which reflects personal attitudes or limited experience.
>
> (Herzberg, 1959)

Herzberg (1923–2000) was a clinical psychologist who believed that 'mental health is the core issue of our times'. One can see from the quotation above that Herzberg believed that an understanding of the psychology of motivation at work was of crucial importance – yet, at that time, little objective evidence was available to explain how increased motivation could be achieved. It was for both those reasons that he, along with colleagues Bernard Mausner and Barbara Bloch Snyderman, undertook the first of his research projects in this area, culminating in the publication of his seminal book *The Motivation to Work* in 1959.

It is interesting to compare the economic picture Herzberg painted in the book's preface, cited below, with that experienced by the Western world in the early years of the 21st century:

> Our economy is so variable that it would be foolish to predict its state when this volume reaches the public, but right now we are faced by significant unemployment, by an under-utilization of our industrial plant, and by a shift of interest from the problem of boredom and a surfeit of material things to a concern for the serious social problems of unemployment and industrial crisis. Yet the problem of people's relationships with their work continues to be a basic one. We should not overlook the fact that although the ebb and flow of our economy would produce occasional periods of over and of underemployment the problem of an individual's attitudes towards his job remains constant. In fact, it may be that during hard times the edge that will determine whether a concern will survive will be given by the level of morale within the personnel.

I believe, and will later substantiate, that not only has the socio-economic landscape described by Herzberg been experienced during the international economic crisis that began in 2007, but that his approach to understanding and developing motivation in the workplace remains relevant to this day.

The purpose of his study was relatively straightforward: 'To discover and then reinforce the kind of things that make people happier – to discover and then diminish the kind of things that make people unhappy', and involved interviewing 204 engineers and accountants from nine companies from Pittsburgh, which was a regional centre for heavy industry. Eight of the companies were manufacturers of differing size and nature of activity, and one was a major utility company. Each of the subjects were asked to recall any times when they felt exceptionally good or bad about their job – either because of a long-term sequence of events or a short-term incident – and how serious their feelings had been. On average, each person recalled between two and three experiences and all were encouraged to include both positive and negative attitudinal experiences. The researchers attempted to identify the relationships between the actual events, the feelings that were expressed by the workers and the effects that resulted. Essentially, the researchers wanted to determine why the attitude of the respondents had changed: what had happened and why that occurrence had affected their morale. Put simply, the sequence of investigation was: factor → attitudes → effects.

Table 3.2 lists the factors in order of their appearance, as a percentage, in the analysis of the respondents' reported events that produced high motivation.

TABLE 3.2 Percentages of factors in reported high-motivational events

Factor	%
1. Achievement	41
2. Recognition	33
3. The work itself	26
4. Responsibility	23
5. Advancement	20
6. Salary	15
7. Possibility of growth	6
8. Interpersonal relations – subordinate	6
9. Status	4
10. Interpersonal relations – superior	4
11. Interpersonal relations – peers	3
12. Supervision – technical	3
13. Company policy and administration	3
14. Working conditions	1
15. Personal life	1
16. Job security	1

The percentages total more than 100 per cent as more than one factor sometimes appeared for a single event.

Factors 1–5 are grouped together as 'high frequency' factors; factors 7–16 as 'low frequency'; with factor 6, salary, in a category of its own. The high-frequency factors were explained as:

- *Achievement* appeared in 41 per cent of the events that accompanied favourable job attitudes. Each one of the stories told by respondents (in Herzberg's study these were either male engineers or male accountants) involved the successful completion of a job.

BEST leadership quote

'People love success and everyone in this firm loves the fact that we were the best-performing law firm in The Sunday Times' survey and also Law Firm of the Year. These accolades are important but, personally, I am most proud of The Sunday Times' award as it demonstrates that our employees think that we are good.'

Kevin Gold
Managing Partner
Mishcon de Reya

- *Recognition* came from many sources, including supervisors, peers, customers or subordinates but was usually associated with achieving some sort of task.

BEST leadership quote

'I realize the value of all our staff and will often go to the receptionist or the administrator as they are as important as anyone else within the company. Being an inclusive business, our management teams are represented by all levels of staff.'

Carmen Watson
Chief Executive
Pertemps

- *The work itself* produced greater job satisfaction – either the specific nature of the work, or from achievement or recognition associated with it. Creativity, challenge, variation and an opportunity to see a job through to its conclusion were often mentioned as providing enhanced satisfaction.

BEST leadership quote

'It's about enjoying what you are doing; being given the opportunity to try new things and innovate; it's about interacting with supportive colleagues; being told you are doing a good job; being helped to train and develop for the next job; it's about having fun at work – it's a whole combination of things that make people believe that their self-worth is valued.'

Ian Munro
Group Chief Executive
New Charter Housing

- *Responsibility* included being allowed to work without supervision; being responsible for one's own efforts; being given responsibility for the work of others; and being given a new job with different responsibilities, but with no formal advancement.

BEST leadership quote

'We maximize the level of authority and autonomy that our managers and teams have in our individual businesses. This is because the more responsibility you give people, the more you trust them, the more explanation you give them, the greater the commitment they will have, because they are seriously engaged with the business. It is not just about saying,

'This is what the company is doing. This is where we are going.' You have to give people some responsibility and authority to make those decisions.'

William Rogers
Chief Executive
UKRD

- *Advancement* is self-explanatory in meaning that the employee was promoted – often unexpectedly. This factor was often related to feelings of growth, recognition, achievement and responsibility.

BEST leadership quote

'Our people strategy is rooted in two very simple questions: 'What does the business need from our people?' and 'What do our people value about working for us?' One of the answers to the first question is 'well-trained employees', and an answer to the second is 'being able to develop workplace skills'. Neither of those insights are particularly surprising in themselves, but fuse them together and the power is immense, because delivering what our business needs simultaneously delivers real value for our people, hence creating a powerful, virtuous circle.'

David Fairhurst
Chief People Officer, Europe
McDonald's Restaurants

Herzberg noted that these top five factors were associated with the job itself, whilst factors 7–16 were more about the characteristics of the context in which the job is done, explaining: 'The satisfiers related to the actual job. Those factors that do not act as satisfiers describe the job situation.' The latter group were described as:

- *The possibility of growth* increasing or decreasing was experienced by some subjects as their situation at work changed. A change of role may have offered promotion potential, although alternatively an employee could have been told that his or her lack of qualifications precluded any further advancement.
- *Interpersonal relations* related only to conversations of a non-social nature between the subject and another employee, be they superior, subordinate or peer.
- *Status* changes, such as reflected in the provision of a secretary or a company car, were only recorded when they were mentioned as being a factor in a respondent's feelings about his or her job.

- *Supervision* – technically this refers to instances where the competence or incompetence, fairness or unfairness of the supervisor was influential. Examples quoted involved a willingness, or otherwise, to delegate or to teach new skills.

- *Company policy and administration* took the form of two example types: one regarding the organization of their company, for example how effective lines of communication were; the second involving more harmful or beneficial effects of company policy, especially HR regulations.

- *Working conditions* included factors such as ventilation, lighting, tools, space and other environmental characteristics.

- *Personal life* included only instances where some aspect of the job affected the respondent's attitude towards his or her job. For example, enforced relocation that the employee's family were unhappy about.

- *Job security* or insecurity caused by the company's stability was recorded under this factor.

The researchers sought to determine whether all factors were major contributors to both job satisfaction and dissatisfaction. They had originally predicted that the factors influencing job satisfaction (1–5) would feature very infrequently in the stories involving job dissatisfaction, whilst the remaining factors would be major contributors to low motivation – which was proved to be the case. The factors involved in producing job satisfaction and high motivation are separate and distinct from those leading to negative feelings: the factors are not opposites of each other. The opposite of job satisfaction is not job dissatisfaction but, rather, no satisfaction; and similarly, the opposite of job dissatisfaction is not job satisfaction, but no job dissatisfaction.

It was for this reason that Herzberg coined the term 'motivation factors' for those that are intrinsic to the job, namely achievement, recognition for achievement, the work itself, responsibility, and growth or advancement. The remaining factors, being extrinsic to the job, he termed 'hygiene factors': 'for they act in a manner analogous to the principles of medical hygiene'. Good hygiene does not, in itself, produce good health, but a lack of it will cause disease. Moreover, in a medical facility, good hygiene is regarded as an expectation: few patients will comment on how clean a hospital ward is, yet will complain vigorously if it is *not* clean. As Maslow had previously stated, 'gratified needs are not active motivators'.

The final analysis of the data sought to identify how long the positive attitudinal changes lasted – and the findings suggested that factors relating to the work itself, responsibility and advancement, almost always result in long-term changes in positive job attitudes. However, changes in job attitude involving achievement or recognition are significantly more often short term. This does not mean that achievement and recognition are not important to positive job attitudes: they are still amongst the most frequently appearing factors resulting in long-term motivation.

Salary

In *The Motivation to Work*, Herzberg considered salary as a separate factor. In the interviews, the issue of financial compensation virtually always involved either wage or salary increases or unfulfilled expectations of such. As we see from Table 3.2 above, salary was the only factor – other than the five that Herzberg termed as motivators – that appeared in any significant frequency in the stories that described high points in job satisfaction. Further results showed that salary is about equal for long- and short-term positive attitudinal changes. However, the research also identified that for negative changes, salary appeared almost three times as often as a long-term effect as compared to a short-term one. The researchers concluded, therefore, that as an affecter of job attitudes, salary has more potency as a job dissatisfier than as a job satisfier.

Moreover, when salary was usually mentioned as producing low motivation it was associated with a feeling of unfairness of the remuneration system within the company. The system was often criticized as only offering wage increases grudgingly, or given too late; or in terms of inequitable pay differentials. In contrast, when salary was included in stories involving increased motivation it was associated with a person's achievement and resulting recognition – which meant more than the money itself. The researchers determined salary as a hygiene factor because it meets two kinds of avoidance needs for the employee. First, it helps avoid economic deprivation due to insufficient income. Second, and generally considered more significant for the respondents in their study, it negates the feeling of being treated unfairly. Salary and wages are, Herzberg suggested, very frequently at the top of the list of answers to the question 'What don't you like about your job?' but generally mid-table in response to the question 'What do you want from your job?' He also reported that in two other surveys into morale at work, comments on the equity of salary greatly outnumbered those on the absolute amount of remuneration. It was concluded, therefore, that, taking all the data into consideration, salary is more of a hygiene factor than a motivator.

BEST leadership quote

'People use money as a measurement tool: "I am a £30,000 person" or "I am a £50,000 person". If you are not happy where you are and you get more money, for a while you think, "Wow, now I feel better". But when you are not happy somewhere, this wears off very fast. Money is a base, but it is a less powerful motivational tool than pride, success, achievement and appreciation.'

Henry Engelhardt
Chief Executive
Admiral Group

It should be mentioned that salary, as reported in *The Motivation to Work*, was defined as the workers' weekly or monthly predetermined pay, not including any bonuses or other financial incentive schemes. Herzberg does, however, seek to explain the success of some incentive schemes and gives examples of companies where they have increased production, job satisfaction and company loyalty. He makes the point, however, that in many cases the plans were often associated with the workers accepting greater *responsibility* and were given in *recognition* of resulting *achievements*: thus meeting more than one motivational factor.

Self-actualization

Recall that self-actualization was the highest level in Maslow's hierarchy of needs, which he described as 'everything one is capable of becoming'. He equated it with what he called 'psychological health' – a universal urge in any person to develop and realize all his or her human potential, 'the full use and exploitation of talents, capacities, potentialities etc'. In his book *The Farther Reaches of Human Nature* (1971) Maslow explained that:

> Self-actualizing people are, without one single exception, involved in a cause outside their own skin, in something outside of themselves. They are devoted, working at something, something that is very precious to them – some calling or vocation in the old sense, the priestly sense. They are working at something which fate has called them to somehow and which they work at and which they love, so that the work–joy dichotomy in them disappears.

Herzberg takes up the term self-actualization, stating that the factors that lead to positive job attitudes, the five motivational factors, do so because they satisfy the individual's need for self-actualization in his or her work:

> Man tends to actualize himself in every area of his life, and his job is one of the most important areas. The conditions that surround the doing of the job cannot give him this basic satisfaction; they do not have this potentiality. It is only from the performance of a task that the individual can get the rewards that will reinforce his aspirations.

He explained that, whilst, the extrinsic factors surrounding the context of the job (hygiene factors) meet the needs of the individual for avoiding un-pleasant situations, it is the motivational factors that offer the opportunity to reach one's potential. The former encourage avoidance behaviour, the latter fulfilling the actuating need. Both kinds of factors meet the needs of the employee but it is the motivators that bring about job satisfaction and increased performance at work.

Relating Herzberg's proposition directly to Maslow's hierarchy of needs: physiological, safety and social needs will cause dissatisfaction if not met but have little potential to motivate, whilst meeting the needs of self-esteem and self-actualization could result in more positive and enduring job satis-faction. Both Maslow and Herzberg, therefore, combine to reinforce the onus on leaders to use motivational factors to empower and enable their people to achieve their higher needs within their workplace.

Subsequent research

Herzberg's study, the subject of his book *The Motivation to Work*, involved interviews with only two worker profiles: male engineers and male accountants. However, the results recorded few significant differences in their reported causes of job dissatisfaction and satisfaction, which led the researchers to argue that the findings could be applied beyond the small sample of 204 respondents they used. They did, though, recognize that this was merely an inference – one that should be tested on larger samples over a broader spectrum of educational and occupational backgrounds.

In Herzberg's paper, 'One more time: how do you motivate employees?', printed in the *Harvard Business Review* in 1968, he reported the findings of 12 different investigations undertaken subsequent to his original research. The same methodology was used by different research teams interviewing 1,685 male and female employees from a wide range of industries and across many countries.

The results, summarized in Figure 3.2, confirmed Herzberg's original findings that motivational factors were the primary cause of satisfaction, whilst hygiene factors were the primary cause of unhappiness at work.

With a view to further testing Herzberg's theory, Bassett-Jones and Lloyd (2005) surveyed 3,200 workers, using work-based suggestion schemes as a research model and found that: 'money and recognition do not appear to be primary sources of motivation in stimulating employees to contribute ideas. However, in line with Herzberg's predictions, factors associated with intrinsic satisfaction play a more important part.'

More recently, a global survey of 1,047 executives, managers and employees from a range of sectors, undertaken by *McKinsey Quarterly* in 2009, reinforced the fact that non-financial motivators such as praise, communications with one's leader, and being given the opportunity to adopt a leadership role were more effective than financial incentives, as detailed in Table 3.3.

FIGURE 3.2 Factors affecting job attitudes, as reported in 12 investigations

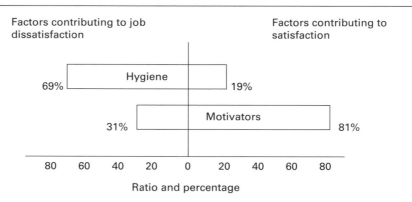

TABLE 3.3   June 2009 McKinsey global survey

	Effectiveness (percentage of respondents answering 'extremely' or 'very effective')
Non-Financial Incentives	
Praise from immediate manager	67
Attention from leaders	63
Opportunities to lead projects or teams	62
Financial Incentives	
Performance-based cash bonuses	60
Increase in base pay	52
Stock or stock options	35

Conclusions

Herzberg's research, subsequently supported by similar studies involving a wider diversity of sample size, offers the following conclusions:

1   Workers are motivated to a greater extent, and for longer periods, by factors that are intrinsic to their job and offer the opportunity for psychological growth and self-actualization. Moreover, they have little impact on job dissatisfaction. These motivational factors are achievement, recognition, the work itself, responsibility and advancement.

2   Factors that are extrinsic to the job, termed hygiene factors, meet basic biological needs and cause dissatisfaction if not met. However, they have little motivational effect as increases to – or improvement of – these factors quickly become regarded as an expectation or entitlement. They include supervision, status, job security, working conditions and company policy.

3   Salary was found to be more powerful as a job dissatisfier than a satisfier, as it was often related to a feeling of inequality, inequity or inefficient company administration. For these reasons it was included within the list of hygiene factors.

4   Hygiene and motivational factors are separate and distinct as they meet different sets of needs: they are not opposites. Consequently, the opposite of job satisfaction is not dissatisfaction, it is 'no satisfaction'.

My findings

I have spent a lifetime leading teams within UK service industries and have always found that people are more highly motivated by intrinsic factors than those relating directly to the job they undertake. The effect of receiving praise from those they serve, resulting in formal and informal recognition for the extra effort they have expended to delight the customer, is what makes work in the hospitality industry, for example, so potentially rewarding. For the last 15 years or so, I have been delivering leadership training across different sectors and to different levels of management and have had opportunities to test my beliefs with the delegates. Near the commencement of most courses I ask them to consider a list of 11 factors and to grade them in terms of how motivational they are to them as individuals, in their current employment role. The factors, listed in alphabetical order, are, in fact, Herzberg's hygiene and motivational factors – although the trainees are unaware of that, or their significance as a motivational theory.

The factors are explained to them and then they are asked to score 1 for the factor that motivates them most – through to 11 for the one that has the least effect. The questionnaires are collected and analysed, in advance of a session devoted to Herzberg's theory later in the course. All the individual scores for each factor are added up and then divided by the number of returns in order to produce group average scores that the respondents can compare with their own individual rankings.

The results, over many courses, are remarkably consistent: whilst individual scores vary according to the views of each person, without exception the top five factors that the group as a whole register as being the most motivational are Herzberg's motivational factors. Their relative positions within the top five vary, but a hygiene factor has never featured in the top five group scores. I believe that this is a very strong endorsement of my experience and beliefs, as confirmed by Herzberg's theory. It reinforces the imperative that, whilst leaders must seek to understand the personal motivational factors of each individual team member, they must also provide every opportunity for followers to grow and achieve their potential.

In 2013, I worked with all levels of management employed in the UK properties of a large international group of luxury hotels. In separate sessions with team leaders, departmental heads and the executive team I invited participants to complete the questionnaire, as detailed above. Table 3.4 details the results in terms of relative ranking and scoring, with the scores being the average for all respondents within the group stated, bearing in mind that they allocated one point to the most motivational factor, through to the least factor receiving 11 points.

Whilst it is appreciated that, in terms of sample size and specific industry sector, these results should not be considered to be of authoritative value, they are remarkably consistent and offer a persuasive indication of the psychological principles that leaders should use to underpin strategies designed to enrich the working lives of their people and thus create high levels of lasting motivation.

TABLE 3.4 Results of motivational questionnaire completed by three levels of management of a luxury hotel group

Executive Team		Departmental Heads		Team Leaders	
Score	Factor	Score	Factor	Score	Factor
1.2	Achievement	1.6	Achievement	2.9	Achievement
2.2	Work itself	3.4	Work itself	3.2	Work itself
4.2	Responsibility	4.0	Recognition	4.3	Responsibility
4.4	Recognition	5.7	Advancement	4.6	Advancement
5.8	Advancement	5.8	Responsibility	5.0	Recognition
6.2	Supervision	6.1	Salary	6.5	Salary
7.6	Status	6.5	Status	6.9	Supervision
7.8	Job security	6.9	Job security	7.3	Status
8.0	Salary	8.4	Supervision	7.3	Job security
8.4	Working conditions	8.6	Working conditions	8.6	Working conditions
10.2	Company policy	9.1	Company policy	9.3	Company policy

Positive psychology

For Herzberg, the words 'motivation' and 'happiness' were virtually interchangeable. When explaining one aspect of the interrelationship between hygiene and motivation factors he stated: 'The factors in our study that made people happy with their jobs turned out to be different from the factors that made people unhappy with their jobs.' Happiness contributed to job satisfaction, which in turn enhanced job performance.

The extent of happiness in a person is one of the measures of a branch of psychology that has emerged in the 21st century, entitled positive psychology. Interestingly, the term was, in fact, first coined by Maslow (1954) when he entitled one of the chapters of his book *Motivation and Personality* 'Towards a Positive Psychology'. The modern movement was, though, advanced by former president of the American Psychology Association, Martin Seligman, in his 2002 book *Authentic Happiness: Using the New Positive Psychology to Realise Your Potential for Lasting Fulfilment*.

Seligman, a recognized authority on issues such as depression, pessimism and self-help, kick-started the movement by controversially proposing that psychology should reverse its direction: from focusing on a 'disease' model, which sought to determine what was wrong with people and then to find solutions to the problem, to concentrate on what was going right and to find ways of increasing people's happiness, satisfaction and well-being. Positive psychology promotes the benefits of positive emotions and individual strengths that are linked to successful outcomes. How people behave, at work and elsewhere, is influenced by the way they think and feel. If individuals are demoralized and unhappy they are likely to be less creative and productive than those who are engaged, happy and motivated – less likely to achieve any level of self-actualization.

In essence, positive psychology means concentrating on people's strengths, rather than their weaknesses, and it is a concept that is gaining momentum in many areas of life. Indeed, in July 2011 Seligman encouraged the British prime minister David Cameron to consider measuring well-being, in addition to financial wealth, as a means of assessing the prosperity of the nation. Seligman lists the three pillars of his model to be:

- *Positive experiences:* in the past – well-being, contentment and satisfaction; in the present – experiences of happiness; and in the future – optimism.
- *Positive individual traits:* enabling people to enjoy 'a good life' due to the expression of, for example, vocation, wisdom, integrity, meaning and future-mindedness.
- *Positive institutions:* fostering and encouraging positive experiences through providing engaging and meaningful work.

It is this last pillar that we will be exploring here – how leaders should apply positive psychology as a means of motivating their people, and enabling them to realize their potential within the workplace, thus resulting in better productivity, engagement and retention. Proponents argue that focusing on positive emotions is not about creating a 'happy-clappy', pink and fluffy environment where employees wander around continually smiling at each other. Psychologist Dr Robert Biswas-Diener, managing director of Positive Acorn and lecturer at Portland State University explains:

> Organizations don't have some kind of moral necessity to ensure that their employees are happy all the time. That just isn't realistic: people have bad days, get stuck in traffic, get parking tickets and have to deal with all sorts of emotional setbacks. However, I do think that organizations do bear some responsibility for creating a non-toxic workplace – and when they do so, what they get as an almost natural by-product is positive workers and that pays off for them!

BEST leadership quote

'I believe in fun. I believe that people should come to work and have a good time. I believe that because when people are having fun they are more productive: they work harder and they are more engaged. It may cost more up front but it pays off on the bottom line many times over.'

Kevin Gold
Managing Partner
Mishcon de Reya

John Lewis's happiness principle

One of the best-known proponents of the 'happiness principle' is the John Lewis Partnership. It was conceived by Spedan Lewis, whose father had opened the John Lewis department store in Oxford Street, London. Whilst convalescing from a riding accident, Spedan Lewis began to formulate ideas about the future of the business, based upon better working conditions for employees and a more equitable share of its profits. In 1920 the first profit-sharing scheme was introduced, along with a representative staff council. It would appear that he was an inspirational leader with views well in advance of his time.

The concept of employees being partners in the company continues to the present day, with the organization's stated purpose is 'the ultimate happiness of all its members, through their worthwhile and satisfying employment in a successful business'. Sir Stuart Hampson, chairman of the partnership between 1982 and 2007, explained:

> In retailing, some jobs can be very routine and hard. Our ownership structure, which allows our partners (employees) to share the responsibilities of ownership as well as its rewards – profit, knowledge and power – helps create job satisfaction and engagement. People who are very commercial but have no sense of staff engagement are not judged to be successful managers here. Our reward development and promotion strategies are geared towards these twin attributes.

This approach is, in spirit, the very opposite of the hard-nosed adoption of the 'shareholder value' model of capitalism. Rather than assuming that everyone is motivated by financial return, the John Lewis Partnership assumes that people, whilst seeking and expecting a reasonable return from their labour, are motivated by higher principles, such as contributing towards the success of an organization in which they share ownership. By making employee well-being its core purpose, it conceives happiness as being of inestimable value in itself, as well as being the foundation of a successful and sustainable business.

Some would say that it is just this alternative view that has seen the John Lewis Partnership ride out the economic crises over the turn of the 21st century better than many other retailers that place shareholder value above all other factors.

Strengths-based approach

In Seligman's initial exploration of the concept of positive psychology he sought to identify what human strengths exist that could counterbalance human frailty. He concluded that there are, indeed, a discreet number of human character strengths that are a-cultural, a-historical, universal and quantifiable (Peterson and Seligman, 2004). In 2006 he suggested that some strengths – such as zest, hope, curiosity, gratuity and love – positively predict happiness and life satisfaction across one's entire life. Therefore, it would be in a person's interest to cultivate such strengths, which he termed 'signature strengths', just as it would be for a workplace leader.

Alex Linley, founding director of the Centre for Applied Positive Psychology (CAPP), in his book *Average to A+* (2008) presents a performance-based view of strengths, which he defines as: 'a pre-existing capacity for a particular way of behaving, thinking or feeling that is authentic, energizing to the user, and enables optimal functioning, development and performance'. Whilst accepting Seligman's list of strengths as being universal, he goes on to suggest that humanity has also developed niche strengths, of which his team at CAPP have identified over 100. He suggests that all people will possess elements of both signature or niche strengths, and how they are expressed is infinite, as each person brings to any particular situation a unique combination of strengths, experience and personality.

Linley's approach to positive psychology is that leaders should identify and harness people's natural strengths as a route to increasing levels of happiness and, as a result, enhancing performance: 'Positive psychology focuses on what people can do well, what they are exceptionally good at, and what it takes for people to flourish so they can perform at their best and give their best contribution.' Linley contends that two common approaches to HR management actually mitigate against this approach, namely:

- *Performance appraisals* – Linley estimates that these typically involve leaders spending 20 per cent of the time discussing what the employee is good at, and the remaining time considering the areas he or she needs to improve in. 'It is a debilitating, demotivating and disengaging process,' says Linley. He further suggests that decades of research have proved that people don't tend to change much over time. Hence, if a person has been with an organization for 10 years, and has had 10 annual appraisals, the same developmental issues will tend to be repeated every time.

- *Competency frameworks* – these can also be counterproductive as they are based upon the principle that everyone needs to be competent in all aspects of his or her role. Linley argues that this broad-brush approach has led to 'the curse of mediocrity' in British industry.

Whilst areas of serious underperformance should be addressed, action should only be taken when they are relevant and crucial to task outcomes. Clearly, a team leader needs to inspire his or her team members – but perhaps less important is an ability to write detailed, grammatically correct reports.

The concept of realizing strengths is linked to that of intrinsic motivation – doing things willingly and enthusiastically because we enjoy doing them, as opposed to being encouraged by some external, extrinsic incentive. The sense of engagement experienced when we are working to our strengths manifests itself through rapid learning, losing a sense of time, repeated and effective task completion, an attraction towards certain tasks, and a real pleasure in performing them.

Sarah Lewis in her book *Positive Psychology at Work* (2011) lists the fundamentals of the strengths-based approach as:

1 Focusing on what is right, what is working, what is strong.

2 Recognizing strengths as part of our basic nature; hence every person has strengths and deserves respect for them.

3 Believing our areas of greatest potential are in the areas of our greatest strengths.

4 Believing that we succeed by addressing our weaknesses only when we are also making the most of our strengths.

5 Believing that using our strengths is the smallest thing we can do to make the biggest difference.

Applying the motivational principle of strength-based positive psychology requires leaders to take a strategic look at the individuals within their team in order to identify particular capabilities. Sometimes they will be readily apparent – but not always. People who have opportunities to use their strengths will show a real sense of energy and engagement, sometimes being so engrossed in the task in hand that time flies by unnoticed. They may also demonstrate a tendency to prioritize tasks that require them to utilize their strengths over those that do not.

There are a number of tools that help leaders identify employees' strengths, as well as their own. One is the online questionnaire offered by the VIA Institute of Character, which can be found at **www.viastrengths.org**. On completion of the questionnaire, respondents are provided with a printout of their top five 'signature strengths' such as: perseverance, love, gratitude, honesty and hope.

Once identified, it is the leader's responsibility to allow people the opportunity to use their strengths to the best degree. That may mean simply reallocating tasks or reorganizing job roles so that people can spend more of their time doing what they are good at. Employees with complementary strengths could be paired together, or teams could be assembled for specific tasks requiring particular strengths.

Alex Linley and Nicky Page from CAPP propose a five-step approach to building a strengths-based organization:

1 *Ensure that you have a deep and mature understanding of strengths.* Strengths are not just the 'things that people are good at' but, as we define them, 'pre-existing capacities for a particular way to behaving, thinking or feeling that is authentic and energizing to the user and enable optimal functioning, development and performance'.

2 *Know where the best place is for you to begin.* All organizations are collections of teams. As such, building a strengths-based organization can begin with building a strengths-based culture within a specific team. If you have the option, make this the leadership team.

3 *Understand your options for taking the approach more widely into the organization.* These can include a traditional cascade model;

taking a 'deep slice' of the organization, using a particular business unit or geographical location; or 'lighting fires' – following people's enthusiasm from the ground up.

4 *Recognize the parameters.* Do existing appraisal processes fit with a strengths approach? What about performance management processes? Consider a strengths audit to help you answer these questions and explore your options for what you can do about them. Simple shifts in philosophy and emphasis can be all that is needed.

5 *Be patient.* Creating a strengths-focus in an individual, a team or an organization does not happen overnight. Take your time, understand what works for you, and progress and embed accordingly. Ensure success by evaluating your approach at each stage and refining or refocusing as appropriate.

An example of how this approach has been applied to change the leadership culture of an organization undergoing far-reaching change is detailed in the case study below.

CASE STUDY   Positive psychology

BAE Systems

In 2007 several senior HR executives from BAE attended a consultancy course delivered by Alex Linley, founding director of the Centre for Applied Positive Psychology (CAPP), and, following the event, the head of HR at BAE Air Support approached Linley to discuss how positive psychology could help with her company's business challenges. Its traditional centralized business model was changing in that, rather than clients going to the company, it was beginning to provide services at clients' locations.

BAE Systems is a global defence, security and aerospace company with approximately 107,000 employees worldwide. The company delivers a full range of products and services for air, land and naval forces, as well as advanced electronics, security, information technology solutions and customer support services. Its Air Support business unit was essentially a traditional engineering organization that designed and built aircraft, but was moving to become a more customer-oriented function that provided maintenance and support. This meant that some of its 12,000 people were moving from its two major engineering centres to work on specific RAF bases across the UK: working alongside RAF personnel and, in some cases, managing RAF personnel in the process. The company recognized that this required a significant cultural shift in leadership mentality and practice.

Described by Sean Watts, head of HR, Resourcing and Organizational Development, as 'a challenging HR agenda', the business transformation process began by working with an industrial artist to produce a poster that illustrated for managers and staff the challenges ahead – The Big Picture Project. From this it became clear that, as Watts explained: 'Leadership development was the success priority for us. Board members came to us and said: "Yep, we're up for this, but it is going to be a different leadership challenge and we need help in order to understand what we have to do differently."'

Hence, Linley and his team from CAPP were brought in to work with the company's senior management team (SMT), as recommended by step two of his and colleague Nicky Page's five-step approach detailed above.

The CAPP consultants interviewed all 16 board members, 20 other senior executives and a few other key stakeholders, including the HR director, in order to gauge perceptions of what leadership success meant for BAE, both now and in the future. This led to the production of a 'leadership strengths profile' for the board, which included several indicators for each of the identified strengths. Board members were then invited to score themselves against these indicators, both in terms of performance and the extent to which they were an area of strength.

As a result of this exercise, the board was allocated several key business tasks: ones that had been on the agenda for a while but had never been tackled successfully. However, rather than being shared out according to job function, they were allocated according to identified personal strengths, with a requirement to report back in one month's time. Members still had their normal, challenging job roles but the additional projects they had been given were things they would have been naturally drawn to and involved tasks they found enjoyable and energizing.

Linley recalls: 'It was a fantastic experience going back a month later. It was like getting a grade-A report at school, as all the projects were moving on positively. This was the big validation point for this approach, where the board told me "Yes, we like this; we want to take this forward."' Whilst starting with such a radical approach at board level may be considered to be risky, Watts explained: 'It is a case of risk versus return. What we have found is that because they have embraced it so well, we've got a degree of buy-in now.'

Subsequent application included:

- individual and team development from a strengths perspective;

- leadership masterclasses on topics including engagement and communication, strategic management and focus, and strengths-based leadership development;

- individual strengths coaching, including the design, development and delivery of a coach selection and matching process, leading to the provision of one-to-one coaching over a 6- or 12-month period;

- senior team coaching and board facilitation for the SMT as a whole over an 18-month period.

Linley and his team received a good deal of encouraging anecdotal feedback: 'It's been very positive. People have talked about ways in which they have made subtle changes that have had a profound impact and of more substantial changes that they are now trying to embed.' More specifically, CAPP recorded that, as a result of the project:

- There was significantly greater teaming across the SMT, with people combining in a variety of different ways to deliver the outcomes that were needed.
- There were observable behavioural differences reported by peers, staff and direct reports.
- Management team members reported feeling more authentic, engaged, energized and happier.
- They were focused on what needed to be delivered, and sharper in their decision-making.
- Above all, they delivered better leadership performance – and that was what the project was all about.

However, whilst one of the stated outcomes was increased happiness within the workforce, Linley made the point that a strengths-based approach is not merely an extension of the current understanding of the importance of happiness and well-being at work. 'As Aristotle described it, happiness is something that comes about through doing the right thing, rather than something that you pursue and achieve for its own ends,' he says. 'So I would argue – and the data supports this – that when you adopt a strengths approach, increased engagement and happiness is one of the results. But was that what we set about to achieve with BAE? No, it was about business performance.'

Watt supports this position, explaining: 'If someone were the greatest strategist in the world but terrible at people management, we wouldn't be able to tolerate that, no matter how strong they were in other areas. So it's about playing to people's strengths where possible, but it is also recognizing that you need to be fairly robust, particularly at board level. It's common sense.' Linley describes it as different to the traditional competency framework, where all tasks have to be completed to the highest standard: 'Get your strengths up to an A grade – absolutely make the most of them. But if there is a discipline that you're not so good at, but that you need, then get that up to a pass, a C grade.' Ideally, a job should be balanced so that the worker does less of the things he or she is not so good at and spends more time on things he or she excels at.

Chapter summary

This is an extended summary, which I hope will be seen as a nine-point blue-print for leaders to apply as a means of enhancing the levels of motivation of their people:

1 *Ensure that all followers' needs are met.* Consider those human needs defined by Maslow – suggested practical applications of which are listed in Table 3.1 – but not necessarily in the consecutive ascending order of his hierarchy. Each person will have a unique set of motivational stimuli and it is the leader's responsibility to understand what motivates each member of the team and then to actively apply measures to maximize that motivational potential.

2 *Believe in your people.* Adopt the assumptions of a McDonald's 'theory Y' manager, namely:
    - most people take an interest in their job;
    - creativity and ingenuity are common qualities amongst workers;
    - people usually willingly accept, and often seek, additional responsibility;
    - people respond well to rewards associated with achieving objectives.

3 *Set a personal example.* Be acutely aware of the need for a certain personal quality, explained by Adair (1996) as being: 'The first and golden rule of motivation is that you will never inspire others unless you are inspired yourself. Only a motivated leader motivates others. Example is the great seducer. Enthusiasm inspires, especially when combined with trust. For motivation is a virus: it is caught, not taught. If a leader is enthusiastic and motivated it is contagious!'

4 *Find ways to create high levels of job satisfaction within your team members* by:
    - adding variety and interest to their work by, for example, rotating their roles and tasks;
    - providing work that is challenging but where objectives and targets can be achieved;
    - reducing bureaucracy and controls to the lowest risk levels possible;
    - allow people the opportunity to use and develop their skills;
    - stress the fact that they are contributing to the success of their team and organization;
    - ensure that supervisor–worker relationships are positive and constructive;
    - create a fun working environment;
    - encourage positive work–life balance.

5 *Offer additional responsibility* to those who desire it and, with support, are capable of embracing it. Leaders should not be afraid

of delegating some of their responsibilities to capable junior staff – transferring the ownership of a specific task, along with the authority to carry it out. Even more motivational in terms of giving additional responsibility is empowerment – giving a junior member of staff the authority to make decisions on his or her own, without having to seek the approval of a manager. As Adair (1996) says: 'The more that people share in the decisions which directly affect them the more they are motivated to carry them out.'

Considering the possibility of employees adopting the responsibility of a leadership role is another powerful way of motivating selected staff and of developing their leadership skills. One HR manager was quoted in *McKinsey Quarterly* for November 2009 as explaining that involvement in special projects: 'makes people feel like they're part of the answer – and part of the company's future'.

Not only are these suggestions related to Herzberg's motivation factor of responsibility, they also offer the opportunity of using a second factor, advancement, as a creator of enhanced employee motivation. By taking on additional roles and/or tasks, and developing the skills necessary to successfully complete them, the person is being offered the potential to grow as an individual, an employee and a team member. Whether or not such development leads to actual promotion, the person will be motivated in the knowledge that he or she is advancing personally and within his or her work environment: moving towards Maslow's state of self-actualization.

6   *Allow followers to succeed.* A sense of achievement was the most frequently mentioned factor in Herzberg's interviews (Table 3.2) as well as the one resulting in the longest-lasting motivational feelings. It was also the most motivational factor stated by all three groups of respondents in my own survey (Table 3.4). In Herzberg's study, he explained that 'each one of this group of stories revolves about successful completion of a job'. It is therefore the leader's responsibility to facilitate a feeling of successful job achievement by setting challenging but attainable goals and then removing the barriers that may prevent their successful achievement. Recall that House's (1997) path–goal model of leadership, as explained in Chapter 1, included the achievement-oriented style, in which the leader sets challenging goals and has the confidence in followers to achieve them.

Too often, employees are faced with the demoralizing fate of Sisyphus, a king in Greek mythology who offended the gods and was thus punished by being required to roll a huge stone up a steep hill in Hades, only to watch it roll back down again – whereupon he would begin the task again, indefinitely. Yet leaders are in a position to review organizational processes in order to ensure that employees have the opportunity to achieve meaningful – and hence, motivational – job completion.

7 *Recognize and celebrate achievement.* Herzberg analysed the interrelationships between the five motivational factors: that is, how often they appeared together in the stories told by the respondents. He found that in the stories in which recognition was coded as a factor, achievement was also mentioned 61 per cent of the time – the highest relationship between any of the factors. Hence, the motivational potential of an employee achieving a task is amplified greatly by having that achievement recognized by practical means such as:

- day-to-day recognition such as handwritten notes, team lunches or on-the-spot award certificates that are low-cost but high-touch methods;
- above-and-beyond recognition relating to an employee's exceptional work that has contributed to the organization's goals;
- career recognition celebrates employees' length of service within the organization;
- celebration events provide an opportunity to formally thank individuals and teams for their contribution to key projects or the meeting of company targets.

Also see Table 3.5 overleaf for an exercise, entitled 'Reap the rewards of recognition', which I use within my leadership training courses to encourage delegates to consider ways of recognizing the value of their team members.

8 *Provide fair financial rewards.* Herzberg's research found that money has more power to make workers dissatisfied and unhappy than it has to motivate them. Generous pay increases tend to have less effect as we psychologically adjust to the new level of income. Although Herzberg concluded that the impact of salary on dissatisfaction was more significant than its effect as a motivator, its powerful influence as a demotivator warrants inclusion in this list. Leaders must ensure that a perceived inequitable pay structure does not mitigate against other policies and practices designed to increase workplace motivation and, hence, performance.

9 *Identify people's strengths and utilize their potential.* Only seek to address their weaknesses – by, for example, focusing heavily on improvement areas during appraisals or expecting all employees to be competent, or better, in all aspects of their jobs – when the shortcomings are critical to the execution of their primary role.

People are happiest and most motivated when they feel they are fully utilizing their inherent or learnt strengths. Leaders should, therefore, be continually aware of high-level capabilities that may, or may not, be evident within employees' current job responsibility. Once identified, it is the leader's responsibility to ensure that the person is given the opportunity to fully employ their strengths for the benefit of the organization.

TABLE 3.5   'Reap the rewards of recognition' leadership exercise

Please tick the boxes of the actions that could NOT be taken to recognize the value of your team members:

☐ Ask if they enjoyed their days off or holidays
☐ Send a letter of appreciation to, or telephone, their family
☐ Provide recognition boards in the workplace for colleagues to record good work
☐ Publish examples of individual or team success on company website, newsletter, etc
☐ Remember special days, eg birthdays or anniversaries
☐ When thanking people, link the praise to company values
☐ Include all staff, eg part-timers, support staff, those from other departments
☐ Provide photographs of them at work for them to take home
☐ Publish customer compliments
☐ 'Catch someone doing something right!'
☐ Show an interest in their family
☐ Provide opportunities for people to shine
☐ Send a hand-written letter to recognize a particular achievement
☐ Introduce Employee of the Month/Week scheme
☐ Use training opportunities as a reward for good work
☐ Consult with the employee's family, friends or colleagues to identify the best reward
☐ Every year, celebrate the date the employee started with the company
☐ Organize formal or informal staff get-togethers to celebrate team successes
☐ Use extra time off as a reward
☐ Set challenging but achievable goals and then celebrate their achievement
☐ Use experienced staff as coaches or mentors for those less experienced or new starters
☐ Ask for their ideas and input
☐ Use personalized 'Thank You' cards
☐ Demonstrate that you understand the challenges of their jobs
☐ Involve senior staff in recruiting new team members – formally or informally
☐ Offer additional responsibility to recognize potential for advancement
☐ Give them an extra day off for their birthday/wedding anniversary, etc
☐ Send experienced staff to check up on the competition
☐ Recognize achievement by a free meal at your establishment for employee and partner
☐ Tell your boss when one of your staff does well (and make sure he/she is aware you did)
☐ Make a note of examples of good work for their next annual appraisal
☐ Invite your boss to be involved in recognizing individual and team successes
☐ Use humorous lapel badges

How many actions did you tick as being impossible to introduce?
How many are left for you to consider using in order to
Reap the Rewards of Recognizing the value of your team members?

The emotionally intelligent leader

– identifying and controlling emotions

Here I continue the theme contained in the previous chapter, which explained how positive psychology seeks to increase people's happiness, optimism and a feeling of well-being. Positive emotions are seen to be linked to successful outcomes at individual, team and organizational levels. Optimists, for example, are more likely to maintain a positive attitude in the face of adversity and, hence, face up to and overcome challenges in their personal and working lives.

Emotions, positive or negative, heavily influence how we conduct our lives: they largely determine how we see ourselves, our self-awareness; how we manage ourselves, for example how we react to stressful situations; and how we build relationships in family, social or working environments. Hence, the ability to express and control our feelings is crucial to our emotional well-being, but so is our ability to receive, interpret and respond to other people's emotions. Imagine the potential problems of not being able to identify that a friend was sad or an employee was angry. This ability to perceive, evaluate and control one's own emotions, and those of others, is called emotional intelligence (EI), or sometimes emotional quotient (EQ), and is a crucial skill required of leaders at all levels.

Recognition of the importance of emotions to the human psyche dates back to humanistic psychologists such as Abraham Maslow, who described how people can build emotional strength. The term emotional intelligence was, however, first introduced to mainstream reading by psychologists Peter Salovey and John Mayer (1989). Many books on the subject have followed, most notably Daniel Goleman's *Emotional Intelligence: Why It Can Matter More Than IQ*, first published in 1995. Goleman proposed that EI was a better forecaster of excellence than general intelligence, in that it may be used to predict up to 80 per cent of a person's success in life. China's *quote 1*

President Xi Jinping, as reported in *China Daily* on 15 May 2013, also confirmed the importance of EI when he said: 'Intelligence quotient and emotional quotient, which is more important? EQ is important for adapting to society, although it should be used together with professional knowledge and techniques.'

IQ is a measure of a person's intellectual abilities: it measures how easily we learn new things; focus on tasks and exercises; retain and recall information; can reason and think abstractly as well as analytically; handle numbers; and solve problems by using prior knowledge. Those with a high IQ, well above the average of 100, are capable of high academic success – but that does not necessarily mean that they make a success of their personal or working lives. Many of us will have experienced highly intelligent people at work, often in a leadership position, who find it hard to relate to, work with or inspire colleagues or subordinates. The reason is likely to be that their high IQ is not coupled with high levels of EI. However, whilst IQ is relatively easy to measure, EI is not as straightforward to quantify.

Measuring emotional intelligence

Recent years have seen significant research activity designed to define and measure EI, resulting in several proposals but no one single, generally accepted model. The *Encyclopaedia of Applied Psychology* (Spielberger, 2004) does, however, suggest two of the most significant EI models to be the Bar-On EQ-i model and Goleman's four dimensions of emotional intelligence.

The Bar-On EQ-i model

The American-born Israeli psychologist Dr Reuven Bar-On began working in the field of EI in 1980 and created his EQ-i measure – standing for emotional quotient inventory – in 1997. He proposed that EI was made up of a series of overlapping, but different, skills and attitudes that could be grouped under five general 'realms' that are further subdivided into 15 'scales'. The EQ-i is a self-reporting questionnaire containing 133 short sentences requiring a response from a five-point scale ranging from 'very seldom or not true of me' to 'very often true of me or true of me'. Resulting average to above-average EQ scores suggest that the respondent is effective in emotional and social functioning; with low scores suggesting an inability to be effective and the possible existence of emotional, social and/or behavioural problems. The higher the scores, the more positive the prediction for effective functioning in meeting daily demands and challenges. A personalized EQ-i leadership report can be obtained from **www.psychological-consultancy.com** for £60 plus VAT (price current at time of writing).

The five 'realms' and 15 'scales' are:

- *Intrapersonal:*
  - self-regard;
  - emotional self-awareness;
  - assertiveness;
  - independence;
  - self-actualization.
- *Interpersonal:*
  - empathy;
  - social responsibility;
  - interpersonal relations.
- *Stress management:*
  - stress tolerance;
  - impulse control.
- *Adaptability:*
  - flexibility;
  - reality-testing;
  - problem-solving.
- *General mood:*
  - optimism;
  - happiness.

Goleman's four dimensions of emotional intelligence

Daniel Goleman's model has a number of competences and skills grouped under four 'domains' that, he proposes, contribute specifically to managerial performance, measured by multi-rater, 360-degree, assessment. Goleman, Boyatzis and McKee's (2002) book *Primal Leadership* describes the competences as an emotional competence inventory (ECI) that high-potential leaders tend to score very highly in. The authors stress also that the EI competences within the list are not innate talents, but learnt abilities, each of which has a unique contribution to making leaders more effective. Moreover, they have never met or measured for EI any leaders, no matter how outstanding, who have strengths in every one of the competences. Highly effective leaders typically exhibit a critical mass of strength in half a dozen or so, usually having at least one strong competence from each of the four domains, which are listed below:

- *Self-awareness:*
  - emotional self-awareness;
  - accurate self-awareness;
  - self-confidence.

- *Self-management:*
  - emotional self-control;
  - transparency;
  - adaptability;
  - achievement orientation;
  - initiative;
  - optimism.
- *Social awareness:*
  - empathy;
  - organizational awareness;
  - service orientation.
- *Relationship management:*
  - developing others;
  - inspirational leadership;
  - change catalyst;
  - influence;
  - conflict management;
  - teamwork and collaboration.

It is apparent that there is significant overlap between the Bar-On and Goleman models, with several competencies appearing on both scales. Emotional self-awareness, adaptability, empathy and optimism are specific words used in both, whilst others, such as Bar-On's self-regard and Goleman's self-confidence, suggest similar concepts. One aspect that does differentiate both lists, however, is that Goleman focuses much more heavily on competencies required of leaders. Indeed, when expounding the 18 competencies in *Primal Leadership* the authors refer each to their impact on leaders' effectiveness. Hence, for me, Goleman's model is more appropriate for leaders of this book to consider.

Leaders operating at any level – team, operational or strategic – determine to a large extent the emotional health of their people: they are the group's emotional guide. The leader has the power, indeed the responsibility, to drive collective emotions in a positive direction, whilst addressing the consequences of toxic emotions. If people's emotions are directed towards enthusiasm, happiness and optimism, their performance will soar, whilst if negative emotions such as anxiety and animosity prevail then individual and collective potential will never be realized. Moreover, followers look to their leader for supportive, positive emotional connections and will largely mirror what they perceive the leader's emotional health to be. Team members generally view the leader's emotional reaction as the most authoritative response to situations, especially those that are ambiguous, and will model their own reactions accordingly. The extent to which a leader praises/criticizes, supports/disregards, encourages/ignores determines his or her emotional impact.

History abounds with demagogic leaders who have had huge impact creating mass destructive emotions based upon anger and fear – for exam Hitler, Pol Pot, Milosovic. Typically, they create feelings of national threat where is it 'us' against 'them' – where 'they' are defined in cultural, national or ethnic terms. Demagoguery generates destructive emotions that challenge hope and optimism, and encourage hatred and the denial of basic altruistic motivations. On the other hand, there are many alternative examples on the world stage where leaders have engendered positive emotions based upon shared aspirations and collective, mutual values. For example, Winston Churchill, one of history's greatest exponents of EI, appealed to the hopes of a nation during the Second World War (how he did this is explored in more detail in Chapter 8).

Thankfully, demagogues are rare at an organizational level, although business leaders have been known to mobilize a workforce towards a goal by means of fear, hatred or uncertainty. Such emotions, however, tend to be unsustainable over the long haul: anger and fear may be effective emotions to overcome short-term obstacles but will exhaust themselves over time, leaving the leader facing the consequences of confused, demoralized followers.

EI has, however, been proved to be a significant factor in leadership success within companies. One study, detailed in Howard Book and Steven Stein's *The EQ Edge* (2001), saw researchers apply Bar-On's EQ-i assessment to members of America's Young President's Organization (YPO). The YPO only accepts as members those who are less than 40 years old and are presidents or CEOs of companies that employ at least 60 people and generate $5 million or more in annual revenue. Results from the test showed that several emotional skills differentiated this successful group of entrepreneurs from other managers that the researchers had tested previously. One was their high level of flexibility: being ready to identify opportunities and move quickly to grasp them. Another high-scoring scale, from the intrapersonal realm, was that of independence. Many of the respondents, some of whom had started their businesses in their early twenties, had no role models to emulate yet had the emotional strength to make important business decisions at a very early age. These business founders were also found to be particularly assertive when conducting business negotiations.

Within the UK, Slaski and Cartwright (2002), again using the EQ-i model, studied the relationship between EI and leadership and management ability amongst 224 middle managers from the retailer Tesco. The company's own competency framework was used to rate performance, which included factors such as setting objectives, organizing and decision-making. The researchers also collected information on physical and psychological health, as well as subjective assessment of stress. The results found a significantly high correlation between EI and overall managerial performance. Moreover, the more emotionally intelligent managers experienced less stress, were healthier, and enjoyed their jobs more than those with lower EI scores.

For me, a more significant study into the relationship between EI and business leadership is Stein *et al* (2009) in which the researchers applied the EQ-i measure to 186 executives (159 males and 27 females) from the YPO and the Innovators' Alliance (IA). The objective was to compare the EI scores of these high-profile executive groups with the general public, and also in relation to various business outcomes such as net profit, growth management, and employee management and retention. In respect of the business outcomes, the researchers tested three hypotheses, their findings for which were:

- *Hypothesis 1* – higher scores on EI will be positively related to the degree to which managing others was perceived as less challenging.
- *Hypothesis 2* – higher scores on EI will be positively related to the degree to which a business challenge was perceived as less challenging.

  Results showed that total EI was positively related to the degree to which a challenge was perceived as easy with respect to managing growth, managing others, training employees and retaining employees. Not surprisingly, the relationship between EI and interpersonal/social challenges was significantly more related than to more task-orientated challenges such as raising capital and technological advancement. The finding suggested that top executives are aware of their own emotions, and those of the people they lead, and use these skills in communications at a personal and organization level, which in turn enabled them to increase staff motivation and commitment. Adaptability was also shown to be positively related to managing growth, coping with technological challenge, managing people and staff training. Other components that impacted on the leaders' ability to manage change were flexibility, optimism, self-regard and self-actualization.

- *Hypothesis 3* – executives who possess high levels of EI will yield higher profit.

  To test this hypothesis the participants were divided into two categories: the high profit group and the non-high profit group. The findings suggested that there were three facets to EI that differentiated those who belonged to highly profitable organizations, namely:

  - Empathy: to demonstrate their understanding of how others feel, thus strengthening working relationships and developing high-performing teams.
  - Self-regard: the ability to respect and accept others as basically good, with general feelings of security, inner strength and self-assuredness. Leaders who project a strong sense of identity will be more likely to motivate their people to perform at higher levels, thus resulting in greater profits.
  - Adaptability: especially reality-testing and problem-solving, was also found to be related to enhance profitability. Hence, business leaders who can realistically and accurately construe external events and solve related issues tend to be better able to generate higher financial returns.

Stein *et al* concluded that:

1 Executives tend to use a variety of EI skills in order to meet the business challenges they face. Hence, EI testing should be applied as a functional

tool in the assessment and development of present or future busine
leaders – in the case of this study, using Bar-On's EQ-i model.

2 Specific EI skills relate to social challenges, whilst others relate to
task-oriented challenges. As the executive's ability to meet both sets
of demands is critical to role success, it would be very advantageous
to understand what skills are most suitable to different situations.

3 Overall, the research supported the notion that high EI skills are
present in top executives and are related to high performance.
Hence, leadership development programmes should include the
identification, enhancement and application of EI skills – a
proposition that will be developed in the next chapter of this book.

Organizational climate

One of the most important roles of a leader is to create a culture within the
organization where employees' beliefs, values and attitudes contribute towards
successful outcomes in terms of relationships, product and service quality,
and financial returns. Whereas an organization's culture remains reasonably
constant over the short term, and takes significant effort to change, organizational climate is easier to influence as it defines the employees' perceptions
and attitudes towards their organization at a given time. Momeni (2009)
suggests that the behaviour of managers has a great influence on staff perceptions to create a positive organizational climate. Organizational climate
has been defined as 'a set of characteristics that describe an organization and
that (a) distinguish it from other organizations, (b) are relatively enduring
over time, and (c) influence the behaviour of people in the organization'
(Forehand and Von Haller, 1964). Put more colloquially, it is likely to be the
answer to the question: 'What is it like to work here?' – a question that,
from my experience, many business leaders would benefit from having asked
of their employees.

BEST leadership quote

'The cultural maturity of people is critical
and it takes a long time. You don't get a
culture immediately: you have got to live
and breathe it. So the pace at which we
will move will be the pace at which we
will steadily grow the culture.'

Karen Forrester
Chief Executive
TGI Friday's

Amy Lyman, co-founder of Great Place to Work, which produces the annual 'FORTUNE 100 Best Companies to Work For' survey in the United States, proposes the following three components of how an employee feels about their workplace:

- Feelings about management: an employee should trust the people for whom he or she works.
- Feelings about the job: an employee should have pride in what he or she does.
- Feelings about other employees: an employee should enjoy the people with whom he or she works.

BEST leadership quote

'We have to know from our people: what are we doing; what are we doing that's wrong; what's silly; what's stupid; how do they feel; do they have trouble getting to work; do they enjoy the environment. All these things. That's one big package of knowledge that management must have in order to run the business.'

Henry Engelhardt
Chief Executive
Admiral Group

Whilst the link between organizational climate and leadership is evident from the first of Amy Lyman's three components, leaders are also prime influencers of the other two. Goleman, Boyatzis and McKee's (2001) research with private organizations showed that organizational climate influenced one-third of the returns measured by the Standard & Poor's 500 Index, the remainder being a result of economic situations and competitive dynamics. Goleman *et al* (2002) suggested that employees who feel upbeat are likely to go the extra mile to delight customers, and therefore improve the financial return – and proposed that for every 1 per cent improvement in the service climate, there is a 2 per cent increase in revenue. Their research also found that it is the leader's mood and behaviour, above all other factors, that was the greatest influence on bottom-line performance in private organizations. There is a powerful chain reaction in which the leader's mood drives the moods and behaviours of everyone else in direct or indirect contact with the leader.

The more emotionally demanding the work, the more empathetic, ι and supportive the leader needs to be. Especially with customer-. staff, where conflict situations can emerge, the leader's understandinǥ application of EI will create a climate conducive to high levels of service delivery. In short, leaders' emotional states and resulting behaviour affect how their followers feel and, therefore, perform. How well leaders manage their own moods affects everyone else's moods and, thus, the climate of the whole organization.

Momeni (2009) found that the relationship between EI and organizational climate had four implications:

1 Rather than focusing solely on skills and knowledge when recruiting new staff, organizations should also consider EI, especially for leaders and other staff whose jobs require social skills.

2 When leaders are appraised, the climate they create within their own teams and with other departments should be assessed and considered.

3 Leaders' EI should be evaluated by a range of methods, including 360-degree feedback.

4 The EI of different leaders across different levels and departments should be compared with the organizational climate of their workplaces.

Team norms

Whilst we recognize the importance of culture and climate at an organizational level, the behaviours and habits of teams are due, to a large extent, to what are called *norms*. Leaders who understand a group's norms, and the crucial importance they have on how the group is likely to react and behave, can create highly emotionally intelligent teams: teams that co-operate, collaborate and cultivate trust and group identity. Collective EI is what sets apart high-performing teams from the 'also-rans'.

Team norms are immensely powerful as they largely determine how a team performs. They are the rules, stated or merely understood, to which members will adhere when faced with a situation. In some teams, confrontation and intolerance are the default interpersonal reactions; in others there may be a charade of civility and mutual interest. Conversely, in others, members listen to each other with respect and true interest, offer support and work through disagreements openly and constructively. Whatever the ground rules, team members automatically sense them and behave accordingly. Norms dictate what feels to be the right thing to do in all given circumstances.

A group's EI competences are the same as those for an emotionally intelligent individual, expressed by Goleman as self-awareness, self-management, social awareness and relationship management. The competences of the constituent members combine to influence the group as a whole: when team members practise self-awareness, for example, and, hence, notice the group's moods and needs, they are more likely to respond to each other with greater empathy. Indeed, being mutually empathetic creates powerful, positive norms that enable the team to build relationships not only within itself, but with the organization as a whole. Listening to the perspective of a member who does not share others' views, or recognizing the feelings of another who is angry or upset, are the norms of a group that is at ease with itself and in tune with the emotions of its members.

As we have seen, how employees feel about their work is determined by their feelings about their leader, their actual job role and their fellow employees – all of which are heavily affected by the mood and behaviour of their leader.

Consider this hypothetical scenario:

John, a proven successful manager in a large insurance company, is tasked to take over a department that, whilst working together well, has not reached its potential. He begins with the force of a tornado and a refusal to accept how things were done previously and who did them. Existing roles and responsibilities are reassessed. People are pressurized to conform to the new working arrangements and practices, and those who do not agree with his plans are made well aware that there is no place for them in the new regime.

What are the likely outcomes of John's intervention and approach? How are the individuals and teams likely to react?

The issues here are John's failure to take into consideration his lack of EI and the impact that this will have on group norms. It is not an unusual scenario: many of us will have experienced a leader who, intent on forcing through change, continues blindly ahead without any consideration of how it will impact on the feelings of those involved and affected. It is an all-too-common mistake: ignoring the realities of the team ground rules and the collective emotions of the group whilst assuming that the leader's authority alone will change people's attitude and behaviour. More likely, it will result in a toxic and rebellious workplace. In John's case, his lack of emotional awareness did mobilize the team – but not in the way he desired. The team came together with the shared and powerful objective of seeing him fail, at any price. It was the team versus John, the leader. What John had failed to take into account were the unspoken, but powerful, norms that had influenced the department before his arrival. These included a strong sense of loyalty between team members, who prided themselves in their sense of personal support for each other. When faced with conflict, they found ways to ensure that members were not emotionally hurt. By treating them uncaringly, John was violating those core team norms. He was challenging their guiding principles of collaboration, unity and mutual support – and they fought back by coming together against a common enemy. His position and authority were challenged and the organization, facing rebellion along with deteriorating departmental performance, replaced him – hopefully with a leader with greater emotional understanding.

More than anyone else in a team, the leader has the power to influence norms. He or she does that by continually monitoring the emotional tone – how it 'feels' to be part of the team. That means not only observing what members are doing and saying but assessing the undercurrent of their behaviour: what is really going on under the surface. The best leaders act on their sense of what the team is feeling and use subtle messages, not least by their own behaviour, to create common ground rules regarding team norms. Positive visions, optimistic interpretations and personal interventions such as encouraging members to listen to and respect others' views during meetings will, over time, move the group towards higher emotionally intelligent group understanding.

Goleman's four dimensions

Let us now look in more detail at Goleman's four dimensions of emotional intelligence, as represented in Figure 4.1.

FIGURE 4.1   The four dimensions of emotional intelligence (Goleman, Boyatzis and McKee, 2001)

	What I see	What I do
With me	Self-awareness	Self-management
With others	Social awareness	Relationship management

Self-awareness

This includes emotion self-awareness, a measure that is also included in Bar-On's EQ-i model, which Book and Stein (2001) define as 'the ability to recognize your feelings and to differentiate between them to know what you are feeling and why, and to know what caused the feelings'. Goleman, Boyatzis and McKee (2002) go on to explain that emotionally self-aware leaders can be candid and true, being able to speak openly about their feelings and with conviction about their guiding values. They are conscious of their strengths and weaknesses and are able and willing to receive constructive critical feedback about the areas they need to improve. Accurate self-assessment enables leaders to seek help to develop new leadership skills where necessary. They do, however, have the self-confidence to play to their strengths and often exhibit a presence that makes them stand out in a group.

BEST leadership quote

'*Reflection is part of leadership. Reflective learning is what you see when you hold up the mirror. It may be gender-specific, but if you hold up the mirror and always see Brad Pitt, then you are not reflecting! A lot of people fall into that trap.*'

Phil Loach
Chief Fire Officer
West Midlands Fire Service

Self-management

This includes adaptability and a sense of optimism that are also listed in Bar-On's model. Adaptable leaders can manage multiple demands without losing their energy or direction, and can adjust to new challenges effortlessly. An innate sense of optimism allows leaders to see others positively and expect the best from them. Setbacks are seen as opportunities, rather than threats, which will offer the potential for future improvement.

Those who score highly in the self-management domain exhibit high levels of emotional self-control: they stay calm and clear-headed during periods of stress. They find ways to manage negative emotions and seek to channel them to positive effect. They have a determination to achieve results through improved performance for themselves and their followers. They set challenging, but achievable, goals that they perceive as reflecting their personal values. A dominant feature of the achievement competence is the continual search for learning, and the teaching of ways to perform better.

The final competence listed in the self-management group is transparency: an authentic and willing openness to others about one's personal feelings, beliefs and values. Transparent leaders are able to admit their own mistakes and failings, whilst also possessing the strength to challenge unethical behaviour in others.

BEST leadership quote

'Everyone is strong in some areas and weak in others and, as a leader, you need to understand your own weaknesses. Knowing your own weaknesses is a strength in itself because you can then build on that.'

Mark Wood
Explorer

Although not specifically included as a competence by Goleman, a requirement of emotionally intelligent leaders is to self-manage their mood, in the understanding of how it affects the emotions of those around them. Goleman, Boyatzis and McKee (2001) explain this effect as being associated with the open-loop nature of the brain's limbic system – our emotional centre. Whilst a closed-loop system is self-regulating, an open-loop depends on external sources, hence we rely on connections with those around us to determine our mood. The open-loop limbic system was formed early in human evolution as it enabled people to recognize others' emotions (those of a crying baby, for example) and to take supportive action. Its effect is as powerful today, as studies have shown that the comforting presence of someone tending to a seriously ill patient can not only lower his or her blood pressure, but also slow the secretion of fatty acids that threaten to block arteries. The signal that a person transmits to others can have a range of significant physiological, as well as emotional, effects – positively or negatively. Our limbic system's open-loop design allows other people to change us physically and emotionally. Seeing someone laugh, for instance, exerts a strong impulse for us to smile or laugh in response. Indeed, laughter is one of the most contagious of all displays of emotion.

Moods displayed by those with authority tend to be contagious as everyone watches leaders and takes their emotional cues from them. Even if strategic leaders are not readily visible to everyone in the organization, their mood affects those around them, which in turn cascades to all levels.

'People go to my PA and ask, "What's he like this morning. Is he in a good mood?" People do pick up on how you are, so it is important to have the right attitude when you come into the room. It's an important component to people seeing you as genuine.'

Ian Munro
Group Chief Executive
New Charter Housing

Adair (1996) beautifully encapsulates the impact that a self-managed leader can have on others:

> The first and golden rule of motivation is that you will never inspire others unless you are inspired yourself. Only a motivated leader motivates others. Example is the great seducer. Enthusiasm inspires, especially when combined with trust. For motivation is a virus: it is caught, not taught. If a leader is enthusiastic and motivated it is contagious.

Knowing John Adair personally, I can confirm that his enthusiasm to enhance the quality of leadership within UK industry has certainly inspired me in my work. Try this the next time someone asks you how you are feeling today. Most people would respond with something like 'Oh, OK', or 'Oh, could be better', or 'Not too bad, thanks'. See what the reaction is if you say 'Great, thanks' or 'Fantastic'. I can tell you from personal experience that the enquirer's reaction will be something approaching incredulity! 'Really, my goodness, that is very positive,' they may reply. The truth is that highly motivated individuals can, and do, have a powerful effect on others: enthusiasm is, as Adair states, contagious.

Social awareness

This includes organizational awareness, where a leader is in touch with the political and social relationships that work within a company; and also the service competence that creates the emotional climate that bonds front-line staff and their customers together in a mutually beneficial service relationship.

However, perhaps the most influential quality of social awareness relates to leaders having the ability to tune in to the emotional signals given off by a person or a group – empathy, again a competence included in both Goleman's and Bar-On's models. Empathetic leaders care about their people; they show interest in and concern for them, whatever their backgrounds or cultural diversity. They have the ability to see the world from another person's perspective, regardless of how that view may differ from their own. For such a powerful tool, empathy is sometimes misunderstood and often underutilized for three main reasons:

1 Empathy is sometimes interpreted as being 'nice' – with making a polite and pleasant statement. It is much more than that.

2 Some people confuse empathy with sympathy, but they are quite distinct emotional responses. Sympathy is an expression of one's reaction to another person's unfortunate or distressing situation. Responses often begin with 'I' or 'my' and reflect the speaker's position, as in 'I am very sorry to hear that'. Whilst perhaps welcome sentiments, they are different to empathetic statements that are more likely to being with 'you', as in 'you must be feeling (a certain way)'. Empathy is an expression of understanding, not sympathy.

3 It is a mistake to believe that by empathizing with someone you will necessarily be agreeing, or approving of, another person's position when, in fact, you may be opposed to it. Empathy is simply an acknowledgement that another person holds a specific view: admitting its existence, without passing judgement on its reasonableness or validity.

It creates a strong emotional impact when a leader displays an understanding of a team member's psychological drivers and can be extremely influential in developing supportive personal relationships.

BEST leadership quote

'I think the ability to emotionally engage with your teams is becoming increasingly important. Sometimes things are tough and it's fine for leaders to get up and talk in corporate sentences, but if they cannot empathize with their people on the ground they may as well not open their mouths because it is pointless and meaningless.'

William Rogers
Chief Executive
UKRD

Relationship management

This is Goleman's fourth domain and contains six competences, which in a sense are the practical applications of the first three domains. By a leader being self-aware, having a high degree of self-management, and being socially aware, he or she is in a strong position to create powerful relationships at individual and team levels. Managing relationships is, in essence, influencing others' emotions, which in turn requires leaders to be on top of their own emotions. Managing relationships, Goleman points out, is not just a matter of being friendly: it is friendliness with the purpose of influencing people in a positive manner. Inspirational leaders get people excited about a shared vision that promises shared benefits. Collaborative effort can only be achieved on a foundation of strong personal relationships. It requires a leader to exert appropriate influence in order to achieve buy-in at an individual and collective level. Influential leaders are persuasive and engaging when they interact with others, often when addressing a group. EI leaders care about their people and seek every opportunity to develop their abilities in order for them to reach their potential. They are also natural mentors or coaches as they show an interest in others' personal and professional progression by giving timely and constructive advice and feedback.

However, there are times when leaders have to face up to difficult situations, especially when they recognize the need for change. They need to have the ability to advocate the benefits of a new order, even in the face of strong opposition, making emotionally compelling arguments that can overcome followers' natural inclination to resist the status quo. Conflict management is also one of the competencies in the relationship management domain, requiring leaders to communicate effectively with all parties, evaluate the different perspectives and find a common solution that everyone can find acceptable. Conflicts invariably have emotional components – an emotionally intelligent leader has the skills to navigate through them to a successful conclusion.

Goleman's final competence within the relationship management domain is about collaborative team-working and calls for leaders to be team players themselves. By acting as role models for collaboration, through mutual respect and co-operation, they generate an atmosphere conducive to enthusiastic commitment to shared objectives. Although having the strength of character to impose their authority if required, their main contribution is to develop the spirit and shared identity of the team – from within it, rather than as an outsider.

BEST leadership quote

'A leader's personality does spread out, partly because you hire people who you get along with, so it's self-perpetuating. If you go to our claims department it has a different personality than our sales department; if you go to Swansea it has a different personality than Cardiff, because the people leading those areas are different. So we believe in differences, we believe in tribalism, but at the same time we believe in the team and everybody working together for one goal. As we say, "There's only one share price." Everyone is a shareholder. It's not as though the marketing department gets a different share price to IT, so you're in this together.'

Henry Engelhardt
Chief Executive
Admiral Group

The above paragraphs describe how leaders can, and should, apply EI to inspire their people to ever-greater performance – using largely the four domains of Goleman's ECI as the model best suited to the practice of leadership. The domains should not be viewed in isolation, as there is an obvious relationship between them. Leaders cannot, for example, manage their emotions if they are not aware of them; nor can they manage relationships unless their emotions support and complement their efforts in doing so. Goleman, Boyatzis and McKee (2002) explain the system that underpins the relationship between the domains and listed competences. Their research has indicated that self-awareness facilitates both empathy and self-management, and these two combine to facilitate effective relationship management. It is, therefore, upon a sound foundation of self-awareness that EI leadership is built. Self-awareness, not necessarily a skill heavily promoted in traditional leadership literature, allows leaders to recognize the power of their own emotions and, hence, allows them to be more able to connect with the emotions of those they lead. Leaders not attuned to their own inner feelings may allow their outward manifestations – anger or indifference, for example – to alienate or demotivate those around them. The impact of doing so at the strategic leadership level could have devastating consequences for the organization as a whole.

The gender factor

When it comes to emotions, a common perception is that women are more 'in tune' with their feelings and are willing to display and share them, whilst men are more likely to raise the barriers and change the subject if their emotions are threatened to be explored and displayed for others to see – 'real men don't cry!'. To what extent do these gender stereotypes prove to be accurate when measured by EI research? Studies show that women are, indeed, more emotionally intelligent in some competencies, but often only to a limited extent, whilst men score higher in others. Book and Stein (2001), using the Bar-On EQ-i model, constantly find that men and women have remarkably similar overall scores, although women consistently score higher in terms of social responsibility and empathy – whilst men excelled in stress tolerance. Indeed, Stein *et al* (2009), in the survey detailed earlier in this chapter, found that women had significantly higher levels of EI in social responsibility and emotional self-awareness.

Goleman (2011) supported the assertion that women are more skilled at emotional empathy – feeling what the other person feels – than men and are, therefore, better suited for occupations such as counselling, teaching and team leadership. He explains that the reason for this gender difference originates in a region of the brain called the insula, which senses signals from the body as a whole. When we empathize with someone, our brain mimics what that person is feeling and the insula interprets that pattern and informs us what that feeling is. Here is where the gender difference lies: women's brains tend to linger longer with the feelings of someone who is upset, whilst the male brain tends to quickly tune out of the emotions and reverts to other brain areas that focus on solving the cause of the disturbance. Both reactions have advantages: the women's tendency to stay tuned in to others' emotions helps to support them during their emotional distress, whilst men can more easily distance themselves from the emotional turmoil surround them and, hence, stay calm.

A study by Garcia-Retamero, Lopez-Zafra and Pilar Berrios Martos (2012) involving 431 Spanish undergraduates in three different disciplines found that emotional clarity (understanding one's own emotions) and emotional repair (an ability to regulate one's own emotions) were highly correlated to transformational leadership. Moreover, the individual's feminine characteristics of emotional clarity and emotional repair predict the extent to which they can become transformational leaders. Finally, high scores in transformational leadership correlated with contingent reward (support for followers in exchange for their efforts and performance), which was predicted by femininity, as were those factors that most contribute to interpersonal relations.

A more extensive study (Freedman, 2012) of over 24,000 leaders and workers from across the world sought to identify factors connecting EI, gender and leadership. It used an EI model used by Freedman's company, 6seconds, although its components are similar to the other models referred to within this chapter. Results from all the study's respondents show that in their 'know yourself' domain (similar to Goleman's 'self-awareness') women scored 1.8 per cent higher than men, and 0.4 per cent higher in 'choose yourself' (Goleman's 'self-management'). This does not, however, mean that every woman has higher EI in these two aspects, rather that they are higher on average. Drilling down further into the actual competences that make up the domains, the results again found that women and men have strengths in specific competencies. The biggest gender gap was in 'applied consequential thinking' that enables people to pause and evaluate all factual and emotional data before taking an appropriate decision. Women, on average, scored 4.5 per cent higher in this crucial area, suggesting that they are more likely to take a more considered approach. They also scored more highly, although not as significantly, in:

- 'enhance emotional literacy' – identifying and understanding feelings;
- 'recognize patterns' – acknowledging frequently recurring patterns;
- 'increase empathy' – the ability to engage with and influence others.

Men, on the other hand, had an advantage in 'navigate emotions' – harnessing the insight and energy of feelings to move forward intentionally: responding rather than reacting.

Freedman's research is particularly useful in that it sought to identify any links between the EI scores of male and female leaders. His report's findings relate to all the 24,436 people surveyed, but 6,236 of those held senior leadership roles – 40 per cent of those being female. Of these, the gender gap relating to EI widens from 1 per cent to nearly 2 per cent, with specific differences in some competencies. In 'pursue noble goals', for instance, no gender difference exists amongst the leaders, whilst males had an edge in this particular competency in the wider survey. In 'enhance emotional literacy', 'apply consequential thinking' and 'increase empathy' the gap widens further, suggesting that female leaders are more emotionally insightful, empathetic and careful in their responses. Indeed, 'increase empathy' was one of the lowest-scoring areas for male leaders in Freedman's research. It does appear, therefore, that competencies surrounding empathy, in particular, are found by more than one study to be an emotionally intelligent quality found more often in women than in men.

Emotional intelligence and business success

In Thomas Stanley's *The Millionaire Mind* (2001) the author details the responses of 733 multimillionaires in the United States when asked to rate the factors (out of 30) that were most responsible for their success. The top three were all reflections of EI:

1 Being honest with all people.
2 Being well-disciplined.
3 Getting along with people.

In comparison, IQ was twenty-first on the list, only being endorsed by 20 per cent of the respondents! So what is the connection between EI and business performance? Bar-On (2006), using his EQ-I model, posits that 30 per cent of occupation performance is based on EI, but when leadership is assessed separately the figure increases to 67 per cent; hence around two-thirds of leadership performance relies on the application of EI skills.

In Book and Stein's *The EQ Edge* (2001), the authors detail the results of a questionnaire completed by 4,888 people across the United States, which asked them – according to Bar-On's model – about their success at work. What is particularly interesting is that the results were presented according to the professions of the respondents, the following of which may be of interest to readers of this book. The five most important factors they believed that contributed to their success were:

Overall (4,888 respondents):

1 self-actualization;
2 happiness;
3 optimism;
4 self-regard;
5 assertiveness.

Senior managers (260):

1 self-regard;
2 happiness;
3 interpersonal relationships;
4 reality-testing;
5 self-actualization.

Business managers (general) (145):

1 interpersonal relationships;
2 assertiveness;
3 happiness;
4 self-regard;
5 emotional self-awareness.

Psychologists (52):

1 reality-testing;
2 independence;
3 happiness;
4 stress tolerance;
5 flexibility.

CASE STUDY   Emotional intelligence development programme

Orme and Langhorn (2002) describe how Whitbread, one of the UK's leading suppliers of services to the hospitality sector, undertook a major project to develop the EI competences of their Beefeater restaurant general managers. Part of the project was to identify any relationships between EI and productivity. It showed that restaurants managed by managers, male and female, with high EI skills produced annual profit growth of 22 per cent, compared with 15 per cent average growth for the same period: amounting to an additional £110 million. More specifically, female managers with high EI produced 28 per cent. The EI factors that underpinned these enhanced levels of profitability were found to be emotional self-awareness, interpersonal relationships, social responsibility, reality-testing and happiness.

The next chapter contains a case study detailing how New Charter Housing – its group chief executive Ian Munro being one of the leaders interviewed for this book – introduced a development programme entitled 'Courage and Spark', based upon the principles of EI, to prepare selected junior managers for more senior positions within the group.

Chapter summary

Emotions heavily influence how we conduct our lives and, for leaders, they are a crucial tool in determining the relationships they have with their followers. Not only do they need to control and positively express their own feelings, but they must be able to receive, interpret and respond to the emotions of those they lead: that is, have a high level of emotional intelligence (EI). Indeed, the benefits of recognizing the powerful influence that emotions have on interpersonal relations apply to everyone, not just those holding leadership positions. This chapter explained and developed two measures of EI – the Bar-On EQ-i model, and Goleman's four dimensions model – the latter of which is most useful in applying to the role of leadership. Several studies were considered, especially in relation to the impact that EI can have on positive leadership. The chapter also contained sections devoted to organizational climate, how employees perceive their work environment; team norms, the unwritten rules that groups will adhere to when faced with specific situations; the gender factor, areas of EI that men and women are particularly strong in; and, finally, the impact of EI on business performance.

Leader development – identifying and promoting the inner self

05

The business case for investing in leadership development is clear. For example, a paper produced by the UK's Department for Business, Innovation and Skills (BIS) entitled 'Leadership & Management in the UK – The Key to Sustainable Growth' provides stark research showing that:

- Ineffective leadership and management is estimated to cost UK businesses over £19 million per year in lost working hours.
- In the UK 43 per cent of managers rate their own line manager as ineffective.
- Only one in five managers are qualified.
- Nearly three-quarters of organizations in England reported a deficit in management and leadership skills in 2012, which is contributing to a productivity gap with countries such as the United States, Germany and Japan.
- Incompetence or bad leadership by company directors causes 56 per cent of corporate failures.

Yet the benefits of effective leadership are equally compelling:

- Best-practice management and leadership development can result in a 23 per cent increase in organizational performance.
- A single-point improvement in management practices (rated on a five-point scale) is associated with the same increase in output as a 25 per cent increase in the labour force or a 65 per cent increase in invested capital.

The report makes the point that the quality of leadership and management has been improving in the UK over the past 10 years – but so has it in other competing countries. The UK does produce some good business leaders but the evidence proves that the business community needs to place more emphasis on leadership development if it is to compete effectively on the world stage. The same applies to other countries in the 21st-century global economy.

BEST leadership quote

'My role as Vice President – Global Leadership Development is about making sure all our leaders know what good leadership looks like: what standards are expected; what activities are expected; what levels of leadership we have within the business, and how there are transitions from one to the next. Different things are expected of different levels so you have to have the tools to act as a good leader for the level you are at, as well as the next level you might be aspiring to.'

Gregor Thain
VP Global Leadership Development
InterContinental Hotels

Whilst the BIS report does, within some statistics, combine leadership and management together, it also differentiates the key requirements of both, explaining:

All managers need to be effective leaders. While a command and control culture will ensure that employees comply with organizational procedures and the terms of their employment contract, it does not create the enthusiasm, innovation and engagement that modern organizations need to compete effectively in a global marketplace. By developing their leadership capability, managers can achieve outstanding results from ordinary people and businesses, getting the best out of their employees and benefiting from the knowledge and skills that often they are not even aware that they possess. Above all, leaders need to inspire trust in their capability to take the organization in the right direction.

Leadership *BEST* practice

Every quarter the managing directors of UKRD spend three days together sharing best practice, talking about cultural values and dealing with commercial issues, as well as reflecting on the development of their own skill sets in terms of managing, coaching and leading. The company invests in external facilitation to help the MDs create the right strategy and environment for their own businesses – which is then translated down the management chain. As William Rogers says, 'It is not just sufficient to lead by example, albeit that is the most important factor, you also have to back that up with some hard-nosed investment in time and money that focuses on your middle management, so that they can push that culture further themselves.'

In terms of management and leadership development, Day (2000) makes the following differentiation:

- Management development:
  - primarily includes managerial education and training with an emphasis on acquiring specific types of knowledge, skills and abilities;
  - applies proven solutions to known problems, which gives it mainly a training orientation;
  - focuses on enhancing task performance in formal management roles;
  - tends to relate to processes that are position- and/or organization-specific.
- Leadership development:
  - seeks to expand the capacity to engage in leadership roles that may, or may not, come with formal authority;
  - develops processes that enable groups of people to work together in meaningful ways;
  - involves building the capacity for groups of people to learn their way out of problems that could not have been predicted, or that arise from the disintegration of traditional organizational structures and the associated loss of sense-making;
  - is oriented towards developing the ability to anticipate unforeseen challenges.

Day goes on to differentiate between leader and leadership development, cautioning against the assumption that, by training those in leadership positions in a set of skills or abilities, effective leadership will result.

Leader development emphasizes individual-based knowledge, skills and abilities that enable people to think and act in new ways, thus providing a meaningful investment in human capital. The primary emphasis of a leader development strategy is to build the intrapersonal competences needed to form an accurate model of oneself; to engage in healthy attitude and identity development; and to use that self-model to perform effectively in a range of organization roles.

Leadership development, on the other hand, seeks to enhance social, as opposed to human, capital. Here, the emphasis is on building individual relationships that enhance co-operation and resource exchange to create value for the organization: hence, interpersonal skills. The foundation of such relationships is mutual obligation supported by mutual trust and respect. Day (2000) makes the point, however, that, whilst trust is a requirement of successful interpersonal relationships, trustworthiness is an intrapersonal quality. Thus, leader development must go hand-in-hand with leadership development in enhancing intrapersonal and interpersonal competences. Organizations that seek to reap the benefits of inspirational leadership should, therefore, engage in programmes that develop both human and social capital. Enhancing the skills of individual leaders without recognizing the need for them to relate effectively with others in a broader social context ignores the fact that the practice of leadership is a complex interaction between individuals and their social and workplace environments. The differences between leader and leadership development are summarized in Table 5.1.

It is interesting to compare the skills listed in Table 5.1 with the four dimensions of Goleman's ECI and the model of emotional intelligence expounded in Chapter 4, namely social awareness, self-management, social awareness and relationship management. Remember that Goleman proposed his model as being particularly relevant to the development of leaders' emotional intelligence qualities. It would appear that Day's proposal adds weight to the validity of Goleman's model as a sound basis for the development of leaders' intrapersonal competences as well as the interpersonal competences required of effective leadership.

Notwithstanding the differentiation between the two development focuses, for the remainder of this chapter I will concentrate mainly on the psychological aspects and implications of the subject, many of which lean towards an emphasis on human capital, rather than social capital: intrapersonal, rather than interpersonal competences.

Two questions must be addressed before we move forward to consider the development of leaders in more detail: 1) Does everyone have the potential to be an inspirational leader? 2) Can leadership be taught and learnt?

In Adair's *Great Leaders* (1989) he wrote: 'The commonsense conclusion of this book is that leadership potential can be developed, but it does have

TABLE 5.1 Summary of differences between leader development and leadership development (Day, 2000)

	Leader Development	Leadership Development
Capital Type	Human	Social
Leadership Model	Individual: Personal power Knowledge Trustworthiness	Relational: Commitments Mutual respect Trust
Competence Base	Intrapersonal	Interpersonal
Skills	Self-awareness: Emotional awareness Self-confidence Accurate self-image Self-regulation: Self-control Trustworthiness Personal responsibility Adaptability Self-motivation: Initiative Commitment Optimism	Social awareness: Empathy Service orientation Political awareness Social skills: Building bonds Team orientation Change catalyst Conflict management

to be there in the first place.' Many of us will have experienced a situation in a school playground where there is one child to whom others are drawn. She is the one who decides which game 'her' group will play, who takes which roles within it, etc. The other children want to be around her and are comfortable being directed by her: there is a cachet associated with being part of her group. She will have no understanding of the concept of leadership, she certainly will never have been on a leadership course, but she is demonstrating the potential to develop the qualities necessary to become an inspirational leader in her future adult life. That is not to say that one of the other children in that playground will also take a similar path: only that she has shown exceptional potential in her early life.

Many people have – and demonstrate – the potential to be effective leaders. They may exhibit the necessary qualities in their private or professional lives, some of which could be:

- good communicators and listeners;
- energetic and enthusiastic;
- calm under pressure;
- self-confident;
- prepared to take personal responsibility for decisions;
- comfortable in other people's company;
- good team player;
- convincing and persuasive;
- adaptable;
- recognizes own strengths and weaknesses.

There are, of course, many other qualities, but a person who demonstrates those listed above will certainly have leadership potential. However, the fact that some people lack many of these characteristics casts doubt on their potential. Some of the necessary skills can certainly be taught and learnt, but as Bennis (2009) wrote: 'Leadership courses can only teach skills. They cannot teach character or vision.' If, for example, a sense of humour and integrity are highly desirable leadership qualities, one cannot imagine any developmental intervention being successful in enhancing those. No one will make a competent musician from someone who is tone deaf and without any ability to recognize and differentiate between notes.

BEST leadership quote

'Even ethics can be learnt in the sense that when you are made aware that you are being too task-focused at work and that you need to be more caring, you can access that part of yourself.'

Ann Francke
Chief Executive
Chartered Management Institute

Yet, for those with the potential to develop their leadership skills, the application of appropriate learning will realize their inherent capabilities. Recall from Chapter 1 that Arvey *et al* (2006) determined that approximately 70 per cent of leadership skills are learnt. The challenge is first to identify that latent potential and then to develop both their intrapersonal and inter-personal competences. For many who are taking a first step on their leader-ship ladder, or indeed those already holding executive positions, it can be a journey of self-discovery. Effective leadership development programmes will include opportunities for participants to examine their own characters, values, behaviours and motivations, and I know from personal experience that classroom-style leadership courses can greatly enhance interpersonal skills. Leadership psychology, as this book seeks to explore, suggests the need for a deeper level of introspective learning. Understanding who you are as a leader will help you develop both yourself and those around you. Let us, therefore, consider opportunities available to identify and develop the intrapersonal qualities necessary for inspirational leadership.

Psychometric tests

Psychometric tests fall under a number of categories, one of which is the assessment of personality as a means of identifying an individual's preferred or typical way of behaving. Personality is seen as a set of traits that are relatively consistent over time and situations. These individual traits represent a person's thinking, feeling and pattern of behaviour and provide an insight into how a person is likely to act when placed in a certain situation. The number of previously researched and recorded traits is vast and, in an attempt to reduce the number, Goldberg (1990) reduced them to what is now commonly known and accepted as the 'big five', namely:

1 openness to experience (inventive/curious versus consistent/cautious);
2 conscientiousness (efficient/organized versus easy-going/careless);
3 extroversion (outgoing/energetic versus solitary/reserved);
4 agreeableness (friendly/compassionate versus cold/unkind);
5 neuroticism (sensitive/nervous versus secure/confident).

Judge *et al* (2002) undertook a quantitative review of the relationship between personality and leadership, using the big five model as a basis for their study. They also sought to differentiate between leadership emergence and leader effectiveness: the former being associated with someone who is recognized by others as having leadership potential; the latter measuring how someone holding a leadership position performs in terms of motivating a team to achieve stated goals.

Their research found a strong multiple correlation between the big five traits and leadership criteria, suggesting that the specified traits are a fruitful basis for examining the predictors of leadership characteristics. Specifically, *extraversion* was seen as the most consistent influence on effective leadership, and even more so on leader emergence. As both sociable and dominant people are more likely to assert themselves in group situations, the pre-eminence of extraversion, especially in leader emergence, is understandable.

The next most strongly correlated trait to leadership was *conscientiousness*, being more related to leader emergence than effectiveness. The researchers concluded that the organizing activities of conscientious individuals, such as note-taking and facilitating processes, may allow them to quickly emerge as leaders.

Openness to experience was the third trait most related to leadership, especially in a business setting, where it was found, along with extraversion, to have the strongest dispositional relationship.

Neuroticism failed to emerge as a significant predictor of leadership, although it was actually *agreeableness* that was found to be the least relevant of the big five traits. The researchers argued that, because agreeable individuals tend to be passive and compliant, it is less likely that they would emerge as leaders. This was found to be particularly true in business, government or military situations, where the 'conforming to others' wishes' nature of agreeable individuals may be most likely to present itself.

The Myers-Briggs Type Indicator (MBTI) is one of the most commonly used tests to assess a person's personality type. Originally designed by Katharine Cook Briggs and her daughter Isabel Briggs Myers, it uses the typological theories proposed by Jung, first published in his book *Psychological Types* (1921), the test being first published as a questionnaire in 1962.

Jung believed that we all have two kinds of functions in our lives: how we take in information; and how we perceive things. Within the two categories there are two opposite ways of functioning: we either perceive information from our senses or based on our intuition; and we make decisions based upon either objective logic or subjective feelings. He further suggested that we use all four functions in our lives and that each person has a primary mode of operation within four preferences – the combination of which determines our personality. The four preferences are:

- *Extraversion (E) or introversion (I)*. If you prefer to deal with people, things, situations, or 'the outer world', then your preference is for extraversion. If, however, you prefer to use your energy to deal with ideas, information, explanations, beliefs, or 'the inner world', then you tend towards introversion.

- *Sensing (S) or intuition (N)*. Those who like clarity, facts, or to describe what they see have a preference for sensing. Alternatively, for those who would rather handle ideas, look into the unknown, or anticipate what is not obvious, their tendency is towards intuition.

- *Thinking (T) or feeling (F)*. These preferences relate to making decisions, with thinkers more likely to use objective logic, along with an analytic and detached approach. On the other hand, those with a preference for feeling will decide using values and/or personal beliefs, on the basis of what they feel is important and what they care about.

- *Judgement (J) or perception (P)*. If you wish your life to be planned, stable and organized your preference is for judgement (not to be confused with judgemental). If, however, you prefer to be flexible and respond to things as they arise you are classed as preferring perception.

FIGURE 5.1   Myers-Briggs personality types

ISTJ	ISFJ	INFJ	INTJ
ISTP	ISFP	INFP	INTP
ESTP	ESFP	ENFP	ENTP
ESTJ	ESFJ	ENFJ	ENTJ

Hence, the two alternatives within the four preferences offer 16 combinations, or personality types (see Figure 5.1). Thus, a personality type classified as INTJ prefers introversion, intuition, thinking and judging. Note, however, that such an individual only *prefers* to use these – they will also use extraversion, sensing, feeling and perception if necessary.

Whilst the MBTI is a recognized and respected method of assessing personality, one cannot apply it directly to the requirements and performance of leaders. Whilst it will accurately point to the preferences of an individual, one cannot directly translate those to determine whether they will make a leader more or less effective in any specific circumstance. It is not a case of saying that sensing is better than intuition, or perception is better than judgement – not least because these options are preferences, rather than absolute determinants of behaviour. All personality types can be effective leaders because all preferences are valuable and have important contributions to make. Equally, all types can be less than effective in certain circumstances or environments. Understanding one's own preferences can, however, be useful in developing self-awareness and emotional intelligence, and for appreciating the impact of one's behaviour on others.

Having said that specific personality types cannot be unquestionably related to leadership effectiveness, studies worldwide have shown some profile types to be more predominant in those holding leadership positions. In one study of 26,477 delegates having undergone leadership development programmes at the Centre for Creative Leadership, the following high percentage frequencies were reported:

ISTJ   –   18.2 per cent

ESTJ   –   16.0 per cent

ENTJ   –   13.1 per cent

INTJ   –   10.8 per cent

This suggests that leaders tend to prefer thinking and judgement (over feeling and perception), which is perhaps not surprising as organizations are likely to require their leaders to adopt logical and planned behaviours.

In a presentation made by Professor Philip Copeland from Stanford University on 1 February 2012 he proposed that combinations of the middle two preferences were particularly relevant to leadership styles in terms of potential strengths and weaknesses, as detailed in Table 5.2.

TABLE 5.2   Myers-Briggs preferences in relation to leadership styles

Leadership Style	Preferences	Potential Strength	Potential Weakness
Co-operation	Sensing/feeling	Encourages people to work together to help one another achieve common goals	'Management by committee', directionless, unaccountable
Consistent	Sensing/thinking	Establishes rules and systems to help people achieve consistent results efficiently and effectively	'Clubby', low-performing
Inspiration	Intuition/feeling	Inspires people due to strong beliefs in the organization's values of serving social needs and helping people grow and develop	Blindly ambitious
Achievement	Intuition/thinking	Motivates people to perform at high levels and work towards being the best and achieving excellence	Controlling, autocratic

360-degree assessments

Most business leaders value commercial data as it provides objective evidence that facilitates decision-making. The same reasoning could be applied to their own development: if they can be provided with evidence, even if largely subjective, of their own strengths and weaknesses they are more likely to 'buy in' to a process of development, which is, therefore, more likely to be effective. If that data offers an opportunity to compare their own assessment of their leadership with that of others who connect and interact with them professionally and personally, then it is all the more objective. Comparing the two assessments (personal and external) can provide a powerful wake-up call if there are significant divergences. Conversely, for those whose self-assessment matches how others evaluate their personality and behaviours, the experience can provide a positive validation of their leadership abilities.

Undertaking 360-degree feedback is one of the most efficacious aspects of a leader development programme as it requires executives to evaluate themselves against a set of criteria, which are also used in questionnaires completed by selected other respondents, often including line managers, peers and direct reports. Respondents are also usually offered the opportunity to provide qualitative comments as well as their quantitative scoring. The subjects subsequently receive a report that allows them to conduct a gap analysis to identify any differences between how they perceive themselves, compared with the other respondents. Follow-up action should contain subsequent discussions with, for example, an executive coach with a view to agreeing a developmental action plan, taking into account the feedback results.

Leadership *BEST* practice

An annual questionnaire is filled out on Henry Engelhardt, chief executive of Admiral Group, by about 9 or 10 direct reportees and a similar number of senior managers who do not report directly to him. The HR manager and IT manager then analyse the returns and speak to the respondents before briefing Henry on the qualitative and quantitative results. Henry says: 'It is hugely important to me because these are the people who are running the business and are closest to me, so if I am not meeting their needs I am in real trouble.'

Thus, the following benefits for leaders are offered by 360-degree feedback:

- *Offers multiple perspectives* from those who can evaluate, and are impacted by, a leader's performance.

- *Enhances skills and behaviours* as a result of identifying specific shortcomings. Key leadership competencies can be addressed with a view to enhancing performance and offering opportunities for advancement.

- *Enables customized development programmes* to be drawn up, taking into consideration the individual's specific learning needs, as opposed to participating in generic, broad-brush programmes.

- *Creates a culture of learning* and continual improvement. This will be particularly powerful if the entire senior leadership team is prepared to participate in 360-degree feedback.

Feedback results can also be used to compare with those from other leaders, either within the same organization or from competencies, behaviours or traits found through research to be common in successful leaders across other sectors and in other countries. Two sources of such research instruments are Kets de Vries's (2004) Global Executive Leadership Inventory (GELI); and Kouzes and Posner's (2001) Leadership Practices Inventory (LPI). Another is Kets de Vries's Personality Audit, which we will consider in more depth later in this chapter.

Whilst I stress the importance of senior leaders within an organization supporting 360-degree feedback in the most powerful way – by their own participation – it appears that they are the *least* likely to participate. Kets de Vries (2004), designer of the GELI, suggests:

> All leaders need feedback to do their best work and continue their development. Unfortunately, the higher you are in an organization, the less likely it is you will receive frank, constructive feedback. It has been estimated that only ten per cent of executives accurately assess themselves. In fact, surveys show that approximately 70 per cent of executives think they are in the top 25 per cent of the people in their profession, and many are honestly unaware of behaviour that impedes effective organizational functioning. We tend to accept feedback that is consistent with the way we see ourselves, and reject feedback that is inconsistent with our self-perceptions. That's why you need 360-degree feedback systems and assessment tools which allow you to compare your perceptions of your leadership behaviour with those of others who are familiar with your leadership styles.

These are persuasive words, from a clinical professor of leadership development holding the Raoul de Vitry d'Avancourt Chair of Leadership Development at INSEAD, France, Singapore and Abu Dhabi and being founder of its Global Leadership Center.

The Johari Window, devised by American psychologists Joseph Luft and Harry Ingham in 1955, is a well-recognized tool for improving self-awareness and mutual understanding between individuals and groups, as well as interpreting the psychological contract between employers and employee relationships – to be expanded in Chapter 6. Essentially, it takes the form of a matrix that categorizes the potential differences between how we perceive ourselves, as compared to how the world around us perceives us (see Figure 5.2). Applying it to 360-degree feedback, in particular the difficulties

FIGURE 5.2   The Johari Window

Known to self Known to others	Known to self Unknown to others
Unknown to self Known to others	Unknown to self Unknown to others

surrounding senior leaders suggested by Kets de Vries, above, executives and their coaches can explore the 'unknown to self / known to others' area with a view to increasing levels of self-awareness. Feedback can also be used to expand the 'known to self / unknown others' box in order to communicate more widely what was previously unproductively hidden from the wider community. The leaders may, for example, assume that their people are aware of their personal values – only to find, through formal feedback, that they are either unaware, or have misinterpreted them.

The Personality Audit

As mentioned above, Kets de Vries *et al*'s (2006) Personality Audit is another multiple feedback instrument – one designed to clarify the various motivational needs of executives. It uses a psychodynamic approach to leadership: the interaction of various conscious and unconscious mental or emotional processes as they influence personality, attitudes and behaviour. Participants are able to assess themselves against seven personality dimensions important in human behaviour, with a view to using identified short-comings as a basis for a leader development programme. The dimensions are formulated to provide a deeper understanding of the psychodynamic and psychosocial forces driving behaviour, especially important in terms of interpersonal relations.

The designers expanded the Johari Window concept of a possible divide between self-perception and the perception of others to include assessment from both the public and private sides of the subject's life. Hence, the number of 'observers' who complete the audit should include at least three from both public and private spheres, in the belief that individuals may be perceived differently inside and outside of work. At the time of publishing their 2006 paper introducing the audit, this was the only questionnaire or personality test to included public and private input.

The Personality Audit uses personality characteristics that determine human functioning that are most helpful in explaining executive leadership behaviour, as well as evidence of personality traits of various existing leaders. This data was used to identify the seven dimensions of personality that the respondents are asked to consider in relation to the audit's subject, on a scale from one to seven. The dimensions are:

1 *Low self-esteem – high self-esteem*. The term self-esteem reflects an evaluative self-judgement centring on identify formation – an individual's desire to articulate his or her self in relation to the outside world. People who have high levels of self-esteem portray positive self-assurance, assertiveness and confidence; whilst low self-esteem suggests insecurity. The audit included scales in this dimension with extreme options such as:

   – *I think other people find me: boring ↔ extremely interesting;*
   – *Looking at myself: I am self-critical ↔ I accept myself fully.*

2 *Vigilant – trustful*. This is essentially a psychosocial personality dimension as it affects a leader's interpersonal relationships. Individuals high on trust tend to be considerate and supportive of others, and possessing a generally hopeful attitude towards life experiences. It suggests one's openness to social interactions and a tendency towards extroversion. On the other hand, overly vigilant people tend to be distrustful and may appear more distant and cold-hearted. Moreover, the amount of trust one is prepared to offer people and situations will influence the degree of adventurousness one displays:

   – *When people hurt me: it is difficult for me to forgive them ↔ it is easy for me to forgive them;*
   – *I reveal myself to others: very little ↔ completely.*

3 *Laissez-faire – conscientious*. People who score high on the conscientious continuum are more likely to be systematic, methodical and efficient. They often seek and achieve social approval and outcomes accepted by others. They may not be spontaneous in behaviour, but compensate by being thorough and correct in detail. Conversely, a laissez-faire personality engenders a happy-go-lucky approach to life, with scant regard to rules, regulations and detail. The danger is they tend to let things slip, thus reducing their perceived value as relational partners and team members:

   – *When I don't do what I promised: I don't worry about it ↔ I feel guilty;*
   – *I pay: little attention to details ↔ great attention to details.*

4 *Self-effacing – assertive*. Assertiveness is about a desire to decide what one does and to deal with the world with a sense of purpose. People who verge towards the self-effacing extreme of the scale, however, tend to be reflective, less competitive and ambitious, and

more socially uncomfortable – they will weigh up all options before making a decision:

- *I defend my point of view: rarely ↔ almost always;*
- *For me, winning is: unimportant ↔ extremely important.*

5 *Introverted – extroverted.* Extroverts are more likely to direct their attention and energy towards the external world, as represented by people and external situations, whilst introverts focus more on their own inner world:

- *I would prefer to spend most of my time: alone ↔ with other people;*
- *I seek the company of other people: rarely ↔ quite often.*

6 *Low-spirited – high-spirited.* Our mood colours our perception of the world and serves as both an internal and external signalling system – the latter influencing how others perceive our emotional state. High-spirited people display strong emotions and are highly expressive, as opposed to the flat, changeable or irritable expressions portrayed by low-spirited individuals. Both extremes may be a reflection of their levels of self-esteem:

- *I am optimistic: rarely ↔ almost always;*
- *I feel hopeless: often ↔ rarely.*

7 *Prudent – adventurous.* Adventurous people tend to be unconventional, imaginative, creative and eager to experiment with new things. More prudent individuals are likely to be more conservative, conventional and conforming, which can in some cases be an indication of a more healthy mental state:

- *In my life I need a great deal of: stability ↔ variety;*
- *I seek new thrills: rarely ↔ very often.*

The designers of the Personality Audit concluded that it identified four major factors influencing the behaviour of executive leaders in both public and private life. They are: mood; extroversion and sociability; assertiveness; and conscientiousness. There is also a noted similarity between some of the dimensions and those of the 'big five' personality model (Goldberg, 1990), although those specifically included in the Personality Audit are more important for the functioning of senior leaders within organizations.

The application of instruments such as psychometric tests, 360-degree assessment, and the Personality Audit will provide a wealth of insights regarding the subject's inner self, which can then be used as the foundation of a development programme. Most organizations' immediate reaction, once a need for leadership development is recognized, is to search for the most appropriate training course on which to send their managers. There are, indeed, many highly recommended programmes, from those lasting a mere few days, to full MBA courses. However, many focus strongly on the management roles of the delegates, and less so on their emotional intelligence (EI). Moreover, improvements in EI skills as a result of formal training courses can be limited and short-lasting. Noe and Schmitt (1986) applied a 360-degree multi-source assessment of the behaviours, such as sensitivity towards others and leadership, of people before and after attending a leadership training course. Results showed an improvement of only 8 per cent on a broad array of such skills three months after the course. This figure is consistent with several other studies of a similar nature: most showing around a 10 per cent improvement in EI skills measured between three months and 18 months after training. Specht and Sandlin (1991) found the half-life of knowledge learnt in an MBA course to be about six weeks.

One is tempted to wonder if the money and effort invested in formal management and leadership training courses is well spent in terms of developing both the intrapersonal and interpersonal skills required of leaders, for example those listed in Table 5.1 earlier in this chapter. Often, managers who attend formal training courses, where they are taught advanced management strategies, financial controls, performance assessment, etc, return to work better equipped to manage their workplaces and are then subsequently propelled into senior leadership roles. Though good at controlling resources and delivering operational results, they may be less prepared for the human and social aspects of their role. For operational benefits to be long-lasting, leaders must create environments where highly engaged followers strive together to achieve the leader's vision.

A proven solution to supplementing formal management and leadership training in order to provide long-lasting benefits for organizations is to follow up the training with a programme of coaching for participants. Coaches can help to both interpret the data provided by the self-discovery instruments discussed earlier, and to enhance any formal training received – hence developing their individual (intrapersonal) and relational (interpersonal) leadership skills.

A study by the Centre for Excellence for Leadership and Management Skills in Wales (2013) that interviewed owner-managers and HR directors of businesses found that, whilst they reported that classroom-based training had a positive impact on participants – in terms of increased confidence, team-working and collaboration, individuals' awareness of roles and responsibilities, and financial performance – subsequent coaching was found to be more effective. When explaining this finding one respondent stated:

> You can see the learning happening, almost like a light's gone on, but when they get back to their workplace what we are finding is that they are finding it difficult to change their behaviour. I think that is where we are struggling to find a way of ensuring that learning continues in the workplace, because while I'm stood in front of them it is easy, but when I am not there, and suddenly the pressure of the job takes over, then their ability to manage – and I mean that in a nice way – comes second to the job that they have to do.

Indeed, one-quarter of the survey's informants highlighted the positive impact of coaching an individual behaviour, one stating:

A lot of the themes coming up through coaching are relationship-building, interpersonal skills, not technical stuff... 23 per cent of the cohort that we've coached so far have had a promotion, and that's rising.

When asked which form of learning was more effective in their organization, another respondent was unequivocal:

Definitely through coaching. We were not getting that through the classroom... it is actually behaviour self-reinforcing. We had an operations manager with a very high authoritarian, control type of management style; through his coaching, he said, 'I got tired. I got tired of trying to make people do things and through my coaching I learnt to actually allow them to think for themselves.' All standard, simple stuff on reflection, but a massive issue for him to let go, provide a bit of input for them, transform people. One of his staff said: 'We don't understand what's happened to him, he's a delight to work with.'

The report concluded by reinforcing a key message from all interviews – the difficulties associated with transferring learning in the classroom to application in the workplace through changes in leadership behaviour. Hence, for leadership and management courses to be fully effective they should be coupled with coaching programmes – either at individual or group levels.

Executive coaching

Although there is a general lack of agreement amongst coaching professionals about precise definitions, the Chartered Institute for Personnel and Development proposes the following agreed characteristics:

- It is essentially a form of development, in that it is less prescribed, though this is not a hard and fast rule.
- It focuses on improving performance and developing individuals' skills.
- Personal issues may be discussed but the emphasis is on performance at work.
- Coaching activities have both organizational and individual goals.
- It provides people with feedback on both their strengths and their weaknesses.

Whilst mentoring has the same broad characteristics, it tends to involve an experienced colleague from the same workplace supporting the development of a more junior or inexperienced member of staff. Mentoring relationships also tend to be conducted over a longer term than coaching arrangements.

The broad aims of coaching are to assist in improving performance and to advance learning and development. It can be applied to individual leaders or within a group learning environment, which we will consider later in the chapter. With regard to one-to-one coaching of leaders, often referred to as executive coaching, it is often used by organizations when a leader has been appointed to a new role or has been identified for one in the near future. Alternatively, a senior executive may require new skills to address a specific performance problem or to make difficult strategic or operational decisions. For a coaching programme to effect sustained behavioural and performance improvements it should:

- *Provide insight into current leadership style.* Here the feedback from tools such as psychometric tests, personality audits and 360-degree reporting will provide a most useful foundation for discussion.
- *Clarify inner strengths and values.* The effectiveness of a leader will be heavily dependent upon his or her levels of EI. Improvements in leadership skills result by recognizing and bolstering one's own emotions, as well as those of one's followers.
- *Improve interpersonal relationships.* Issues such as empathy, influence, conflict management and team development will feature large in coaching discussions.
- *Broaden perspectives.* Coaching will help leaders to conceptualize and to think strategically. The ability to recognize and understand complex situations is essential in senior leadership roles.
- *Identify and overcome barriers to change.* Coaches will help leaders to address and overcome ingrained resistance to new ways of working amongst colleagues and staff. They may also perform a role in enabling leaders to recognize and address similar resistances within their own personality and resulting behaviour.
- *Enhance a learning mentality.* One of coaching's most important goals is to develop a questioning, enquiring and learning mentality. This involves stepping back and reflecting on one's actions; being prepared to accept external feedback and advice; and to be continually seeking ways to enhance one's performance.

BEST leadership quote

'One of the keys to our success is having a very clear coaching culture. All my managers and supervisors are coach-trained from a psychological perspective. Coaching conversations are a feature of how the organization operates: giving and receiving feedback; telling people that they have done well or need to improve; and identifying blockages to success.'

Ian Munro
Group Chief Executive
New Charter Housing

Good coaching provides an environment where issues can be discussed in total confidentiality; where people are heard but never judged. Trust is quickly developed between coach and client, which is used as a foundation for successful exploration, ownership and positive change. An effective coach attempts to see the world as the client sees it, which in turn acts as a mirror to enable the client to reflect on issues and behaviours more clearly. Hence, coaches must:

- be continually aware how their own inner feelings and behaviours could influence the one-to-one relationship;
- be authentic and truthful, never trying to hide or dodge difficult issues;
- leave their personal egos outside the room – facilitating the discussions, not acting the role of expert;
- be empathetic to the emotions of the client;
- remain detached and not get personally involved with the client's world. Being detached is not being cold or aloof; rather acting as an objective observer.

However, as the essence of coaching is the formation of productive one-to-one relationships, the client also has a responsibility to make the relationship work by being:

- Open to constructive feedback, either from the coach, or from the comments and results from the multiple feedback instruments covered previously in this chapter.
- Committed to the process and not just acting as a willing participant. Coaching will be of little value unless the client really wants to explore the potentiality of change and is prepared to devote the time and energy to realize it.
- Prepared to reveal personal weaknesses to others. Leaders, especially those holding senior positions, strive continually to project an aura of confidence and infallibility. Moreover, a preparedness to admit shortcomings to others must first begin by doing so to oneself.
- Brave enough to consider modifying a leadership style that has previously been effective, but may not be fully appropriate to changing circumstances.
- Prepared to have his or her assumptions, motives and behaviours challenged by the coach. This may require an 'ego check' whereby the extent to which a leader's high level of self-confidence reasonably affects decision-making and interpersonal relationships is explored.

Kets de Vries *et al* (2010) describe the relationship between coach and client in the form of a two-by-two matrix. One dimension signifies the degree of transference awareness the client has of his or her inner feelings and thoughts; with the other relating to that of the coach (as shown in Figure 5.3).

FIGURE 5.3   The transference/counter-transference interface
(Kets de Vries *et al*, 2010)

	Unaware (COACH)	Aware (COACH)
Aware	3. Acting out: coach	4. Working alliance: the 'good' intervention
Unaware	1. Wild intervention: folie à deux	2. Acting out: client

CLIENT (row labels: Aware / Unaware)

Unaware   **Aware**
COACH

The matrix reflects the fact that coaches must feel and experience what is going on within the client's inner feelings and thoughts by not only listening to the explicit content of the conversation, but also the implicit one – as reflected by body language, demeanour, tone of voice, etc. In addition, they must also be aware of the influence of their own thoughts, associations, even prejudices on the client relationship. It is the impact of both parties' awareness of their inner consciousness that is classified in Figure 5.3.

In quadrant 1 both parties are unaware of the other's feelings, hence stick to their own agenda without any degree of empathetic listening. Coaches offer advice without considering the client's legitimate needs, often according to general coaching practice. Because they are largely driven by their own needs, the specificity of their input is extremely low. The clients themselves have little awareness of the influences on their behaviours and actions. Hence, although a brief honeymoon period of limited productivity may occur, it never continues to a meaningful relationship, quickly degenerating towards a speedy termination. With mutually reinforcing lack of empathy, both parties operate independently in a dangerous *folie à deux* (delusion shared by two parties in close association).

Quadrant 2 sees the coach having a degree of awareness of the client's psychological make-up – not matched by the client's own personal awareness. This poses a severe challenge for the coach: one for which no solution is apparent. Rather than recognize the futility of the process, they may elect to act out the relationship, regardless of meaningful progress. Because confronting the client with difficult issues results merely in a stonewall reaction, coaches operating in this quadrant may choose to readily agree with whatever position the client takes – acting almost as a 'popular friend of the family' who steers away from any issues that may rock the relational boat.

Clients in quadrant 3 have an insightful awareness of their own personality and behaviour, although this degree of self-awareness is not reflected in the coach. The coach is a poor listener, yet quick to give reassurance and advice regardless of whether it is really appropriate and helpful. Ironically, such coaches may appear most charismatic, almost seductive, in their persona –

often delighting in dramatizing certain situations. Given this apparently attractive appearance and ready advice, the client may be easily swayed by their pseudo-expertise – sometimes towards destructive consequences. In essence, however, the coach is merely acting out his or her role, often offering the same advice time and time again, like a broken record. The termination of the relationship is often prompted by the emotionally intelligent client, who eventually realizes that he or she is being used by one not so attuned to the inner self.

Quadrant 4 represents a positive working alliance where both parties are genuinely aware of, and interested in, the other's perspectives. They know how to truly listen and benefit from the insight gained by doing so. They embark on a mutually reinforcing learning curve that inevitably leads to an authentic relationship. From the coaches' perspective, they know how to create an atmosphere for their clients to gain awareness and insight, whilst continually being aware of their own emotions.

The coaching process

The phases of the coaching process are fairly standard, namely:

1 *Contracting*, where the coach and client (be it a person or an organization) agree issues such as development goals, resources, time span, confidentiality, methods and cost.

2 *Data-gathering*, including the feedback instruments discussed previously in this chapter.

3 *Feedback* from coach to client, from which the client's strengths and areas for development will be discussed and agreed.

4 *Coaching sessions* in which the coach works with the client to monitor and reinforce development plans. Depending on the background and experience of the coach, these sessions may be conducted according to different approaches (see below).

5 *Evaluation* should commence once the sessions have concluded, according to the original contract agreement. This may be conducted between coach and client or, if the programme has been commissioned by the client's organization, the HR department may be involved. Either way, an evaluation should be made of both the coach's effectiveness and the degree to which the client's performance has been improved as a result of the programme. It may be that some of the feedback instruments, such as the 360-degree questionnaire, are rerun to compare the respondents' assessment of the leader before and after the coaching intervention.

Although the five stages above will apply to most coaching programmes, the approach taken by the coach will depend to a large extent on his or her background and intellectual traditions. Peltier (2001) identified five main approaches, summarized in Table 5.3 and listed on page 125:

TABLE 5.3   Summary of approaches by Peltier (2001) (from Feldman and Lankau, 2005)

Coaching Approach	Focus	Elements of Intervention	Evaluation Criteria
Psychodynamic	Client's unconscious thoughts and internal psychological states	Psychoanalysis – uncovering gap between ideal 'ego' and reality; defence mechanisms; transference; counter-transference; family dynamics	Increased self-awareness of thoughts, feelings and reactions
Behavourist	Client's observable behaviours	Intrinsic/extrinsic reinforcement; primary/secondary reinforcement; positive/negative reinforcement; punishment	Increased understanding of causes and consequences of behaviour; behaviour change
Person-centred	Client's understanding of self without direct intervention by coach	Creating a trusting and empathetic therapeutic relationship	Personal growth and change
Cognitive therapy	Client's conscious thinking	Identification of distorted thinking and irrational thoughts	New thinking that leads to positive feelings and effective behaviour
Systems-oriented	Individual, group and organizational influences on client's behaviour	Data-gathering and analysis of client's interactions with other individuals; requirements of role; group and intergroup relations; direct intervention within the organization	Improved job, group and organization effectiveness

- *Psychodynamic approach.* Psychoanalysis is used to help leaders explore unconscious thoughts that may influence how they think, feel and perform at work. Discussions may include defence mechanisms that distort leaders' perceptions of themselves and others; ways they unconsciously handicap themselves at work; and methods for identifying and addressing dysfunctional relationships or personal behaviours.

- *Behaviourist approach.* Here the focus is on observable behaviours, rather than internal psychological drivers, and what influences reinforce (positively or negatively) the leader's behaviours. The objective is for the client to become more effective in communicating with others, and in understanding the impact their own behaviour can have on others within the organization.

- *Person-centred approach.* The coach aims to have the client take more responsibility for what happens within his or her work environment, as opposed to attributing positive and negative outcomes to external influences. Rather than diagnosing issues and offering advice, this approach requires coaches to create a climate where clients discover for themselves what changes are needed, along with engendering the desire to influence them.

- *Cognitive therapy approach.* Cognitive psychology assumes that people can learn to notice and change their own thoughts. Hence, using this approach, coaches can explore with clients what thoughts initiated their emotions at work, often unproductively. Then, rather than seeking to change their emotional reactions, the clients are taught techniques for blocking or rechannelling negative thoughts.

- *Systems-oriented approach.* This assumes that the leader's behaviour can only be understood in the context of the multiple (often unreasonable) demands imposed upon him or her at work. The coach seeks to understand the individual, group and organizational influences affecting the leader's performance in order to offer advice as to more effective ways of dealing with them. This tends to be the most complex and comprehensive approach to coaching as it involves other members of the organization who have an influence on the client.

It is apparent that all the coaching approaches, except perhaps the systems-oriented approach, require the leader to embark on a journey of self-discovery: the psychodynamic approach explores unconscious thoughts; the behaviourist approach focuses on observable behaviours; the person-centred approach looks at taking responsibility for personal actions; and the cognitive therapy approach encourages leaders to identify what thoughts influence their emotions at work. Self-discovery may be necessary, because it is unlikely that an executive will receive much (if any) informal feedback from his or her subordinates regarding his intrapersonal and interpersonal competences. Moreover, it is often the case that senior leaders do not have a full appreciation of the impact that their emotions and behaviours have on others. It may not mean that they do not care, rather that they assume someone will tell them if something is going wrong. However, this may not be the case as subordinates may not feel confident enough to act as bearers of bad news, especially if it involves issues surrounding the leader's personal characteristics and behaviours. Goleman, Boyatzis and McKee (2001) quote a CEO as explaining:

> I so often feel I'm not getting the truth. I can never put my finger on it, because no one is actually lying to me. But I can sense that people are hiding information or camouflaging key facts. They aren't lying, but neither are they telling me everything I need to know. I'm always second-guessing.

BEST leadership quote

'My management team tell me when I am being ambiguous or contradicting our values. They give me the feedback that gets me back on track, and they feel confident with being able to do that.'

Ian Munro
Group Chief Executive
New Charter Housing

In *Primal Leadership* (2001), Goleman and colleagues explain their five-part process of self-discovery and personal reinvention, which could easily be included as part of a coaching process. It is designed to rewire the brain towards more emotionally intelligent behaviours that impact positively on the emotions of those that come in contact with the leader. The process of five questions begins with imagining your ideal self and then, secondly, understanding your real self, as others see you. The third step involves creating a plan to bridge the gap between the ideal and real self, which is practised in the final stage. The process concludes with the creation of a community of supporters to keep the process alive and continuous.

In more detail, the steps are:

1   *'Who do I want to be?'* Identifying your ideal self, including what you want from your life, requires deep introspection, along with an understanding that achieving that vision may entail fundamental changes to previous thoughts, learning and behaviours. This is an important first stage because it involves the creation of a vision that encapsulates the deepest expression of one's life's desires – which becomes both a guide for future decisions and a barometer of our sense of personal satisfaction.

2 *'Who am I now?'* This step of the discovery process entails you coming to assess your leadership style as others do, although, as previously suggested, eliciting others' views, informally at least, may prove less than straightforward. Leaders should encourage open critiques from as many sources as possible, as well as evaluating available 360-degree feedback in terms of EI. For example, when people rate how well a leader listens, they are really assessing how well they feel he or she hears them. However, not only should you be seeking areas of weakness – a dispiriting process – but also confirming your strengths, which is an aspect of positive psychology discussed in the previous chapter.

3 *'How do I get from here to there?'* Bridging the gap between the ideal self and the near self requires the creation of an action plan, ideally in consultation with a coach. Goleman proposes that its goals should be written in terms of learning objectives, rather than performance improvement objectives that the leader has to prove conclusively. The best kind of learning focuses on your own ideal self, rather than someone else's model of what you should be. Moreover, learning goals should be designed to enhance existing strengths, rather than addressing areas of weakness that may be adequate for the roles and responsibilities of the leader.

4 *'How do I make change stick?'* Creating long-lasting change requires a leader to rehearse new behaviours again and again until he or she has mastered them at the level of implicit learning. Repeating actions eventually triggers in our brains the neutral connections necessary for genuine, lasting change to occur. Implicit learning is what cognitive psychologists call the automatic strengthening of those neutral connections as a result of repeated behaviours. Goleman, Boyatzis and McKee (2002) propose that, for the most part, the brain masters leadership competences – from self-confidence and emotional self-management to empathy and persuasion – through implicit learning rather than the explicit variety provided in classroom-based courses. Hence, the key to learning new leadership skills lies in practice to the point of mastery: when you can sustain the new skills over the long term.

5 *'Who can help?'* Leadership is intrinsically stressful, and when people feel stressed they no longer feel comfortable and safe – not a situation conducive to learning and development. Leadership can be a lonely place where every action is scrutinized, which in turn discourages the exploration of new behaviours. Conversely, if leaders feel psychologically safe they are much more likely to experiment with less risk of embarrassment, or fear of failure. Having a community of supportive fellow leaders, for example, can offer a more comfortable arena for continual development. Cultivating special relationships with those who have your personal and professional development at heart is a powerful force for encouraging change. We cannot improve our EI or leadership style in isolation. We need to get feedback on the impact that our actions have on others in order to assess our progress towards our learning objectives. Be it as a member of a supportive group or in a coach–client relationship, leaders need the help of others on the journey from the real self to the ideal self.

Group coaching

Continuing the theme of how leaders can benefit from the support of fellow leaders, let us consider an alternative to one-to-one executive coaching: group coaching. Coaching in groups can offer participants a number of different perspectives from fellow leaders who may be facing similar challenges. Groups, if facilitated well, provide lively, challenging and interactive supported learning environments. Moreover, group members are encouraged to hold other members to account for the agreed behavioural changes, which can result in long-term positive benefits. Kets de Vries *et al* (2008) recorded positive self- and observer-assessments up to a year after group coaching, particularly in terms of self-awareness, coaching behaviour, rewarding feedback and team-building.

The group size, with leaders from a single organization, will typically be between 4 and 10 and the group session will last between one and three days. A well-designed programme will include the following elements:

- introduction/ice-breaker;
- exercises to encourage open discussion about their true selves;
- discussions and analysis of multi-respondent feedback instruments;
- action-planning;
- follow-up support arrangements.

Introduction

It is important at the onset of the programme that the facilitator attempts to put participants at ease by stressing that all discussions and written material will be treated in the utmost confidentiality. Everyone will be expected to participate, both personally and as a group member, offering input and advice to fellow members.

The facilitator may begin early interaction by asking the participants what, for example, they view as good and bad leadership; perhaps personal examples of notable leadership experiences are encouraged and discussed.

Discussion exercise

This second stage continues the process of self-discovery by creating what psychologists call 'transitional space', defined as 'the space between the psyche and external reality where intimate relationships and creativity occurs'. It is an environment where people who recognize the need to change can take the time and space to understand where they are and consider what they want to be or do.

An exercise used for this purpose by coaches from the Kets de Vries Institute is to invite participants to draw a self-portrait on a large piece of paper that represents dimensions of their life: for example their future, past, work or leisure. Once finished, their colleagues from the group are invited to comment on or analyse the portrait, with the originator having to listen in silence. Once complete, the subject is then asked to offer his or her own interpretation of the portrait, in terms of past experiences that have influenced its composition. The purpose of this exercise is to help the subject to see his or her world through the lens of others' thoughts and emotions. As Kets de Vries says: 'The empathy and support shown by other participants, the appreciation that other people truly care, encourages participants to embrace experimentation and eventually take control of their executive behaviour.' The 'transitional space' begins to fill.

Considering the multi-respondent feedback

This stage involves revealing to the group each participant's results of previously completed feedback instruments such as 360-degree questionnaires and personality audits. Individual participants are invited to comment and interpret the findings, in particular those that indicate specific strengths and weaknesses. Again, they are asked to consider whether any past experiences have influenced the results of the assessments.

Then follows the group's reflections on the individual's results, with the facilitator encouraging them to consider their own past interaction with him or her and to look for clues as to the sources or triggers of the EI and resulting behaviours exposed by the feedback results. Group members may ask questions to clarify issues or even challenge the presented evidence, offering helpful advice and suggestions as a result. Every participant should therefore experience both challenge and support, leading to a hope that issues can be resolved successfully. Through having examined and reflected upon their own feedback results, and then heard the comments of the group, participants are then better placed to decide whether they want to react to this and change their behaviour.

Action-planning

Participants are required to construct a realistic, measurable action plan focusing largely on the major issues raised during the previous stages. It is important that the individual plans are shared with the group, ideally with the subject explaining the objectives and actions contained therein: what they will do differently when they return to work. This verbal affirmation is an important link to the final stage of the process.

Follow-up support

Before the session finishes each participant is allocated an internal mentor to act as a supportive learning partner to help the leader through the change process that he or she has committed to. Continuing emotional support back in the workplace is essential if the behavioural changes contained within the action plan are to be realized. Goldsmith, Lyons and Freas (2000) demonstrated that 50 per cent of managers who received feedback on their performance with no follow-up were found to be unchanged or less effective 18 months later. Conversely, of those who did receive subsequent support, 89 per cent were assessed as being more effective over the same period.

The final role of the group coach should be to offer some practical advice to the leaders re-entering their work environment, such as:

- Thank the feedback respondents for their helpful input and invite them to expand on any aspects that were not clear.
- Brief your management team on what you have experienced during the group coaching programme.
- Tell people, at home and at work, what you plan to do differently – thus creating a further encouragement to your commitment to behavioural change.
- Keep your action plan visible and refer to it regularly – comparing progress with stated objectives.
- Have regular timetabled conversations with your mentor for support, challenge and encouragement.
- Tell your own manager what you have experienced and share the outcomes with him or her.

The facilitator

Group coaching can offer additional supplementary benefits to one-to-one sessions but the group dynamics and interventions can be much more challenging for participants. It is one thing to share one's inner thoughts with a trusted coach – but quite another to do so with a group of work colleagues! All coaching can awaken deep-seated psychological issues that may pose the threat of unresolved problems lasting long after the coaching process has completed. This is especially relevant where issues have been shared with others who may not be trusted as much as an executive coach. Hence, in selecting a coach to facilitate a group process it is highly recommended that the person has sufficient psychological understanding and practice, along with experience of life within organizations. A coach who does not have that background may not be able to recognize the presence of a psychological problem of a characterological nature within individuals, as well as those associated with the dynamics of a group.

Leadership *BEST* practice

'Courage and Spark' leadership development programme at New Charter

When I interviewed Ian Munro, chief executive of New Charter Housing Group, he told me about the various development programmes the company offers its people. One of them, 'Courage and Spark', was of particular interest to me as it appeared to offer a markedly different approach to leadership development, especially at the leadership level at which it is targeted. Designed and co-delivered by leadership consultant and coach Peter Bluckert (**www.peterbluckertconsulting.com**), at its foundation is the belief that:

> It can make a real difference to young leaders and their organizations if they are able to fast-track their emotional and psychological development through early exposure to an intensive personal growth programme. Behaviours change as we grow and develop and when our awareness and consciousness is raised. Deeper and more sustainable change comes about through developing the inner leader in order to become a great outer leader.

Note the phrases 'emotional and psychological development', 'personal growth' and 'the inner leader'. This is not leadership development based on recognized leadership competencies, rather one that concentrates on emotional intelligence (EI) development, through what it describes as 'a deep-dive personal reflection experience'.

Peter kindly agreed to talk me through the programme and its ethos and commenced by explaining that so many of the senior executives he has coached and trained throughout his career have commented: 'I wish I had experienced this emotional intelligence development much earlier in my life' (sometimes adding 'I would have understood my wife and children much better!'). This led Peter to investigate whether other providers in the UK and overseas offered junior leader development based upon the principle of EI – only to find that there was very little of this style of intervention. Peter was fortunate that he had been working with New Charter for many years – even when it existed as the housing department of Tameside Council. Ian Munro, its visionary leader, took little persuasion to have those identified as future leaders exposed to Peter's new course, which he entitled 'Courage and Spark'.

New Charter has a turnover of £100 million, with 880 staff managing social housing in Greater Manchester, Nottingham and Oldham. It also has a building company charged with maintaining the houses, which in itself has another 200 staff. Hence, the two 'Courage and Spark' programmes currently delivered to New Charter each have 16–18 carefully selected delegates, in their twenties to forties, who range in occupation from administrator, through housing manager, to building trades persons.

The first three-day workshop is preceded by the delegates undertaking the Hay ESCI 360-degree feedback process, based on Goleman, Boyatzis and McKee's (2001) four dimensions of emotional intelligence (see Chapter 4), the results of which the course tutors discuss with each delegate a few days before the programme begins. The stated purpose of the first workshop is to enable the delegates to explore:

- who you are and who you want to be;

- your strengths, values, purpose and personal vision;

- your connection with others;

- whether or not the way you're working (and living) is actually working;

- how 'who you are' shapes 'the leader you are';

- your intentional change agenda.

Peter describes the workshop as a powerful and challenging journey of discovery, approximately half of which offers opportunities for self-learning – including the second day, described as the Deep-Dive Day, which consists of five small group exercises designed for delegates to clarify their personal values, purpose and achievements.

Another unique feature of the three days is the 90-minute 'experiential group' sessions held every afternoon, which provide a space for raising personal awareness issues within a group setting. Hence, the overarching purpose of this first workshop is to encourage delegates to ask themselves if they are the finished product and, if not, what feedback they have received from the group and tutors that will help them be a better, resonant leader. Goleman and colleagues (2001) describe one sign of resonant leadership as 'a group of followers who vibrate with the leader's upbeat and enthusiastic energy'.

There is a gap of four months before the second workshop, during which time each delegate is tasked to ask six to eight people in his or her private and working life a simple question: 'What is the single most important thing I need to do to develop my leadership skills?'

Armed with the responses, delegates attend the second workshop, which continues the self-reflection process towards a greater understanding of the change needed to develop their leadership presence, influence and impact. Day one, entitled 'Immunity to Change', after the book of the same name (Kegan and Lahey, 2009), encourages delegates to identify and challenge the reasons that may prevent them from making the changes necessary to develop their leadership skills. Day two begins with some instruction on a distinctive coaching methodology, after which each delegate holds a coaching session in a small group of four – not only good coaching experience, but also additional peer intervention. The workshop, hence the programme, ends on the third day with structured exercises focusing on their personal leadership impact and influence, after which delegates individually describe to the assembled group what leadership presence they feel they project – to then hear comments and feedback from their fellow delegates and tutors.

I suggested to Peter that the programme as a whole is extremely challenging – not least in terms of the amount of self-reflection, and peer feedback – especially considering the delegates' age and experience. Few of them would have expected to undertake a six-day leadership development programme, let alone one so psychologically challenging: least of all the likes of a plasterer in his mid-twenties! Peter agreed and made the point that selection was key – those attending will have been identified by Ian Munro, Christine Amyses, the HR director, and their senior managers for their capability and potential for career development and possible executive-level succession. He also made the point that a plasterer was one of the 'star delegates' on the previous programme!

Finally, I asked why it was called 'Courage and Spark'. Peter explained that, in his opinion, it takes courage to take the difficult decisions associated with leadership, as well as the emotional energy to make your mark as a leader.

Chapter summary

The case for investing in leadership development is proven by many significant surveys, yet many organizations are failing to reap the rewards of having inspirational leaders who are in tune with both the objectives of the business and those who are the crucial element in realizing those objectives – their followers. This chapter explained the difference between management and leadership development; and then between leadership development, focusing on social capital, and leader development, which seeks to enhance the intrapersonal skills of the leader – the inner-self.

Various instruments designed to evaluate the personality and behaviours of leaders were discussed, notably psychometric tests, 360-degree assessment, and the Personality Audit. Data gathered by personal and multi-feedback assessments provides a wealth of information that can be used to compare how a leader sees himself or herself, with those that they lead and associate with in the workplace. It should also form the starting point for development programmes, especially coaching, which can be individual one-to-one executive coaching, or conducted within a group of leaders from the same organization. The process of both models was explored in depth within the chapter.

The psychological contract

– unwritten expectations of leaders and followers

When employees are recruited to a new organization they will expect to receive a written contract or, at the very least, some form of documented agreement that lays down what is expected from them in terms of their behaviour and performance in relation to their new role. The contract will also detail what they can expect from their new employer such as pay, conditions, holiday entitlement and contract period. The written contract or agreement is a precise document but will, by its very nature, contribute very little to the future working relationship between the organization – represented by its leaders – and the employee. Both parties will have unspoken and tacit expectations of each other that began to be formed during the recruitment process, and will continue and develop throughout their future working association.

BEST leadership quote

'It is very much about trying to establish a standard and a behaviour of intellectual – if you like psychological – commitment to doing things the right way. Hence the reason why we start that process at recruitment: we do not want people to join our company who don't understand that.'

William Rogers
Chief Executive
UKRD

The employee may have been sufficiently encouraged to apply for the job by an advertisement that lauded the organization's dedication to personal development and supportive team-working: factors that particularly appealed to him or her. They will have constructed their application form and CV to stress their commitment to the qualities and values they believe the organization is looking for in its staff. Hence, expectations are being formed by both parties even before they meet, and will be reinforced and expanded throughout the recruitment process. These obligations may not be contained specifically within an employment contract, yet they are understood by both parties and may prove to be more influential to their future working relationships than any written document. It is a contract – a psychological contract (PsyC) – that defines the reality of the relationship between employer and employee covering, for example:

- personal development;
- motivation to work;
- organizational culture and values;
- the ethical code to be adhered to;
- relationships at all levels and in all directions;
- levels of expected support.

Note that several of those bullet points could be applied to both parties: the PsyC is a two-way street.

The concept was first introduced by Edgar Schein who, in his book *Organizational Culture and Leadership*, defined it as 'an unwritten set of expectations operating at all times between every member of an organization and the various managers and others in that organization'. He further stressed that it is essential that both parties' expectations of a contract should accord, if a long-lasting relationship – benefiting both – is to develop.

Guest and Conway (2002) proposed the following key factors associated with a PsyC:

- the extent to which employers adopt HR practices will influence the state of the PsyC;
- the contract is based upon the employees' sense of fairness and trust, and their belief that the employer is honouring the 'deal' between them;
- where the PsyC is positive, increased employee commitment and satisfaction will have a positive impact on business performance.

It is interesting to consider how an understanding between two or more parties, similar to the PsyC, could also influence relationships outside an employment environment. The PsyC is based upon interpersonal qualities such as trust, respect, compassion, empathy, fairness – all features of emotional intelligence – which translate to many other situations where human beings interact, especially where there is a degree of interdependence between them. Be they family or sporting relationships, for example, through to the severe conditions we will consider in extreme leadership (Chapter 8), the degree to which different parties meet the expectations of each other heavily influences the extent to which they will commit to shared objectives. However, for the remainder of this chapter we will focus on how the PsyC impacts on the relationships between employers/employees, leaders/followers.

Whilst I have used the plural, groups, the concept of a PsyC can also be applied to individuals. Whilst individual employees or followers will hold personal views and understandings as to the informal 'contract' that exists, the collective view of group or organization members is usually more significant and, in practice, a senior executive or leader will be more concerned with how the PsyC relates to a collective situation. This would especially apply within large organizations, where their scale will prevent consideration of the complexities of expectations and understandings on a person-to-person basis. That said, it is certainly incumbent on individual leaders to consider the implications of the PsyC in respect of the mutual relationships of those they directly lead. Whether considered or applied at the individual or collective level, the PsyC is formed of unwritten expectations of one party that translate to obligations required of the other.

Employee expectations

Whilst formal employment contracts will include details of pay, working hours, holiday allowance, pensions and other benefits, there are a host of other aspects of employment that may not be covered, such as:

- job security;
- recognition;
- work–life balance;
- status and respect;
- duty of care;
- open communication channels;
- provision of equipment;
- quality of leadership;
- opportunities for delegation and empowerment.

Yet the employee will have levels of expectations in relation to such benefits that may or may not accord with what the employer believes is their obligation. The extent to which the employees' expectations match, and are met by, the employer's perceived obligations is crucial and will be a major factor determining the levels of motivation within the workforce.

BEST leadership quote

'I did a survey 12 months ago asking, "What do you want from your managers and what motivates you at work?" I then did the same thing with some managers, who came back saying: "We think that the teams are motivated by money, working conditions and knowing what is expected from them." However, only one of those features, "knowing what is expected of them" was what the teams said. In fact, one of their top motivators was recognition and praise, whilst salary came only sixth. It is interesting that we have that difference between what the team think and what the management expect them to think.'

Antony Smith
Culture and Development Manager
Bourne Leisure

Let us consider, as an example, an employee's expectation to be treated equitably. When people feel that they are being treated fairly, or even better, advantageously, they will be more highly motivated and, hence, perform better at work. Conversely, if they believe they are not receiving equity of treatment they are more likely to feel disaffection and demotivation – leading to underperformance, unreliability and a host of other unproductive outcomes. People's belief as to whether they are being treated fairly will be formed by two measures: whether they feel they are receiving adequate reward for their input in terms of effort and personal qualities; and also by comparison to work colleagues performing similar roles. Equity of treatment, the second measure of fairness, is not about the relationship between personal reward and effort; it is dependent upon the comparison that a person makes between the rewards he or she receives, and that received by others considered to be in a similar situation. Being treated no worse than work colleagues is a reasonable expectation of all employees and, as such, is a powerful and influential aspect of the PsyC.

Adams' equity theory

Around the time that occupational psychologists such as Maslow, McGregor and Herzberg were publishing their motivational theories, John Stacey Adams created his equity theory, which proposed that an employee's motivation is affected by whether he or she believes that his or her employment benefits and rewards are at least equal to the amount of effort he or she put into their work. His theory, therefore, extends beyond the individual, in that it involves comparison with others in terms of work inputs and outcomes. Adams called those with whom we compare efforts and rewards 'referent others' as they act as reference points for comparison and, hence, determinants of our sense of equity and resulting levels of motivation.

Adams' theory is more fluid than many other motivational theories in that it can be used to explain why a person's degree of motivation can change from day to day, even hour to hour, when there has been no change to his or her own personal circumstances. Reduced motivation could occur, for example, if a colleague was perceived to have received a better reward-to-effort ratio – even worse if applied to an entire group. Creating a universal perception of equity of treatment is an important feature of the PsyC and leaders must be continually conscious of this.

Consider it in the form of scales of justice, where we balance our own inputs with our outputs, and where the degree of fairness or equity is determined by how the scales balance in comparison with the 'referent' others. Inputs include aspects such as:

- effort;
- loyalty;
- commitment;
- skills and ability;
- flexibility;
- tolerance;
- determination;
- enthusiasm;
- personal sacrifice;
- trust placed in leaders, colleagues and subordinates;
- good attendance and punctuality;
- willingness to work extra hours when required;
- courtesy to clients and colleagues;
- honesty;
- input of ideas.

Outputs are aspects such as:

- tangible rewards, such as financial benefits;
- recognition;
- reputation;
- praise;
- level of responsibility;
- development opportunities;

- sense of achievement;
- advancement;
- feedback on performance;
- interesting work;
- respectful treatment;
- reasonable job security;
- pleasant and safe working environment.

How we react to a perceived imbalance will differ according to our own personal priorities. For some people, most of the time, there will be a proportional relationship between the level of demotivation and the perceived disparity with other people, whilst for others the degree of demotivation may be disproportional, resulting in a huge feeling of injustice from an apparent slight tilting of the scales. Moreover, people's reactions will differ – from reduced effort to disobedience or even outright rebellion. Others may make demands for more outputs, which if not forthcoming may encourage a move to other employment. Adams' equity theory provides a reminder to leaders that followers do not only react to how they are treated personally, but also by comparison to other team members.

Leadership *BEST* practice

Each PwC [PricewaterhouseCoopers] employee, from the CEO downwards, has someone called a *people manager*, who may not be their line manager but is responsible for achieving a deeper understanding of that person in terms of expectations and career planning. It is a two-way relationship, with the people manager offering mentoring advice, but also reporting up any identified interests or concerns. The system therefore offers opportunities to use the collected information to inform overall company policy.

Coyle-Shapiro and Neuman (2004) studied 500 public sector employees over a three-year period to identify their perceptions of what they believed their employer owed them in terms of outputs, and the extent to which they had been met; as well as the extent to which their own inputs had been fulfilled. The researchers were particularly interested in exchange and creditor ideologies, and their moderating effect on the PsyC.

Exchange ideology determines the extent to which individuals' work effort is contingent upon how it is perceived that the organization responds to their inputs. Those with a strong exchange ideology will work hard only if treated fairly, whereas those with a weak exchange ideology will continue to work hard even if they perceive themselves to be treated poorly. The extent to which employees perceive that their inputs are reciprocated – by their employer's contribution to the PsyC – will have an effect on measures such as absenteeism and loyalty to the organization. Moreover, individuals may react both in respect of present inducements, as well as proactive reciprocation based on the anticipation of future treatment by their employer. Hence, the strength of an individual's exchange ideology may influence his or her response to the organization's assumed present and future outputs, with the effect being more pronounced in respect of those with a strong exchange ideology. Such employees take a keen interest in what they receive from their employer in exchange for their hard work, prefer high outcomes for themselves, and feel that their organization 'owes' them for their efforts.

Creditor ideology, on the other hand, reflects an inclination to give greater contribution to the PsyC than is received in return. Those with high creditor ideology prefer to have others in their debt, hence willingly work harder than could be expected of them: thus they are rated high in creditor ideology. They prefer to over-reciprocate their input to the contract, rather than feeling that they are the lesser contributor to the exchange. Consequently, creditor ideology determines the extent to which an employee reciprocates the outcomes offered and fulfilled by the employer.

The study concluded that both exchange and creditor ideologies influence what employees feel obligated to contribute to the exchange relationship implicit with a PsyC. Those with a strong exchange ideology are more likely to pay attention to the outcomes they believe their employer is obligated to provide, and moderate their contribution accordingly. On the other hand, those who have a high creditor ideology focus more strongly on what they can contribute to the relationship and will tend to willingly exceed their employer's inducements. The key skill of a leader, in this respect, is to understand the psychological standpoint taken by their followers in order to ensure the optimum exchange contribution, based upon realistic expectations.

A fundamental tenet within the PsyC is how we determine our worth to our employer, as it will influence the depth of expectations we hold. A person who has been seeking employment for some time and finally secures a job may have lower expectations than an existing employee who knows, as does his employer, that he could secure an alternative job, possibly at a higher salary, without much difficulty. The market worth of one is perceived to be significantly greater than the other, yet external factors can affect this perception and, therefore, influence the potency of the PsyC. Imagine, for example, a programme designer working for an internet company in Silicon Valley in the late 1990s: the number of internet users was increasing dramatically, business was booming, attractive bonuses were being paid to computer developers. Our designer was reaping the lavish rewards and was confident that her job was safe and that her experience would be sought by other employers should she decide to move on. She knew she was considered to be a valued member of the company, which would go to great lengths to retain her services – her PsyC expectations of her employer were justifiably high.

Then the dot-com bubble burst! Her company had, unbeknown to her, extended its borrowing in the hope of dominating the market and, hence, hardly had sufficient financial reserves once the market collapsed. Now, all of a sudden, the company was struggling and was having to lay off staff, as were most of its competitors. Our designer was no longer confident of her job security: the balance of power had swung towards the employer. Her relative value had diminished, which was reflected in a different interpretation of her PsyC. She was the same employee; her employer was the same; the conditions of her written employment contract may not have changed – but she would feel the need to demonstrate and reinforce her inputs (loyalty, enthusiasm, personal sacrifice, etc) in the hope of receiving recognition from her employer that she was still a valued member of staff with a continuing future with the company. The scales of justice had reversed, as had the expectations and assumptions within the PsyC.

The above scenario demonstrates how external factors can influence the PsyC, but it can also be affected by the personality traits of the employee. As previously described, a PsyC is an unwritten set of perceptions and expectations regarding obligations within an employment relationship. From the employees' side they will vary from person to person, according (to a large extent) to each individual's personality: especially what sort of PsyC they are seeking; how they perceive the contract and any future breach or violation of it; and how their attitudes influence its enactment. A study by Raja, Johns and Ntalianis (2004) examined the relationship between employee personality and PsyC type, perceptions of contract breach, and feelings of contract violation. They considered how personality characteristics were related to contract type, using three of Goldberg's (1990) five-factor model of personality (discussed in Chapter 5) – neuroticism, extraversion and conscientiousness – along with three others: equity sensitivity, locus of control and self-esteem:

- *Neuroticism* is associated with emotional instability, mistrust, anxiety, self-pity and lack of psychological adjustment, which results in those prone to this personality trait having limited social skills, along with a disinclination to take control of situations. This tends to result in them enjoying limited job satisfaction and performing poorly over a wide variety of jobs. More complex tasks can cause them to experience high anxiety. These characteristics combine to make neurotics unlikely to engage in long-term commitments that demand high social skills, initiative and trust in others. Hence, they are more likely to form PsyCs that are short term and transactional – on a purely financial basis, in exchange for aspects of performance not requiring high levels of initiative and confidence.

- *Extraversion* is the characteristic of extraverts – who are highly social, talkative, enthusiastic, assertive and ambitious. They seek material gain, recognition and power, which combine to create a desire for status and increased financial remuneration. They generally perform well and gain high levels of job satisfaction in doing so. As regards the PsyCs they will seek to create for themselves, they are likely to be long term, as more time-restricted ones will not allow sufficient opportunities for gaining the status, recognition with social networks and power that they desire. The researchers argue that extroverts will form relational PsyCs with more emphasis on material gains in their exchange relationships. Moreover, being highly assertive, energetic and ambitious, they will be very vigilant in monitoring how well their organizations are fulfilling their part of the contract, especially in materialistic measures. They will use their advanced social skills to seek information to ensure they are not being denied the outputs they expect in both the short term and the long term.

- *Conscientiousness* in employees is related to being methodical, dependable and risk averse. Conscientious individuals are generally highly motivated and satisfied in their roles – being more concerned with task completion than with financial reward. They will regard their PsyC as relational in nature and extending over a long-term period, and including opportunities for achievement and personal success. Conscientious people will be very active in monitoring their contracts and, being risk averse, will actively seek reassurance to ensure they do not face any unpleasant surprises, as well as being afforded opportunities for personal development and success.

- *Equity sensitivity* is a personality trait that explains how a person reacts to perceived inequality of treatment. Those with high levels of it are outcome-oriented and expectant of more for their inputs than other colleagues. They have been found to place more emphasis on tangible extrinsic outcomes such as pay, benefits and status. Conversely, those with low equity sensitivity give more attention to their inputs and are less aware of possible inequity in exchange relationships. They are also more concerned with intangible, intrinsic outcomes such as a sense of achievement and personal work, and self-actualization. It is apparent that the needs of people with low equity sensitivity closely match those identified by humanistic psychologists such as Maslow and Herzberg, discussed in Chapter 3. Equity sensitivity was found to be negatively related to job satisfaction, commitment, work ethic and social responsibility; and positively related to a likelihood to leave positions of employment. People with high levels of equity sensitivity are therefore more likely to form PsyCs of a transactional nature, based on expectations of pay, status and material gain. Contracts will generally be short term in nature, with less emphasis on relationships than on extrinsic benefits. Also, as equity of treatment is high on their agenda, they will be especially vigilant in monitoring the maintenance of their PsyCs.

- *Locus of control* is a variable that describes how people perceive the relationship between their own actions and the outcomes resulting from them. Those with internal loci of control believe more strongly that outcomes such as reward and recognition are within their own control. Individuals with external loci of control are more likely to attribute personal success or failure to factors beyond their influence, such as luck, or input from other people. The former, those with an internal locus of control, will probably be committed employees enjoying high levels of job satisfaction, whilst the latter may perform to lower standards and be less motivated. External loci of control encourages a less forward-looking approach, coupled with reduced interest in long-term relationships, resulting in transactional PsyCs that offer quick gains rather than future opportunities, which are perceived as uncertain and potentially problematic. Believing that outcomes are generally out of their personal control, they are not likely to closely monitor the relationship between their inputs and the outputs they receive in return.

- *Self-esteem*, the last personality trait considered by Raja, Johns and Ntalianis (2004), refers to the value one puts on oneself. People with high esteem are confident in their abilities and will seek roles that they believe will offer opportunities for personal development, achievement and self-actualization. They consequently seek to form PsyCs that promise such potential – ones that are long-lasting and relational enough for their status to be recognized on the basis of their high performance. Their high levels of confidence and self-worth will encourage them to closely monitor that their PsyC expectations are being met by their employer.

We can conclude that, in general, relational PsyCs will result in better personal and organizational outcomes than those of a transactional nature, including job commitment, performance and longevity in post. The role of leaders in building powerful, mutually beneficial relationships with their followers is therefore of paramount importance in influencing the formation of the PsyCs between both parties. The dominant position held by leaders, compared to their followers/employees, means that the success of PsyCs at individual, group and organizational levels is largely determined by them. We have seen that the individual personality of employees will determine to a large extent the type, longevity and expectations contained within individual PsyCs, and it is up to leaders to build teams around them who have positive expectations, whilst also showing empathy towards those whose contracts may not totally accord with the leader's expectations. McGregor's theory X leaders – an authoritarian management style (see Chapter 3) – are less likely to be in tune with the concept of PsyCs, let alone exhibit an empathetic approach to them. Indeed, I personally worked as a department mental head under a director who once told me that his staff were 'paid to do their job and I expect them to get on and do it'. A more enlightened leader – a theory Y leader with a more participative management style – is more likely to take the view that 'everyone is different and it is my role to understand their assumptions and expectations and, as far as I can, meet them for our mutual benefit'.

Leadership *BEST* practice

Every Haven caravan park, part of Bourne Leisure, has cultural champions, called *Pioneers*, who are volunteers with a passion for the business. They undertake the induction training for new members of staff at the start of the season, which is based around the cultural values of the company, and then act as, what manager Antony Smith describes as, 'the eyes, ears and voice of the culture throughout the year'.

Organizational culture

To what extent does the culture of an organization influence the PsyCs embraced by its leaders and employees? Research undertaken by Richard *et al* (2009) sought to determine what relationship, if any, there was between organizational culture, PsyCs and organizational commitment – hypothesizing that PsyCs mediate the relationship between the other two factors. In doing so, they defined organizational culture as: 'the pattern of shared values and beliefs that help individuals understand organizational functioning and thus provides them with norms for behaviour in the firm'. In particular, they focused on hierarchical and clan cultures. The former are held together by formal rules, policies and structures, with interactions subject to careful scrutiny, evaluation and control. They are also found not to be very adaptive and are generally resistant to change. Conversely, clan cultures emphasize togetherness, participation and teamwork – encouraging effective horizontal and vertical communications and positive human relations. There is less emphasis on formal structures and controlled decision-making, and more on tradition and loyalty. The researchers make the point that, whilst both culture models appear to be diametrically opposed, organizations can contain characteristics of both.

'Culture is the reflection of leadership behaviour within the organization. Leaders can indeed influence, as well as change, culture for the benefit of the organization. However, we have seen great organizations, which we have measured over many years, fall off the list because the founding principles have not been lived by leadership. In short, great culture can take years to build up but a moment to break.'

Jonathan Austin
Managing Director
Best Companies

As the organization plays a significant role in determining the PsyC it has with its people, it would appear reasonable to assume that its culture would be a major influence in this. Hierarchical cultures, for example, encourage perceptions of a transactional contract based upon limited employee responsibilities, narrow span of control, and clearly defined outcomes relating to the quality of work inputted in the exchange relationship. In contrast, clan cultures, where members are treated much like family, are more likely to encourage relational PsyCs in which employees agree to contribute loyalty and trust to a contract that is matched by the employer (clan leaders) creating a sense of togetherness and belonging. Raja, Johns and Ntalianis (2004) also reported similar findings relating to the differing consequences of relational and transactional contracts in terms of intentions to quit, job satisfaction and affective commitment.

In addition to considering the relationships between cultures (hierarchical and clan) and types of PsyCs (transactional and relational), the study also sought to explore two more factors affecting the exchange relationships between employees and employers, namely commitment and yearly earnings. Previous research had identified that there is a connection between organizational culture and commitment – with (clan) cultures that are based upon mutual respect, teamworking and innovation being related to positive employee responses such as commitment, job satisfaction and low staff turnover. Richard *et al* (2009) introduced an additional criterion, yearly earnings, arguing that organizational culture not only impacts on PsyCs, but also has implications for the reward system. A clan culture, for example, recognizing the value of its members, is more likely to invest in them, including appropriate compensation. In contrast, hierarchical cultures, with their emphasis on cost reduction and efficiency, will probably result in lower levels of compensation, including yearly earnings. Hence, organizations that value long-term relationships with their people are more likely to offer greater rewards, including higher monetary reward, to encourage trust, loyalty and commitment. There are, therefore, direct links between the culture of an organization and the effectiveness of the PsyCs made with its people, measured by the commitment given by employees and the financial reward offered by the employer.

As we have also considered previously in this book, the culture of an organization is determined largely by its senior leaders, who require the operational leaders to cascade the culture throughout the organization, down to the team leaders whose role it is to 'live' the ethos of the culture in their dealings with the front-line staff. Employees in large organizations do not usually identify any single person as their 'employer'. They have little appreciation as to who, if anyone at all, is personally responsible for determining the values upon which the outputs of a PsyC will depend. For this reason, many business leaders have decided that they need to create a corporate personality or identity based upon a set of intangible values that employees can expect to be offered in exchange for the inputs they apply to their side of the scales of justice. Often termed an 'employee value proposition' it is an attempt by employers to clarify the PsyC they hope will be 'signed up to' by their staff.

BEST leadership quote

'This year I appointed a Director of Culture and People Development because culture is about our family values and is absolutely in our DNA.'

Karen Forrester
Chief Executive
TGI Friday's

Moreover, rather than creating a single value proposition for the whole workforce, some organizations have realized that a 'one-size-fits-all' informal contract may not be appropriate and have thus taken a more segmented approach. The expectations of a diverse workforce will vary according to factors such as age, lifestyle, and attitudes to communication in the organization. Hence, the 'contract' is tailored according to the needs of different groups by emphasizing different elements of the value proposition. Flexible benefits packages could be offered to different groups, for example sales teams, technical support or administrative staff. Whilst not tailoring the employer's side of a PsyC to the personality characteristics of individual employees, it is probable that the majority of those employed in sales activities would be extraverts, whilst many administrative staff would have high levels of conscientiousness. Employers who recognize that different work groups will form different informal, unwritten contracts with the organization may, therefore, ensure that their sales teams would be given every opportunity to realize their ambition for status and recognition, as measured by the financial rewards they have achieved. Administrative staff, on the other hand, would be more likely to respond positively to long-term career planning based upon structured development plans. There are exceptions to the rule, of course, but many of us will readily relate these generalized descriptions to colleagues we have worked with ourselves. We will consider the preferred PsyCs of different groups, including those of different generations, in more depth later in this chapter.

The importance of emotional intelligence

Empathy – an emotional intelligence quality recognized in Chapter 4 – is described as 'the ability to engage with and influence others', being one of the key qualities a leader needs to display in order to create a supportive climate: one where employees trust their organization, as represented by its leaders. One normally considers empathy as being displayed by individual people, but in terms of PsyCs it reflects how the organization as a whole engages with its people collectively or in different work groups. A company that appears to understand the needs, concerns, opinions and ambitions of its employees is more likely to create a climate of trust, co-operation and transparency – factors featuring large in PsyCs. The more an employer demonstrates an awareness of the employee situation, the more likely that healthy PsyCs are established and maintained. If, however, things are not going well for a person. he or she will look for someone to blame, especially if he or she has an external locus of control. If the problems are work-associated, the employer will feature high on the blame list and the PsyC will be seen as having been breached. One can also envisage a shift on Goldberg's (1990) neuroticism scale from secure/confidence towards sensitive/nervous. The employee's trust in the employer's best intentions will be eroded and suspicions will multiply.

Trust is a crucial requirement of a fruitful two-way PsyC and is defined in the *Oxford Dictionary* as a 'firm belief in the reliability, truth, ability or strength of someone or something'. Its opposite, suspicion, is often founded upon a belief that the other party is withholding information or actions that would be to one's personal benefit. From my personal research and experience, if employees are asked informally, or within a staff satisfaction survey, what is their organization's greatest failing, they will often say 'poor communications'. *Communications, communications, communications* – perhaps the most important leadership skill of all. How often have we heard people say 'no one tells us anything' or 'wouldn't it be nice if they just listened to us occasionally' or 'one manager tells us one thing; another tells us something completely different'. Within a PsyC it is the responsibility of both parties to communicate effectively: employees to be open and honest about their feelings; and employers to create open, transparent lines of communication throughout the organization. The onus is, however, on the leadership to create a culture of transparency that, in turn, creates a level of trust within their followers to reciprocate. Distrustful employees are a time bomb waiting to explode: their leaders will be blissfully unaware of the simmering discontent until it blows up in their face.

BEST leadership quote

'Leaders must avoid the temptation to "sugar-coat" bad news and "hype" the good news. If leaders communicate well, and communicate often, they will earn the trust of their employees.'

David Fairhurst
Chief People Officer, Europe
McDonald's Restaurants

I have lost count of the number of leaders I have known who 'talk the talk' of open communications, but fail to 'walk the walk'. Could it be that they believe that their people:

- already know?
- don't want to know?
- are incapable of understanding?
- have no right to know?

Or is it that they fear the consequences of being open and transparent? Sharing information risks loss of power and a dilution of unique authority, they may think – an opposite interpretation to Kofi Annan, the UN secretary-general, whose well-known assertion states that: 'Knowledge is power. Information is liberating.'

Leadership transparency encourages mutual trust, whilst also empowering followers with the facts upon which to objectively create their PsyCs. Without the necessary facts they are in danger of being influenced by misinformation, rumour or false perceptions. Ignorance and uncertainty make people feel threatened and vulnerable, neurotic even. A vicious circle begins to form, where secrecy begets greater secrecy, begets greater fear; where trust transforms into suspicion and open, destructive hostility.

Leadership style is an important variable in determining how both parties in a PsyC approach their responsibilities. In Chapter 1 I suggested transformational leadership as an important example of the relationship theory of leadership – and its comparison to transactional leadership in influencing the fulfilment of PsyCs is equally relevant here. The transactional style refers to patterns of actions that influence people in the way they behave, by setting measurable goals, co-ordinating their work and then rewarding or sanctioning them according to the extent that the goals are met. This style works best when the job requirements are clearly understood, consistent and can be communicated in advance. It can be particularly effective where work is done at a distance: with limited interpersonal interaction between leader and employee. It does, however, assume that the task requirements are consistent and that the employee does not have to make any significant decisions individually, or with other team members, in order to achieve the task successfully.

The transformational leadership style, in contrast, works by inspiring followers through appealing to their personal values in order to increase their motivation to achieve mutually supported goals. When leaders behave in a transformational fashion they elevate their followers' aspirations in terms of job achievement. They reinforce common goals and mutual identification, and propose a compelling vision for the future. Followers are encouraged to question old assumptions and to view problems in innovative ways. Transformational leadership requires followers to welcome, and operate, a degree of self-management, especially in a changing environment where the task is not so well-defined or clearly understood. By its very nature, it is most successfully applied where leader and follower are co-located and, hence, can interact freely. Communication through information technology is certainly not conducive to a leader adopting the transformational style.

It is important to realize that both transactional and transformational styles are not mutually exclusive and can both play their parts within the creation and fulfilment of PsyCs. Leaders can employ a combination of both: the latter to communicate an overall vision and to imbue work with meaning; and the former to provide direction and structure to individuals and teams requiring it. Factors that may influence the application of specific leadership styles are:

- mix of generations within teams and departments;
- generational expectations;
- the skills and abilities of individual employees;
- the task to be achieved: routine or fluid;

- external pressures, such as competition or globalization;
- internal pressures, such as downsizing or financial constraints;
- cultural diversity within the workforce, resulting in a variety of approaches affecting leader–follower relationships;
- distance between leader and followers: close contact or geographically dispersed;
- size of the organization, affecting the leader's personal knowledge of each employee.

Whilst we know that the senior leadership within an organization determines its culture, which, to a large extent, underpins the inputs and outputs of its PsyC, it is the team and operational leaders that are the keys to their success. How the leaders heading business units and departments handle their followers on a day-to-day basis determines how the PsyCs are fulfilled. Line managers are the primary contract-makers for employees (McDermott *et al*, 2013). When they act in ways aligned with the unwritten terms of the PsyC, both its inputs and outputs are supported. Good leaders adapt their style, behaviours and communication to convey appropriate and realistic expectations to their followers. In their daily contact they can directly convey what efforts are needed from them and what they can expect in return. By virtue of what leaders pay attention to, measure and control, they exert huge sway over how their people direct their efforts, how well they perform, and how successful the leader's vision is achieved.

Contract violation – from the employee's perspective

Contract violation, or breach, occurs when either party believes that the PsyC has not been honoured. It signals an imbalance in the exchange process, where either the employee or employer does not receive the expected outcomes in return for the inputs they believe they have contributed. From the employees' position, responses to a perceived breach could include:

- altering their own perceived obligations to the PsyC;
- lower job satisfaction and morale;
- reduced commitment to their role or organization;
- reduced task performance;
- breakdown in trust;
- deliberate disruptive behaviour;
- notice to quit.

The employee who believes that his or her organization has failed to meet its side of the bargain by failing to deliver what he or she not only deserves, but what is important to him or her, experiences feelings of anger and betrayal. Such perceptions can occur shortly after the employee joins the organization, if the assumptions gained during the recruitment process fail to materialize, or even after years of satisfactory service if, for example, aggressive downsizing or outsourcing are introduced. Either way, the relationship, which was initially founded upon trust rather than written contract terms, is broken and may be difficult, or impossible, to repair.

It is obviously in leaders' best interests to maintain expectations to reasonable and achievable levels: where they can deliver on their followers' assumptions of outputs in return for their effort, loyalty and commitment. As I have proposed earlier, open communications are crucial to positive work environments, even during difficult periods of change. Indeed, it is during such times when honest communications are required in order to counter followers' suspicions that can so easily lead to reduced morale and feelings of betrayal. All too often, for example, employees believe that internal politics are working insidiously to their disadvantage. Kiewitz *et al* (2009) identified that when employees attribute PsyC breach to external forces, outside the control of their employer, they will be less likely to view it as reneging on the exchange relationship implicit within a PsyC. However, if they believe that the breach was committed intentionally, they will perceive this as a strong signal that their organization does not care about them or value their contribution. Worse still, the two studies contained within Kiewitz *et al* (2009) demonstrated that if employees suspect a political motive behind the contract breach it enhances their assessment of the malevolent nature of the organization. Organizational politics revolve around a subjective belief that the work environment is being influenced by those in power, engaging in self-serving behaviour. Employees who perceive high levels of internal politics are more likely to believe that the PsyC breach reflects badly on the organization.

Managing expectations

Leaders must manage the expectations of their people. Previously in this book, I have extolled the benefits of encouraging employee empowerment, participation and involvement in decision-making – not least in terms of enhanced staff engagement leading to business benefits. Yet encouraging staff involvement can post a dilemma for leaders as the process can have a snowballing effect, as involvement raises staff aspiration and expectations of even greater contribution. This forms part of the PsyC, where the employees' willingness to participate in devolved decision-making is seen as an input – to be matched by the employer's output of the empowerment ethos being continued, or even expanded. Yet personal and situational factors may require a review of the extent to which the ethos can be further developed. The organizational situation, the person(s) involved, or the nature of the work may call for moderation in the extent of staff involvement now or in the future – thus risking a perception of PsyC breach.

Here, I add to research by Paul, Niehoff and Turnley (2000) to propose methods by which leaders can manage expectation relating to staff empowerment, which could be applied more widely for all expectations of employees within a PsyC:

- *Orientation and socialization.* During the recruitment process candidates should be presented with an accurate preview of the job and employer so that their expectations will closely match the reality of the role they are applying for. This should include details of staff involvement programmes, as well as orientation and socialization. Orientation includes an understanding of the mutual obligations within their employment status. Socialization involves an acceptance of what behaviour is acceptable within the organization and the values it upholds.

- *Employee opinion surveys.* Open-ended survey questions that elicit employee interpretations of company practices and policies can provide useful insights as to how the PsyC is viewed, and any breaches that have occurred or are likely to occur in the future.

- *Discussion groups.* Periodic meetings between employer and employee representatives can be used to assess perceptions of the exchange relationships within the PsyC.

- *Review of organization literature.* Company publications, including staff handbooks, can give rise to expectations underpinning PsyCs and create a benchmark for comparison between entitlement beliefs and reality. Such literature should not be allowed to foster false, unreasonable expectations.

- *Leadership training.* All leaders understand that followers expect rewards, financial or otherwise, in return for their efforts, but not all will be conversant with the concept of PsyCs and the crucial importance they have to employee–employer exchange relationships. The concept of a PsyC is rather like that of human love: everyone knows it exists, what a powerful effect it can have on us, and the disastrous consequences of its betrayal. However, unlike love, we can be trained to understand and apply it reciprocally to great effect.

- *Ensure open, two-way communications.* Employees may be prepared to accept actual and anticipated changes when they know the rationale behind them. I have no hesitation in reiterating that communication is one of the most important leadership functions; yet it is one that is practised so badly, so often.

- *Encourage good employee relations.* The purpose of related activities should be to meet the needs of both employees and employers, thus demonstrating a willingness to fulfil obligations within the PsyC.

- *Provide supportive line managers, mentors and role models.* Zagenczyk *et al* (2009) found that organizations that put in place appropriate support mechanisms can moderate employee expectations of the exchange relationships within a PsyC and, if a contract breach is believed to have happened, can reduce the belief that the organization neither values their contribution nor cares about their well-being. The line manager, in particular, is key in terms of 'living' the relationship on a day-to-day basis.

Contract violation – from the employer's perspective

As we have found, a PsyC requires inputs and outputs from both parties in the exchange relationship, which, if not forthcoming due to a breach of the contract, has implications for each. So far we have explored the implications of a breach, perceived or actual, by the employer – but what about contract violation where the employer suffers as a result of employee breach? Perhaps it is not surprising – in an age of economic pressures leading to job insecurity, coupled with the demand for increased flexibility, longer hours and reduced pay in real terms – that much of the recent research into PsyC breach has been conducted from the employees' perspective. Less well considered has been the employer's experience of contract violation.

PsyCs are, at their very core, based upon mutual trust. Hence, when one party is perceived as not fully partaking in the relationship, it is the breakdown of trust that results in the offended party feeling less inclined to invest emotionally and/or behaviourally in the relationship. Moreover, the effect will be more pronounced in relational as opposed to transactional contracts, which are less specific in terms of responsibility and reward, and therefore more dependent upon each contributor trusting the other to fulfil their obligations.

BEST leadership quote

'We have a value that is very simple: "You are obliged to be open, frank and honest with people." Typically in a law firm, if you have an underperforming assistant no one says anything to them. Gradually that assistant is not given work because the internal market does not buy them; they become more miserable and depressed, and things cascade into a difficult situation. Now what will happen is someone will say, "Hang on. The social contract says we have to be frank and honest", and they will have a conversation. Hence, the values have come from something that is merely written down, into a Charter of Rights.'

Kevin Gold
Managing Partner
Mishcon de Reya

In organizations – often in small to medium enterprises (SME) – where it is the employee who breaches the PsyC, the disruption caused can be considerable. Examples of employee contract breach include:

- criminal activity, such as theft;
- leaving the organization without giving prior notice;
- refusal to carry out duties;
- intentional disruptive behaviour;
- lack of team participation.

In relational contracts, more prevalent in SMEs, such violations can result in intense feelings of anger and betrayal on behalf of the business owner, which can result in withdrawal behaviours similar to those of employees who perceive a breach of contract. The employer may well review his or her leadership style and consider a shift from a transformational to a transactional style – a closer examination of which will follow later in this chapter.

The employer will be at pains to limit the damage and disruption to the smooth running of the business caused by employee violations; as well as any fallout due to a resulting change of leadership style in the eyes of other employees. Depending on the actual violation and its consequences, the impact of reputational damage affecting customer confidence may also be of critical concern for the business leader. A study by Nadin and Williams (2012) found that small business owners often reacted to contract breach by one of their staff by deliberately and proactively involving other employees in dealing with such incidents, which served three functions:

- They sought support from other staff members to deal with what was a challenging and personally distressing situation.
- They wished to reaffirm the norms of acceptable behaviour that had been transgressed by the violation: the employee obligations within the PsyC.
- Recognizing that they had more at stake than the practical fallout of the violation, they were at pains to reaffirm their authority in the eyes of their team. The violation was seen as an identity threat, which required considerable effort in order to confirm their leadership status.

The generational factor

Every employee has his or her own individual expectations and assumptions about his or her job: no two people will have exactly the same. Yet certain categorizations will influence these expectations: for example, personality types, levels of education, gender and age groups – all of which merit consideration in terms of the exchange relationships within a PsyC. Whilst I am not suggesting that each employee's age should be considered uniquely in order to arrive at a balanced PsyC, it would be prudent for employers to be aware of the broad needs and feelings of generally recognized generational groups that constitute the large proportion of the workforce. That said, organizations should resist any temptation to 'label' people and thus make assumptions about their attitudes and expectations. There is, however, sufficient evidence to suggest that each generation creates its own traditions and cultures through shared attitudes, preferences and dispositions. These differences can be held throughout one's life and are influenced by a combination of factors, such as those listed in the CIPD report of September 2008, entitled 'Gen Up: How the Four Generations Work', as:

- societal trends around raising and educating children;
- traumatic social events;
- a significant change in the economic cycle;
- influence of significant leaders and entrepreneurs;
- a dramatic shift that influences the distribution of resources in a society.

The three generations that form the vast majority of the current working population – baby boomers, Generation X and Generation Y – along with their characteristics and work-related expectations, are discussed below:

- *Baby boomers* (born circa 1946–64) account for around 30 per cent of the UK workforce. Growing up after the Second World War, for some of them their formative years could have been influenced by rationing and other hardships, although Beetlemania and the pop culture revolution will have had greater impact in their later youth. Other influences include the civil rights movement, the women's movement, nuclear disarmament, union power and soaring inflation. Baby boomers have contributed to all these momentous changes and, as a result, have come to believe that change is possible to an extent that no other generations do. They are idealists and optimists who believe that, through hard work, they can ensure a better future for themselves and their families. Boomers are competitors who dedicated their lives to their jobs, being the first generation to contemplate having dual careers, although many found themselves 'time poor' in their rush to achieve their ambitions. Those born earlier in the time frame had a greater desire for extended job tenure and advancement within one company than the younger members of this generation, although, overall, more than half have spent the last 10 years with their current employer. Socially, many have reached a point in their private and working lives where they no longer have as strong a desire to network and socialize as they once did. Because they have had such a career-dominated existence they may find it difficult to balance work and home life and to nurture relationships in both environments.

- *Generation X* (born circa 1965–78) account for slightly more of the current workforce than baby boomers but are less optimistic in nature. Indeed, although they may have enjoyed a relatively comfortable childhood, they are often thought of as being negative and cynical, and characterized in the media as people who 'sleep together before getting married (if they even do), don't believe in God, question privilege and the royalty, and don't respect their workaholic parents'. In other words, generally anti-establishment. Their formative years would have exposed them to corporate scandals and governmental corruption such as Watergate. They joined the workplace in times of economic turmoil, with many graduating into the worst job market since the Great Depression, with large-scale redundancies, and pay and benefit cuts. They are, therefore, less likely to be loyal to their employers and are requiring of a better work–life balance. They recognize the need for hard work but are committed more to their own careers than their organizations, hence frequently change jobs, preferring creative, entrepreneurial ventures, especially those that promise skills development and a recognition of social and environmental issues, rather than status and a job for life. Half have spent five years with their current employer. Generation X expect employers to promote their people on ability and potential, rather than seniority with the company – and they expect these views to be considered and valued!

- *Generation Y* (born circa 1979–2000), also known as millennials, are the quickest-growing segment of the workplace, increasing from 14 to 21 per cent between 2001and 2005, to a current 27 per cent. Accessible technology has played a huge role in shaping this generation, which, as a result, has developed excellent multitasking skills, often in the role of service or knowledge workers. Like baby boomers, they place high value on hard work and a structured environment, although they expect the new technologies to provide options for flexible working outside traditional hours. Education also features large in the minds of Generation Y workers: they are more likely to have gained qualifications prior to entering the world of work and expect developmental opportunities to be offered by their employer. Expectations for career progress may be high but, as the employment market is flooded with graduates, such hopes may prove to be unrealistic. In contrast to the baby boomer generation, however, Generation Y workers feel the need to socialize and network on a regular basis in order to advance their careers, albeit not necessarily with one employer – perceiving personal connections to be as important to their future as their skills, abilities or even qualifications.

Delcampo *et al* (2011) establish a synopsis of generations, as shown in Table 6.1.

TABLE 6.1 Synopsis of generational values, strengths and weaknesses (Delcampo et al, 2011)

Generation	Personal Values	Work Values	Strengths	Weaknesses
Baby Boomers	idealism; creativity; tolerance; freedom.	workaholism; criticism; innovation; commitment; loyalty.	accountability; adaptability; clear communication; initiative; project management; problem-solving; service orientation; collaborative working.	need for instant gratification; technology; valuing diversity.
Generation X	individualism; scepticism; flexibility; negativity; creativity.	learning; entrepreneurialism; spirit; materialism.	adaptability; resource management; problem-solving; technology; valuing diversity.	self-centred focus; desire quick achievement; lack of plain speaking; project management; service orientation; collaborative working; loyalty to organization.
Generation Y	moralism; confidence; positivity; environmental consciousness; ambition; social responsibility; pragmatism.	passion; balance; leisure; security; team-working; thrive on feedback and praise.	accountability; project management; service orientation; valuing diversity; collaborative working; better educated.	communicating by texting; problem-solving; loyalty to organization; over-reliance on technology.

BEST leadership quote

'If you are going to put millennials in a hierarchical, controlling environment that is all about greed they are not going to last very long. The CEO of the Girls' Day School Trust told me what happened when a successful alumni, a vice-president of Morgan Stanley, came to speak to her girls. The expectation was that they would ask questions such as "You are very successful. How can I get where you are?", but instead the questions were "What about your ethics?", "What are you doing about your communities and the world?", and "Why would I want to work for your organization?". What we want is not to lose that attitude as they grow older.'

Ann Francke
Chief Executive
Chartered Management Institute

By understanding the values and expectations held by different generations, business leaders are better placed to develop compelling value propositions for their staff. However, the 2008 CIPD report referred to above cited numerous employers who were struggling to attract and retain certain generational groups, whilst turnover was very low in others. Baby boomers, for example, were interested in long-term reward packages, whilst Generations X and Y value more short-term benefits. Another example of the generational requirements of the value propositions identified was related to personal development opportunities. Here, boomers and Generation X expect these to include internal job moves, whilst Generation Y is more interested in being given specialist skill training to allow them to grow 'on the job'.

The relationship between age and employees' interpretation of PsyCs was examined by Bellou (2009) who offered an international perspective by studying the needs of 1,145 employees in Greece. She found that Generation Y have generally accepted the reality of modern-day employment relations and PsyCs. Whilst they struggle for balance between work and private life, their expectations are rather restricted by the difficulties experienced in finding suitable employment. Baby boomers, on the other hand, appear rather indifferent, caring less for support and opportunities to contribute to the success of their organization. Bellou suggests that this may be a result of boomers wanting to retire, or simply being intimidated by their overall working experience. Generation X, in contrast, appear to be the most triggered: having been dragged to the contemporary working reality, they are highly demanding. They expect more than the other two generational groups, such as advancement and development opportunities, participation in organizational issues, job security, support and commitment from their employers. Consequently, Generation X are not only uncompromising but also somewhat attached to the better PsyC outputs they experienced when they first entered the employment market. It would be interesting, however, if further research was conducted to ascertain whether generational attitudes have changed since the collapse of the Greek economy that followed shortly after Bellou published her findings in 2009.

Bal *et al* (2008) conducted a meta-analysis of 60 studies to examine the influence of age on job attitudes when a PsyC breach has occurred. Taking as read that a breach will harm employees' trust in their organization, which in turn will result in reduced job satisfaction and commitment, the researchers examined whether age moderates that effect, such that the attitudes of older workers are less affected by contract breach. Of the 60 studies, 75 per cent were conducted among employees, 17 per cent amongst MBA students and the remaining 8 per cent were amongst managers.

The results were interesting and did, indeed, indicate that age was a moderating factor in terms of trust, job satisfaction and commitment when a PsyC was breached – but not consistently across all three reactions. It was found that, as employees grow older, they respond less emotionally to contract breach than younger workers, especially in terms of reduced trust and commitment, because older workers focus more on positive aspects of their relationship with their employer and, hence, are less affected by expectations not being met. However, this was not the case in terms of job satisfaction where the correlation was more negative for older workers. Thus, when they perceive a breach of their PsyC, the level of job satisfaction experienced by older employees reduces more than for younger generational groups.

The researchers proposed several explanations for this job satisfaction–contract breach relationship for older workers, such as:

- Older workers have more experience, therefore their work may be less interesting.
- They have fewer opportunities to change jobs than younger employees.
- Job satisfaction for older workers stems primarily from their relationship with their employer and co-workers: more so than those of a younger age – for whom satisfaction may be derived to a greater extent from the work itself.
- Older workers may receive higher satisfaction from factors outside their work environment, such as family and hobbies, therefore breach of their PsyC at work is of less importance to them.

Present-day workforces present leaders with a complex mix of generational motivations, assumptions and expectations. Moreover, the changing demographic landscape will continue to present challenges as the older generations approach retirement and newer employees join organizations alongside Generations X and Y. The active leadership of cross-generational attitudes, alongside potential misunderstandings and conflict, will be an issue at all levels within organizations. However, avoiding labels and assumptions about followers' attitudes is important, as people may have core values throughout their working lives but life experiences will combine to influence their psychological needs at different times throughout their career path. Leaders need to develop a compelling value proposition that meets the common generational expectations, whilst also being able to adapt PsyCs to reflect individual, sector and cultural differences. The challenges facing leaders are wide and far-reaching, such as: attraction, recruitment, engagement, career development and retention of talent.

Proactively managing the organization's brand values and reflecting generational differences in the offer of PsyCs will be fundamental drivers for the attraction and continuing engagement of talented staff. PsyCs will need to reflect the increasing importance of social responsibility and the different cross-generational attitudes to loyalty and commitment. Emphasis on retention and engagement must be balanced against business needs, in the light of increasing demands for acceptable work–life balance and flexible working arrangements. PsyCs should also take into consideration the younger generations' expectations of opportunities for socializing and networking.

Leadership development will need to include an understanding of the requirement to adapt leadership styles as a result of different generational views of hierarchies, reporting structures and team-working, as well as the younger workers' expectation of increasing responsibility and autonomy. Trust is a crucial factor in PsyCs, which is less easy to establish with Generation X than the age groups either side of them. Managing the potential conflict between the baby boomers' expectations of reward linked to length of service, and the younger generations' aggressive attitude to performance management and reward related to merit will be a significant leadership challenge. The requirement to deliver communications through multiple channels is unlikely to reduce, with some employees wanting it technologically based, with others more interested in its reliability and trustworthiness.

The changing employment relationship

Bellou (2009), referred to above, discussed how Generation Y has generally accepted the realities of the modern-day exchange relationships, as assumed within the PsyCs agreed between employee and employer over the past two decades or so. This period has seen major changes within the workplace (some discussed in Chapter 2) as a result of increasing demands being placed on organizations for greater flexibility and productivity – at less cost.

These economic demands, coupled with organizational restructuring within both the private and public sectors, have led to job losses at all levels, and within all departments. Hence the PsyC offering job security, stability and predictability, enjoyed by baby boomers, has changed significantly. Indeed, it is the expectation of tenure of employment in exchange for reasonable job performance that has been perhaps the greatest change in the PsyC. In the 1950s and 1960s most people were clear about the security and stability of their job – feelings that fostered a sense of commitment to the organization. In return for their loyalty and hard work, the employer would provide good pay, regular advancement, annual wage increases and rewards for loyal and long-standing employees. The PsyC was understood and honoured by both parties.

However, since the 1970s that exchange has been severely strained. The flexible, flatter, slimmer organization, constantly having to adjust to changing markets, can no longer guarantee the PsyC outputs previously offered. The expectations of Generations X through to Y have, in consequence, changed and those boomers still in employment have been forced to believe that the workplace has become much less comfortable than in their earlier years: the PsyC they remember has changed to such an extent that the commitment and loyalty they were previously happy to offer is not now so willingly reciprocated.

For the younger members of the workforce, their expectations are largely different as they seek development opportunities, autonomy, flexibility and to have their views heard and considered. They value independence, creativity, tolerance, responsibility and a better work–life balance. Hence, their PsyC has changed over recent decades: from one that was largely relational in nature, with lifelong rewards for contract adherence, to one that is more short term, situational and with less emphasis on interdependence and mutual commitment.

The link between type of PsyC and employee commitment was explored by McInnis, Meyer and Feldman (2009), who found that a more positive correlation was evident when the contract was trust-based, collective and long term. Conversely, transactional contracts – short term, tangible and explicit – created less feeling of loyalty and commitment from workers. However, the findings of the study raised questions as to whether, in the current world of work, we can so easily define PsyC types as being either transactional or relational. It found 'new' types of contract emerging as the employment picture changes to meet the challenges of the 21st century. The evidence suggested the emergence of what the researchers described as 'organization-centred contracts', which tend to be imposed, and of a short-term nature. They give the organization greater control and might typically be used with peripheral, rather than core, employees who provide an important, but non-permanent, function. By dictating the contract terms and duration, organizations can ensure that important, clearly defined tasks can be completed without creating long-term relationships. Not surprisingly, it was found that the more 'organization-centred' the contract was considered to be, the less commitment the employees demonstrated.

The study also found evidence for an increasing number of 'balanced contracts' that included features from traditional, transactional and relational forms. They tended to be open-ended in nature but also included some tangible performance-reward features. Their objective is to retain many of the benefits of longer-term relational contracts, but with the added flexibility required to adapt to the ever-changing economic environment. In practice, balanced contracts are aimed to meet the needs of both employer and employee.

The final, non-traditional PsyC identified by the research corresponded to what Rousseau (2005) described as I-Deals. Here, employers individually negotiate flexible contracts with the intention of retaining key people. For example, the employee may be able to negotiate unpaid time away to pursue other interests on the understanding that he or she will return once the leave is completed. Whilst one might imagine that an I-Deal offering apparent employee benefits would be viewed by them as attractive, the research suggested that it could result in a level of commitment based upon obligation, rather than desire.

Hence, new PsyCs are emerging in response to demands for flexibility and adaptability in the new global economy – some that place greater control in the hands of organizations; others offering benefits shared between employer and employee. For the employee, contracts that are based upon trust and that treat him or her as an equal partner are, the researchers conclude, of value in the developing world of the contemporary work environment.

How will Generation Y lead?

This is an important question because how organizations attract, develop and retain young leaders in the future will be crucial to their future. Bersin (2013) reported research by Deloitte, in partnership with the Confederation of India Industries, which sought to understand the role of millennials in business, with nearly half of the 2,400 respondents already being in leadership positions. Millennials will rule the world in the future and the following seven research findings suggest that supporting and retaining this talent will require many organizations to rethink the way they do business:

1 *Millennials want leadership and they want it their way.* The principal finding was that they are particularly interested in creating and leading their own businesses. This is probably not too surprising considering the fact that they have seen their elders laid off during recessional times, and have also experienced the growth of new internet companies. Hence, if organizations want to keep their Generation Y talent they will have to offer creative opportunities to innovate and build.

2 *Millennials know they are not ready for leadership, but they still want it.* The research showed that they are very aware that they need to develop their leadership skills. However, modern, flatter

organizations offer less opportunity for promotion so they will need to create special assignments and job rotation programmes to meet the expectations of their millennials. Deloitte describe this as having a corporate lattice, rather than a corporate ladder.

3 *Millennials value open, transparent, inclusive leadership styles.* Young people readily use social media, so companies must also operate accessible, transparent internal communication systems. Moreover, growing up where gender, race, sexual orientation and age diversity is increasingly accepted, millennials will, themselves, also lead in an inclusive way.

4 *Millennials demand career growth, and quickly.* Personal development is very important to them so they will move jobs willingly if their present job does not offer promotion potential – much more so than their generational predecessors, who are more likely to accept career progression over a longer period. Organizations should, therefore, offer a more dynamic career model, including assignments offering opportunities for leadership development.

5 *Millennials want appraisals based upon performance, not length of service.* Organizations that reward employees entirely for their length of service will not meet the needs of Generation Y, who want their performance to be fully and fairly recognized.

6 *Millennials require less role clarity and manager relationships.* Not only do they not seek structured jobs, they are also less committed to strong relationships with one manager. Rather than relying on a single manager for advice and support they are more interested in building up a close network of peers and colleagues. That is not to say that they do not value effective leadership, they do, but they are happy to operate in an open culture that offers support from many sources.

7 *Millennials thrive on change.* Unlike previous generations who were wary of, and uncomfortable with, change, young 21st-century leaders want to work in innovative, dynamic and changing organizations. More established leaders should, therefore, create environments where their younger colleagues have new learning experiences, such as opportunities to work on projects and new business development initiatives.

Figure 6.1 offers an analysis of some statements contained within the Deloitte research, comparing responses from millennials with those from other generations.

FIGURE 6.1   Needs of millennials compared to other generations (Bersin, 2013)

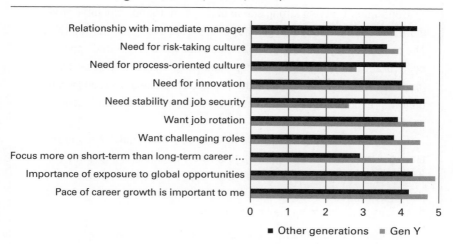

Relationship with immediate manager
Need for risk-taking culture
Need for process-oriented culture
Need for innovation
Need stability and job security
Want job rotation
Want challenging roles
Focus more on short-term than long-term career ...
Importance of exposure to global opportunities
Pace of career growth is important to me

0   1   2   3   4   5

■ Other generations   ■ Gen Y

Leadership *BEST* practice

A good example of an organization recognizing that its PsyC offer should meet the needs of its employees is McDonald's. The Generation Y cohort makes up almost 75 per cent of their workforce who, according to the 2008 CIPD report quoted previously, are more inclined to expect development opportunities on the job than any other generation. In McDonald's case, they have also been found to be more positive about the use of feedback processes to improve performance, and to look to their store leaders to provide them with the support needed to progress along their growth paths. Therefore, training and development plays a fundamental part in McDonald's efforts to attract, engage and retain a large proportion of their workforce. With such a large proportion of younger employees, the company has developed a bespoke training and development programme to meet their specific generational needs, rather than using a more broad-brush approach. The company had identified what expectations their people held and what inputs they could offer to the PsyC and found them to be superb multitaskers, with the ability to quickly absorb information from a myriad of channels, especially those using audio-visual communication. David Fairhurst, McDonald's chief people officer (Europe), told me: 'The work we have done on aligning training to qualifications has transformed lives and is a source of immense pride for me and for the business.'

Generation Y have a strong sense of loyalty to friends and peer groups, more so than their sceptical generational predecessors, Generation X. The bespoke programme that McDonald's designed is founded upon collaborative working, multitasking, audio-visual delivery and real-time feedback. The intention is that if the young workers' expectations are met they will respond with a commitment to deliver high levels of customer service and product quality.

For my book *Aspire to Inspire* I interviewed a McDonald's restaurant manager from Leicester, Pritpal Sagoo, who explained his company's development programme and went on to expound his leadership philosophy in relation to his team. Here is an excerpt from the book that describes how Pritpal applied his philosophy:

> *The leader should create a culture that encourages personal development, in the belief that most people are motivated by achievement. It is the leader's role to create an environment where endeavour is valued and rewarded; where people are respected for the contribution they make to their team and their organization.*
>
> *However, for Pritpal, a successful team can only be created if all members are aware of what is expected of them – hence it is the leader's responsibility to explain what he or she requires from each team member and then to create the structures and processes that allow those expectations to be met. Each person is different and so the leader must not adopt a 'one size fits all' approach; rather identifying individual needs and using the authority vested within the leader to ensure that those needs are met. However, leaders must not shirk from taking corrective action if it is merited. A happy workplace is founded upon an appropriate balance of control and reward: if no discipline exists within a team there will be members who coast along. People need to know what is expected of them and that, Pritpal asserts, is one of the most important responsibilities of leadership. If leaders provide an example of openness, honesty and integrity, those will be the foundations upon which they can reasonably expect their followers to behave.*

Pritpal may, or may not, have realized that his approach concisely describes the exchange relationship contained within a PsyC, but it certainly does. It also goes some way to explain why McDonald's is regularly recognized as a good employer, including in *The Sunday Times'* Best Places to Work survey.

Chapter summary

As opposed to a written contract of employment, the PsyC encompasses the unspoken, but understood, set of expectations that employers and employees have with each other. In exchange for inputs by the employee, such as commitment, flexibility and personal sacrifice, they believe they have a right to expect their employer to reward them appropriately, as well as providing interesting work, a pleasant and safe working environment, and reasonable job security. Equally, an employer expects employees to fulfil their part of the contract in exchange for the benefits, tangible or otherwise, understood to be offered to them. The PsyC is based upon assumptions and expectations that form an exchange relationship that, if breached, can lead to feelings of betrayal and mistrust by either party.

External factors, such as economic pressure on the organization, can influence the contract, as can the personality type of the employee and the culture of the organization itself. Such variable constructs call for leaders to consider the need for different contracts for different individuals and work groups. The chapter explored the very different expectations of the three main generations currently engaged in employment: baby boomers, Generation X and Generation Y. As the effective fulfilment of the perceived obligations within the exchange relationship of a PsyC is crucial to staff engagement and, hence, performance, the leader's role in understanding and managing expectations is critical. This will call for leaders to carefully consider the approach they adopt to meet different individual, group and situational needs.

Strategic leadership

– navigating a course into an uncertain future

With organizations in the 21st century facing a wide array of complex challenges and opportunities, including but not limited to those discussed in Chapter 2, the need for strategic leadership has never been more acute. The focus of this chapter is on research and practice of how strategic leadership can be utilized in directing the organization into an uncertain future. Specifically, we will consider:

- strategic thinking;
- strategic planning;
- the psychology of decision-making.

Strategy is a common term within management literature, however it means different things to different people: from superficial 'navel gazing' to detailed 'all-encompassing planning'. The term 'strategy' is derived from the Greek work *strategia*, which refers to a high-level plan designed to achieve predetermined goals within an environment of uncertainty.

A definition of the strategic element of the strategic leadership role comes from Mintzberg, Ahlstrand and Lampel (1998), containing five aspects and thus highlighting its complexity:

1 Strategy as a plan: is a direction, a guide or course of action into the future.

2 Strategy as a pattern: has consistency in behaviour over time and is informed by past behaviour.

3 Strategy as position: is the location of particular products in specific marketplaces.

4 Strategy as perspective: is the organization's way of doing things.

5 Strategy as a ploy: is a way to beat the competition.

Hence, it can be seen that strategy involves the preparation of a plan that requires an understanding of the internal policies and procedures of the organization, as well as external forces such as the market it operates in, its competitors, relevant legislation, political influences and environmental implications.

Rowe and Nejad (2009) focused on the personal aspect of strategic leadership by defining it as: 'the ability to influence others to voluntarily make day-to-day decisions that enhance the long-term viability of the organization, whilst at the same time maintaining its short-term financial stability'. In doing so, they differentiated it from managerial leadership and visionary leadership. Managerial leaders, they assert, need order and stability to be able to control the tasks they are responsible for. They usually have no involvement in, or preference for, using goals to motivate their people – who they may have little empathy with. Adopting a transactional approach, they use rewards, punishment and other forms of coercion to achieve their objectives. Being acutely aware of the cost-benefit balance of their actions, they will be closely tuned into the short-term financial implications of their leadership decisions. It may be, however, that these short-term gains are as a result of a least-cost approach, which might not be beneficial to long-term sustainability.

Managerial leaders, Rowe and Nejad assert, make many of their decisions based upon past experiences and retrospective analysis, whilst visionary leaders are orientated to the future. Visionary leaders' preferred means of achieving their objectives is to influence followers to join them on a journey towards a shared vision. They articulate a compelling future and then energize their people towards achieving it. Adopting a transformational leadership style, they invest in their people and rely heavily on their personal values, beliefs and sense of identity. The danger is, though, that in taking such a forward-looking perspective, they can pay insufficient attention to the short-term stability and day-to-day functioning of their organization. It is not surprising, therefore, that many companies favour managerial leadership as a less risky, and therefore more attractive, alternative option.

Yet it is fair to assume that all organizations, if questioned, would strongly assert the need for both short-term financial stability and future growth and viability. Hence the call for leaders who are more than the sum of the two styles: those who are acutely aware of the immediate challenges and opportunities facing their organization, whilst also planning for the future – strategic leaders who:

- Pay particular attention to building their organization's resources, capabilities and competencies in order to gain sustained competitive advantage.

- View human capital as an important, indeed critical, factor driving innovation. Hence they seek means of creating new capabilities and competencies required for continuing wealth creation.

- Create learning organizations that spread and reinforce current developmental initiatives, whilst searching for new avenues of learning required to meet future challenges.

Yet, whilst most organizations would espouse the benefits of strategic leadership, not all will endorse and support its application. Indeed, many will implement structures and policies that positively constrain and discourage their leaders from adopting a strategic perspective, rather than offering the autonomy and protection necessary for them to flourish. I personally have seen this occur in the many local government departments I have worked with in the past: where managerial leaders dominate in their determination to impose rigid financial controls that stifle initiative and innovation. That said, the controlling pressure is often imposed from the upper echelons of large, diversified organizations or, in the case of local authorities, from their central government masters. The very fact that political leadership within democratic countries exists for limited terms encourages the use of tight financial controls designed to deliver short-term gains. Outside the party-political environment there are, however, notable examples of business leaders who have combined managerial capabilities with a far-reaching vision to create sustainable businesses, such as Virgin's Richard Branson, Body Shop's Anita Roddick and General Electric's Jack Welch.

Welch described his strategic toolkit as a series of the following five questions, with the answers ultimately leading up to what he called the 'Big Aha':

1 What does the playing field look like now?
2 What has the competition been up to?
3 What have we been up to?
4 What is around the corner?
5 What is our winning move?

There are, of course, other, more detailed, toolkits available to assist senior leaders in their strategic planning, although most will follow the line of Welch's thinking. Some situations require more sophisticated tools due to the complexity and scale of the organization's operations, which call for a high degree of analytic analysis. The leader's role is, however, not just to decide and define the future strategy but also to communicate and manage it through all levels of management, and their staff. Hence, strategic leadership has two dimensions: the *analytic* and the *human*.

The analytic dimension requires the leader to organize and master the available data and provide persuasive arguments as to its interpretation and integration into the strategic plan. Those who see their strength as an analytical leader may feel an obligation to lead from the front, being the ones who identify the best strategic solution, demonstrating their pre-eminence through business skills and market expertise. They are often seen as visionaries, comfortably assuming star status, especially within their exclusive 'inner circle' of like-thinkers. Rather like the in-group concept of the leader–member exchange theory described in Chapter 1, the analytical leader's followers enjoy the exclusive access and understanding of the data and its interpretation. They will appreciate a business strategy that is linear in format, with success being measured as well-defined objectives being 'checked off' as the plan continues towards its completion.

The human dimension encourages the strategic leader to see his or her role as the architect of a process that is continually shaped by customer needs, competitor pressure and input from others within the organization. Recognizing that the strategy will evolve over time, such leaders believe it is important to enable and encourage others to take a longer-term perspective and to contribute their views to the plan. Leaders who embrace the human dimension are comfortable revisiting previous assumptions and decisions: they view strategic change as measures of leadership success, not failure. They recognize that long-term success for their organization will be based upon their strategic guidance to a community of followers who are committed to a strategy they feel they are contributing to.

Rather like my previous assertion that strategic leaders require both managerial and visionary qualities, they also must give due consideration to the analytical and human dimensions in order to navigate their organization and its people to sustainable success.

BEST leadership quote

'One of the things we have found over the past four or five years is that employees are crying out for organizational clarity. Put simply, they want to be clear why the organization exists, beyond making money. They want to be clear about how they are to behave – the values of the organization. They want to be clear about where they are headed – the outrageous ambition. Finally, they want to be clear about the plan that breaks down how they are going to achieve that ambition.'

Jonathan Austin
Managing Director
Best Companies

Strategic thinking – defining the future

Bonn (2005) defines strategic thinking as: 'a way of solving strategic problems that combine a rational and convergent approach with creative and divergent thought processes'. He suggests that the process orientation focuses on how senior managers in an organization understand and take strategic action in a highly complex, ambiguous and competitive environment. This is due mainly to the ever-changing marketplace, advances in technology and changes in the national and global economy. From this it appears that, rather than being planned, strategy emerges over time. As Eisenhardt and Brown (1998) argue: 'While, traditionally, strategy was about building long-term defensible positions, or sustainable competitive advantage, today strategy should focus on continuous adaptation and improvement' and be 'constantly shifting and evolving in ways that surprise and confound the competition.' Thus, leaders need to have an overall view of the big picture; be flexible in their approach; and not provide a strategy that is set in stone, but one that is fluid and can move with changes that are either internal or external to the organization.

BEST leadership quote

'Six years ago we made it very, very clear that we were setting out a people-led strategy. Our vision is – and this is important – "Our people are family; our guests become friends; our competitors envy us; our people come first".'

Karen Forrester
Chief Executive
TGI Friday's

The 'big picture' involves a knowledge of the external factors that may impact on the organization, such as the marketplace it operates in and the other organizations it competes against; as well as broader considerations, including legislation, political direction and environmental challenges. One way of identifying external trends and events, and making sense of them in relation to one's own organization, is environmental scanning. Wikipedia defines the process as: 'the study and interpretation of the political, economic and technological events and trends which influence a business, an industry, or even a total market'. It forms the first process of an external analysis, to be followed by: monitoring specific trends and patterns; forecasting their future direction; and assessing their impact on the organization. The external analysis would be merged with an internal analysis, including reviewing the organization's vision, mission, strengths and weaknesses.

The goal of environmental scanning, according to Morrison (1992), is to alert strategic leaders to potentially significant external changes in sufficient time for them to be included in the strategic planning phase. He identifies three levels of environment for scanning:

- *The task environment* is the organization's customer base, as well as the complete range of its stakeholders.
- *The industry environment* comprises all other organizations that operate within the same market.
- *The macroenvironment* refers to the broadest perspective, where changes in the social, technological, economic, environmental and political (often shortened to the acronym STEEP) sectors affect the organization directly or indirectly.

Hence, environmental scanning can be either passive or active. The former is largely about reading newspapers and journals, hence with no systematic or targeted purpose. It is active scanning, however, that focuses our attention on information resources concerning relevant task and industry environments, as well as the macroenvironment.

In today's competitive business marketplace, where change is a constant, an adaptive approach is required by leaders: one that rises above the routine managerial processes and problems to gain an elevated perspective of the organization and its operational environment.

This different perspective may be achieved through the development of potential future scenarios. An example of this approach was the Foresight Programme, set up in 1994 to help the UK government think about the future. The first programme brought experts together from industry, government and academia, and operated through 15 panels relevant to particular sectors of industry. Today, the Foresight Programme runs through projects that investigate challenges and opportunities arising from science, technology, or issues for society where science and technology play an important role. One such initiative is focusing on the future of manufacturing in the UK up to 2050. The project utilizes industry and academic experts from the UK and abroad who are considering likely scenarios for the future along with actions that can be taken. Whilst this type of programme is run at a government level, a similar approach could be considered within organizations to enable the leader to prepare the organization for the future. For example, the government aims to reduce UK greenhouse gas by 80 per cent by 2050, which may impact on the automotive sector, as transport is a major source of greenhouse gas emissions. The leader of an automotive development organization could, therefore, consider a strategy of developing low-emission vehicles such as electric vehicles, plug-in and hydrogen-powered vehicles in order to meet such environmental challenges. Hence, the strategic leader's role is to clarify the vision, as well as co-ordinating its implementation.

BEST leadership quote

'My vision is for McDonald's in Europe to be one of the region's most progressive employers: creating opportunities which make a positive contribution to the lives of individuals and communities, whilst at the same time driving profitable growth for the business. In short, for McDonald's to be a business that creates social, as well as economic, value.'

David Fairhurst
Chief People Officer, Europe
McDonald's Restaurants

Boal and Hooijberg (2001) state: 'It is in the vision of the leader and the articulation for change that the past, present, and future come together.' They then go further to suggest that visions have both a cognitive and affective component: with the former focusing on outcomes and the means of securing them; and the latter making a direct appeal to the personal values of and belief systems of the person crafting the vision. Hence, the cognitive component largely determines what information is sought and subsequently used, whilst the affective component influences the leader's motivation and commitment to implement his or her vision. Visions, however, like the personalities of those creating them, can be either expansive or restricting, thus determining the future of the organization.

Pre-existing characteristics of the leader (eg locus of control, job involvement and organizational commitment), as well as group and organizational characteristics (eg cohesiveness, technology and structure), will affect the intrinsic and extrinsic validity of the vision. Intrinsic and extrinsic validity are the intervening psychological states between leader behaviour and leader effects that contribute to the context within which the vision is created, and its likely achievement. This factor, Boal and Hooijberg contend, is particularly influential in the adoption of a transformational leadership style.

On the subject of strategic leadership, Millet (2006) makes an interesting differentiation between '*visioning*' and '*futuring*'. *Futuring* requires the leader to consider the future initially from the macroscopic, external environment and continue the process through to the microscopic factors influencing the organization. Consideration of internal issues, such as missions, goals, assets and culture are only examined after market trends and customer preferences are fully understood. It is a process that commences with concerns about global and national economics, public policy, social and demographic trends, consumer behaviour, market dynamics and competitors to determine their implications for the organization. A particular important application of futuring is the identification of the emerging, but yet unarticulated, voice of the customer.

Visioning, on the other hand, addresses the future from the opposite direction: progressing from the micro- to the macro-levels. Millet (2006) describes it as: 'a kind of stretching exercise whereby the question typically asked is how the company will change from its current position to achieve business growth in the future'. It is, he asserts, a more motivational and emotive process than futuring, as it contains a high dose of desire and wishful thinking. The strategic leader should conduct the process like a conductor of an orchestra: he may wield the baton, but relies on other members to contribute to the music, which should arouse their emotions and commitment to the success of the piece. Both the music (vision) and the conductor (leader) must be inspirational.

Millet's argument is that futuring and visioning must be integrated into strategic plans in a way that identifies both the specific operational changes and the resources that will be needed to put them into effect – the thinking has to lead to action. It matters little, he suggests, whether visioning or futuring is commenced in the first instance, so long as the organization does both.

Strategic leaders aim to navigate their organizations and followers through periods of change as a means of achieving the prosperous, sustainable futures they envisage. To the leader, change may mean saving the business through a process of restructuring and cost reduction; whilst to followers it may distil down to whether or not they keep or lose their jobs. Change is profoundly unsettling and, the less control we have over it, the more psychologically unsettling it will be. Leaders, therefore, must understand and reconcile both the organizational and human aspects and consequences of a change programme. They should not respond to external influences without considering the internal repercussions; neither should they force through internal changes that no longer fit the environment that the organization operates within. What strategic leaders should do is to assess the organization's readiness for change at a philosophical level, being amenable to change or not, as well as at a practical level. Jarrett (2008) formulates the change equation as: *internal capabilities + external environment + strategic leadership = a change strategy*. He goes on to describe the 'myth of change' as a belief that it can be undertaken in steps – as a planned, controlled process based upon assumptions of stability, certainty and centralized sources of authority. The reality, he contends, is that:

> We now live in a fast-changing, post-modernist world; complexity, uncertainty and difference are parts of our norm. Sources of power, as well as expectations of employees and consumers, have shifted; today, emergent, interactive processes yield results. Wise leaders avoid simple-step models.

BEST leadership quote

'In order to make change work you have to change not just systems, processes or structures – you also have to change behaviours. The reason most change programmes fail is that leaders do not place sufficient emphasis on managing expectations and being very clear about what behaviours have to change; and in order to change behaviours you have to communicate, communicate, communicate.'

Ann Francke
Chief Executive
Chartered Management Institute

The concept of taking a holistic approach to strategic thinking was described by Kaufmann (1991) as:

A switch from seeing the organization as a splintered conglomerate of disassociated parts (and employees) competing for resources, to seeing and dealing with the corporation as a holistic system that integrates each part in relationship to the whole. Each system, procedure, policy, organizational culture, individuals working within the organization and the leader are related to the whole and should be considered such.

In order to aid senior managers' 'systems thinking' Kaplan and Norton (2000) introduced the concept of strategy maps that: 'give employees a clear line of sight into how their jobs are linked to the overall objective of the organization, enabling them to work in a coordinated collaborative fashion towards the company's desired goals' and 'provide a visual representation of a company's critical objectives and the crucial relationship among them that drives organizational performance'. The map considers employee competencies and technology as assets, as well as corporate culture. Each of these assets cannot be separated from one another: they are all interlinked. With the benefits of a strategy map, senior management can understand how implementing a strategic decision on one part of the organization may have an effect on another. It follows that strategic leadership requires an understanding of the interrelationships and interdependencies of such assets.

It is important that individuals can think beyond, as well as within, the organization and develop novel solutions to survive against their competitors – and that strategic thinkers must be creative. Ford (1996) proposed that: 'creative thinking skills are the ability to generate many alternative solutions to a problem and to develop and identify unusual associations or patterns'.

This suggests that strategic thinking is a mental process, as argued by the Cognitive School of Thought. However, the ability to think strategically is influenced by an individual's interaction with others, from stakeholders to shop-floor workers.

The seminal management thinker Peter Drucker proposed a three-step process for strategic thinking:

1 *Ask penetrating questions to generate creative options.* The two fundamental, yet profound, questions that Drucker suggested would liberate a leader's thinking were: i) What business should we not be in? ii) Knowing what we know, would we enter this business now?

   The first question implies that some previous decisions may not have been appropriate or effective. Perhaps they may have seemed to be at the time but the benefits may have been overestimated or the costs underestimated. Perhaps changes to the business environment had not been accurately forecast. The second question assumes that we know our business intimately and, with that depth of understanding, it encourages us to face reality and question its viability. If we conclude that we really should not be continually struggling to make the business work, then we should deal with the obstacles to getting out, and get out! While strategic planning models and systems may be helpful, Drucker suggests that they may not be sufficient in the face of reality. His universal message is: are you asking the right questions?

2 *Reframe and simplify the prevailing view of the situation.* Referring to Einstein's wisdom that 'Any fool can complicate things, but it takes a genius to simplify them', Drucker encourages leaders to reframe and simplify issues as a means of enhancing understanding, insight and clarity of strategic thinking. An example of this approach was the effect he had in the mid-20th century by calling attention to the critical contribution that white-collar workers had within the US manufacturing sector. Previously they had been viewed as merely an overhead cost required to support the production workers. Introducing the term 'knowledge work', he reframed and expanded management's strategic thinking about organizational culture and the key contribution of creative, innovative (non-production) thinkers. Business leaders began to realize how 'knowledge work' could result in the creation of products and services that contributed to their organization's competitive strategy.

3 *Question the assumptions underpinning current views.* Strategic thinking requires leaders to cultivate constructive dissent and to manage it effectively. Management's premise could be 'we sell what we make', leading to strategic planning based upon the question 'How do we continue selling what we make in the future?'. The dangerous assumption underlying this approach is that 'customers will continue to buy what we make'. Drucker encourages business

leaders to challenge that progression of thinking by proposing a radically different premise, namely: 'The customer defines the business.' This, in turn, leads to a very different set of questions, such as 'Who is the customer?', 'How do we find out what the customer wants?' and 'What does the customer perceive as value and how can we provide that now and in the future?'. It is the strategic leader's responsibility to create a culture that has the willingness and confidence to challenge pre-existing assumptions.

BEST leadership quote

'*I think that too much is expected of leaders to know what is going to happen in 10 years' time. Here [at InterContinental Hotels], we put more emphasis on being able to adapt and change, rather than pretending that we can predict the future. It is better to be really secure about why we are here and what our values are, and then be willing to learn and adapt our plans as situations evolve.'*

Gregor Thain
VP Global Leadership Development
InterContinental Hotels

Encapsulating his three techniques to strategic thinking, Drucker said:

> The job is not to impose yesterday's normal on a changed today; but to change the business, its behaviour, its attitudes, its expectations – as well as its products, its markets and its distribution channels – to fit the new reality.

Strategic leaders need to be highly skilled analytical thinkers who are capable of handling the host of available information in a creative way that leads to thinking 'out of the box'. Gavetti (2011) suggests that they: 'must also be practitioner psychologists who expertly analyse and manage their own and others' thought processes. The difficult quest for distant opportunities require strategic leaders who are good economists and good psychologists.' Advances in behavioural and cognitive disciplines provide strategic leaders with greater knowledge, which can be used to identify, act on, and legitimize opportunities for enhanced performance.

Associative thinking

Gavetti utilizes contemporary research in the cognitive and neurological sciences to demonstrate how strategic leaders can manage several mental processes as a means of overcoming their own and others' cognitive limitations. He asserts that most organizations focus their strategic thinking around a limited number of opportunities, the intense competition for which makes it hard for them to gain attractive returns. Superior opportunities are out there, but as they are 'cognitively distant' they are hard to recognize and act upon – which is doubly unfortunate because other organizations also find them difficult to identify and, therefore, offer little competition for them. Whilst strategic planning models are designed to identify future opportunities they are of limited use, Gavetti asserts, in bringing into focus those that are 'cognitively distant'. Recent research on human cognition suggests that leaders would do better to utilize *associative thinking* for that purpose.

Associative thinking explains that the primary way we make sense of the world is by comparing unfamiliar things with those we have already experienced and logged into our long-term memory. Because associations are fundamental to human cognition, leaders who use associative thinking to create innovative solutions have the potential to gain significant competitive advantage. It does, however, require them to manage their own, and others', mental representations. When we are faced with a new situation, our brains automatically 'google' our long-term memory for similar past experiences and reposition them to the front of our consciousness. They then become the basis upon which we represent and interpret the new situation. Yet associations are influenced by biases, attitudes and emotional states, which must be challenged if the process is to work effectively.

Hence, in practical terms, strategic leaders compare a business situation with one previously experienced. They then form a new mental representation that recasts the current situation in terms of the older one. However, in order to create unique opportunities they must cultivate genuinely novel representations that reinterpret the competitive environment in new, powerful ways. What differentiates associative thinking from other creative approaches, such as brainstorming, is that it can be taught (see Gavetti (2011) for more details). In order to maximize the potential of associative thinking, strategists should be aware of, and challenge, limiting factors, such as drawing superficial similarities between new and previous situations, which can be exacerbated by the human mind's confirmatory nature. Past experiences in one industry sector may, for instance, encourage the thinker to perceive another sector in the same light, even if it may offer completely different opportunities. They should also be aware of any tendency to look for evidence that supports the comparison, rather than evidence that supports and undermines it. Finally, emotional baggage may skew and divert clear strategic associative thinking.

BEST leadership quote

BEST leadership quote

'To find the best answers, leaders need to be innately inquisitive: constantly challenging the status quo; constantly asking, "Can we do this better?". At the same time, however, they must also be mindful of creating unnecessary and distracting "innovations" that deflect resources and attention from what the organization truly needs to be achieving.'

David Fairhurst
Chief People Officer, Europe
McDonald's Restaurants

In essence, what Gavetti is proposing is that, instead of merely trying to think differently (outside the box), strategic leaders should learn how to apply structured associative thinking to access the 'cognitively distant' as a means of reconceptualizing a business. Other researchers have also applied cognitive theory to develop the competencies of strategic leaders, some of them using techniques similar to Gavetti, which they term 'experimental learning' or 'reasoning by analogy'. Chen and Lee (2003) suggested that when individuals make decisions under uncertainty, they compare new problems with past cases or experiences from which they can derive useful information or courses of action. Such thinking is directed towards the future in terms of what would work for the organization to ensure it stays competitive. However, Miettinen (2000) criticized experiential learning for not allowing for reflection, as well as not allowing for new knowledge to be obtained. According to Miettinen, experiential thinking results in false conclusions, does not help understanding of change and new experiences, and may cause laziness and dogmatic thinking. This would mean that characteristics such as creativeness, innovativeness and openness could be hindered.

Strategic competence requires an ability to take on board information and think analytically whilst also being creative, although there is no agreement to what these competencies are. It is the ability to be cognitively versatile that makes good strategic leaders. Thus, what is ultimately needed is the ability to switch back and forth between 'habits-of-the-mind' and 'active thinking', a process referred to as 'switching cognitive gears' (Louis and Sutton, 1991). In practice, the ability to switch from one processing strategy to another is difficult because of strong individual differences in the way in which information is gathered, organized, processed and evaluated. Each individual uses different ways to process information, and Lewis (2002) argues that questions should be asked as to whether there are different approaches that managers choose, depending on their circumstances, objectives and personal preferences, and whether those strategies that an organization adopts are the direct result of managerial choice, constrained by societal, sectoral, environmental and organizational factors.

Individuals think about problems and evaluate possible responses using two complementary processes (Hodgkinson and Sparrow, 2002), namely: i) a largely automatic, preconscious process, which involves developing and using heuristics (eg basic rules of thumb); ii) a deeper, more effortful process involving detailed analysis.

This approach is based on cognitive theory, where individuals construct meaning and make sense by building mental representations that guide their thinking and the direction of their decisions. They visualize the likely situation, the action to be taken and the likely outcome. However, problems can arise when there is too much information to process and individuals become overloaded with complex information. People have limitations on their memory in terms of how much information they can process. One of the key capabilities required of a strategic leader is the ability to see the bigger picture through all the complex detail.

Strategic planning – making the future happen

The vision has been defined, so now the strategic leader has to take decisions and make plans to steer the organization towards what Garry Hogan, MD of Flight Centre (UK) Ltd, once called 'a brightness of future'. Once the thinking has happened, the planning must commence. Aldehayyat and Anchor (2010) define strategic planning as: 'the devising and formulation of organizational level plans which set the broad and flexible objectives, strategies and policies of a business, driving the organization towards its vision of the future'.

The subtitle of this book is 'How the *BEST* leaders inspire their people'. One may be inclined to ask, though, how strategic planning can achieve that objective. How can the planning process influence the motivation of those who will be involved in its implementation? In one of the LES5ONS series of management videos, Dr John Roberts, CEO of United Utilities, tells the story of the formation of his company following privatization of the electricity industry in the UK, a decision made in 1988 by the Conservative government. Prior to that, Roberts describes the organization as being 'inefficient and self-indulgent': it was inwardly focused with no concept of customer service and poor industrial relations. It was a moribund organization, slow to change, with no fear of failure as it was entirely owned by the government.

Then, by the following year, it became United Utilities plc, with Roberts as its CEO, with all the autonomy of any other competitor within the energy sector. As Roberts described it: 'we were free to go into retail, free to go into hotels, free to go into liquidation!', hence in need of a clear strategy. In a very short period of time within this new trading environment he found that the behaviour of his people changed dramatically:

> Giving people a simple cohesive strategic message made all the difference. The sense of belonging, ownership and strategic direction gave our people something to focus on and drove our performance forward. People have within them the innate ability to do a good job. What they need is the proper leadership and proper motivation that turns them on to do it. If you give people direction they respond.

However, it appears that not all organizations are as willing to change as was United Utilities. The strategic thinking may be comprehensive, and a competitive, sustainable future mapped out, but it will only be successful if the plans are implemented effectively. A number of potential barriers to successful implementation can thwart the plans of the strategic leader. Heide, Gronhaug and Johannessen (2002), in a case study on a Norwegian ferry-cruise company, observed 174 barriers under the following categories: communication (123); organizational structure (19); learning (13); personnel management (8); culture (8); and political (3). It is enlightening how, yet again, communications is shown to be such a crucial factor in leader–follower relations.

As John Roberts found at United Utilities, people are much more likely to buy into the inevitable changes associated with the implementation of strategic plans if they feel they are involved in the process. Yet, traditionally, strategic planning is seen as the responsibility of top management – who, all too easily, can interpret this role as both a sign of power and an expression of the scale of the difference between them and the lower echelons of the organization. More recent research has, however, emphasized the role of middle management in strategy formation and enactment. Increased education levels of the younger (Generation Y) managers and the general trends towards decentralization in recent times suggests that a strictly top-down approach may not yield the best strategy. After all, it is the operational leaders who have the responsibility to cascade the strategy to the team leaders and beyond.

BEST leadership quote

'The leader can set the tone and direction but going up to the hill and saying "Follow me" is not going to get people moving if they do not know where the hill is or what direction you are pointing in. Hence, you need leaders at every level; you need leaders of leaders.'

Ian Munro
Group Chief Executive
New Charter Housing

Sharing strategic information with all stakeholders, including lower-tier management, may appear to be the most appropriate course of action, although it comes with certain dangers. Not least, industry competitors may be able to access sensitive information or may lure away those who hold it. Strategic leaders must balance the information needs of those required to implement the strategy against those who would seek competitive advantage by obtaining it. Whilst the balancing act is difficult, Parnell and Lester (2003) propose that: 'distinguishing the most critical and confidential data and decisions from that which is of little value, or cannot be readily concealed, is central to the process'.

The lack of clarity and ownership of strategic plans throughout the organization threatens the efficient usage of resources, whilst wasting management time spent correcting and clarifying misunderstanding – culminating in poor strategy execution due to blurred and differing personal and job priorities. The onus is on the strategic leader to create a broad understanding of both the 'what' and the 'why' within the broader leadership team. One way of doing so is to identify and develop a group of talented, committed operational leaders who can act as champions of the cause to those above and below them. They would not replace the role of the senior leadership team, but rather act as a catalyst for the process and a bridge between conception and implementation – creating momentum and ensuring consistency. This strategy support team could include members who have been identified for promotion and will benefit from the development opportunities arising from their membership. They will emerge as well-equipped managers who have publicly endorsed the strategy and, hence, are in a better position to rise and benefit from its success.

BEST leadership quote

'I've made up my own Pareto-type Principle, which entails spending 20 per cent of your time developing your own understanding so that you can set the vision; 30 per cent doing the process bit, like writing it down; but 50 per cent of your time engaging with your staff at various levels to see if it is working. Indeed, I encourage and expect all my staff to spend 20 per cent of their time on themselves – one day a week. The benefits, the force multiplier, is that once you get people into the mode of doing that, they do it faster and they do it as part of their normal day; and we get better results.'

Phil Loach
Chief Fire Officer
West Midlands Fire Service

Lowering the participation level of strategy formulation and implementation challenges traditional thinking that recognizes the role of the 'chosen few' in driving the organization forward. It encourages the development of an inclusive organizational culture that thrives on shared ownership of shared objectives, and where the strategic leader does not reside in his or her ivory tower but rather is seen as part of the team. Being prepared to include others in one of the most important leadership responsibilities demonstrates the leadership approach of shared social responsibility, which, you may recall from Chapter 1, is founded on four principles:

- The leader must be seen as 'one of us'.
- The leader must be seen to 'do it for us'.
- The leader must 'craft a sense of us'.
- The leader must 'make it matter'.

The human dimension to strategic planning is key to its success. It is, therefore, not surprising that it features in several of the obstacles or barriers to strategy implementation identified by Wessel (1993), namely:

- too many and conflicting priorities;
- the top team does not function well;
- top-down management style;
- inter-functional conflicts;
- poor vertical communications;
- inadequate management development.

The psychology of decision-making

Let us now look in more detail into the psychological requirements and make-up of effective strategic leaders, in particular in respect to the decision-making process involved in making future plans.

The environments, internal and external, in which senior leadership operates is embedded with uncertainty, ambiguity, complexity and, indeed, information overload. Within this context, Boal and Hooijberg (2001) suggest that the essence of strategic leadership is the creation and maintenance of three qualities: absorptive capacity and adaptive capacity, coupled with managerial wisdom:

- *Absorptive capacity* refers to the ability to learn through recognizing and assimilating new information, and then to utilize it in future planning. Sometimes the absorptive process will only lead to minor modifications or adjustments to previous interpretations, whilst, more radically, the new information may cause a shift in *weltanschauung* (interpretation of life, or world view). People continually add or ignore input to their memory, but for strategic leaders the process is particularly important as they are in a unique position to change or reinforce existing policies and procedures within their organization as a means of positioning it competitively within its operational environment.

- *Adaptive capacity* is the ability to change: to be strategically flexible in the face of a changing competitive environment. In order to identify and take advantage of future opportunities, strategic decision-makers require both cognitive and behavioural flexibility, not least an openness to, and embracing of, change.

- *Managerial wisdom* is the capacity to perceive when the environment is changing, and then to take timely action. In classical Greece, it was described as *kairos* – 'a passing instant when an opening appears, which must be driven through with force if success is to be achieved'. That opportune moment may have a human component, which, if so, calls for the leader to have, and apply, high levels of emotional intelligence. Examples of relevant competences from each of the four domains in Goleman's emotional competence inventory (discussed in Chapter 4) could include self-confidence (self-awareness domain); optimism (self-management); empathy (social awareness); and change catalyst (relationship management). Indeed, almost all of the 18 competences would be called for in *kairos* time.

Decision-making is, of course, one of the fundamental requirements of any level of leadership but, perhaps, none more so than that involved in strategic planning and implementation. The entire future of the organization and its people may depend on decisions taken by the strategic leader. It is necessary, therefore, for us to consider here the factors that may help or hinder the appropriateness and resulting success of the decision-making process.

Confirmation and hindsight biases

Imagine a team leader who is in a demanding job, with insufficient time to devote the amount of time he would like to all team members. He therefore spends what time he has on developing and motivating those who he feels will perform the best. This proves to be true as these 'chosen few' do indeed undertake their duties to a high standard. It would appear, therefore, that this strategy is successful: those who he devotes his attentions to are his best workers. However, if their quality of performance is enhanced by the time their leader spends with them, is his decision not a self-fulfilling prophecy? He has certainly not tested the validity of his decision regarding his allocation of time. The only way to do so is to give less time to the 'chosen few', and more attention to those team members he values less; and to then evaluate the results of this alternative course of action. My point is that people tend to consider only positive tests of their views, making them difficult to disprove – a bias towards confirmation, rather than rejection.

The danger is that strategic leaders only seek confirming evidence of the continuing validity of their decisions, rather than rigorously testing them as the strategy unfolds. Fischhoff (1975) conducted an experiment with MBA students, asking them to predict the outcomes of a specified future political event. The students made their forecasts, allocating a quantitative measure of their confidence next to each. Two weeks later, after the event had taken place, the students, who had subsequently heard about the event in the national press, were asked to recall their confidence scores of each of their predictions. Their responses were instructive: if the outcome *had* occurred, the students tended to recollect that they had confidently predicted it would. If, though, it had *not* happened, they either claimed that they had not predicted it would, or had allocated it a low measure of confidence. Hence, they were portraying the hindsight bias as an 'I knew it all along' effect. It would seem, therefore, that as decision-makers we do not always learn from our experience because we do not apportion sufficient value to it: rather our *recollection* of what we did decide confirms our decision to have been well made.

Whilst it has been some time since Fischhoff's experiment was undertaken, the conclusion remains valid to this day: people tend to believe that their judgement is sound – a perception that can be reinforced by both confirmation and/or hindsight bias. These biases give us inappropriate confidence in our decision-making abilities: a dangerous cognitive habit for strategic leaders!

Discretion

Hambrick and Finkelstein (1987) suggest that the extent of the discretion enjoyed by senior leaders will moderate how their strategic choices relate to organizational outcomes: the greater the discretion the more influence on the outcomes. The extent of discretion that a decision-maker has will be influenced by demographic and organizational factors, as well as personality characteristics. The personality factor determines how the leader perceives the extent of discretion he or she has: if leaders are not aware of it they are unlikely to take action in certain circumstances; conversely, if they believe they have more discretion than they have, their decisions may be questioned and resisted.

House and Aditya (1997) relate discretion to 'weak' psychological situations, where wide latitude in decision-making is allowed; and 'strong' situations, where choices and actions would be constrained and the personality characteristics of the leader would not be so influential. Hence, it is in circumstances where a good degree of discretion is allowed that the personality of the leaders will have most impact on their decisions.

Upper echelon theory

Hambrick and Mason (1984) argued that the specific knowledge, experience, values and preferences of top managers influence their assessment of the organizational environment and, hence, the strategic decisions they make.

Finkelstein and Hambrick (1996) developed the theory by examining the psychological make-up of strategic leaders and how that influences information-processing and decision-making. If strategic choices have a large behavioural component, then they will reflect the idiosyncrasies of the decision-makers, including their knowledge or assumptions about future events; their knowledge of alternative courses of action; and their knowledge of the consequences of each alternative decision. How they choose to categorize each alternative and its consequence will also be influenced by the leader's personal values. This process is continually updated by a constant stream of internal and external stimuli, which in turn filter and distort the decision-maker's perception of what should be done. Hambrick and Mason (1984) contend that strategic leaders are faced with complex situations that are impossible to fully comprehend, hence they impose a cognitive base and values to the decision, which impose a screen between the situation and their eventual perception of it.

In sequence, what happens is that the leader, being unable to interpret every aspect of the situation, can only adopt a limited perception of it. His or her perceptions are then further limited by selectively considering only some of the information included in his or her 'field of vision' – those areas to which his or her attention is directed. Finally, the information selected for attention is interpreted through a filter consisting of his or her cognitive understanding and values. The eventual decision is, therefore, founded upon the eventual perception of the situation, combined with a set of personal values.

The idiosyncrasies that influence decision-makers' perception of the problem to be solved, and behaviour in addressing it, include age, tenure within the organization, functional background, education, socio-economic roots and financial stability. Hence, the upper echelon theory emphasizes the leader's background characteristics, rather than any psychological dimensions, as primary influences on his or her decision-making. Organizational outcomes can, therefore, be partially predicted by an assessment of the leader's background.

The use of heuristics

Decision-makers do not have infinite time and resources to gather and analyse information; nor do they have limitless mental capacity to interpret the data potentially available. Thus, even when they do try to make decisions according to a rational and logical process they often need to make simplifying assumptions due to the limited available information and analytical constraints. In such situations they may use heuristics: mental shortcuts that reduce the cognitive burden associated with decision-making. Heuristics offer the user the opportunity to reduce the complexity of decision-making by considering fewer choices and requiring less memory storage and retrieval. Cognitive psychologists have identified a number of heuristics that people use when making decisions, in particular the representative and availability heuristics.

The *representative heuristic* is a mental shortcut that involves comparing a current situation to our prototype of a particular event or behaviour. In the event that one of two alternatives are recognizable, people tend to choose that formative one; hence arriving at a decision with the least amount of information or effort.

The *availability heuristic* encourages people to base their decisions on how easily they can remember similar events happening in the past, thus estimating how likely it is that it will happen again in the future.

Heuristics can be used consciously or subconsciously, and can be beneficial in terms of cognitive economy. However, strategic decision-makers should be aware of the need to override them in favour of more comprehensive processes, not least because they can result in some significant biases, such as:

- *Framing the problem.* The way in which a problem is described can hugely affect how we resolve to address it. For example, financial decisions can be influenced by whether the current position is understood to be positive or negative. If positive, we tend to be risk-averse; if negative, we are more likely to take risks to avoid or recover losses. Indeed, actual words used to describe an issue can influence how we interpret events. Loftus and Palmer (1974) conducted experiments to explore factors that influenced memory of a filmed car accident. They found that the way that the question was posed (using either the word hit, smashed, collided, bumped or contacted) largely determined the research participants' estimate of the speed of the car. Moreover, those who were asked the question containing the word 'smashed' were more likely to believe they had seen (non-existent) broken glass than those whose question included the word 'hit'.

- *Using information.* Not only do we tend to attribute more weight to easily available information, but we also do so for memories that are more easily retrievable. We can also apportion greater weight to information that is self-serving or confirms our existing point of view.

- *Judgement bias.* It is inevitable that we filter the huge amount of sensory information we are faced with every day. If leaders did not do so they would be faced with 'analysis paralysis' – the inability to make sense of any situation. How we filter the information does, however, run the risk of judgement bias due to, for example, our natural over- or under-confidence, or tendency towards optimism or pessimism. This can be mediated to some extent, by revisiting decisions or targets as more information becomes available, although many are hesitant to do so.

- *Post-decision evaluation.* Fundamental attribution bias is a tendency to attribute good results to our own decisions and bad ones to factors outside our orbit of control. Thus, we can filter out, or discount, information that may question our original decision and threaten our self-esteem. We naturally want to control, or appear to control, events affecting us – which can result in us assuming we have more influence over them than we actually do. This can lead to an underestimation of the risks of our actions or decisions; and reduced exponential learning as we filter out information that questions the amount of control we actually have. No one, including strategic leaders, have complete mastery over their environment, so we must not succumb to bias in our judgement as we struggle to come to terms with that inevitability.

Five essential skills for strategic leaders

To close this chapter on strategic leadership, I propose the following five essential skills for leaders who are charged with navigating a positive, sustainable future for their organizations:

1 *Anticipate future threats and opportunities.* The organization may be performing well at present but it is unlikely to continue as such indefinitely. A whole host of external and internal factors are queuing up to push it off course, not least competitors, changing customer needs, and advances in communication technology. Strategic leaders must, therefore, be constantly vigilant, scanning the environment for early signs of change. This will require talking to and listening to customers; conducting or, at the very least, being up-to-date with market research; evaluating emerging sector competitors; and conducting scenario planning to map out alternative futures.

2 *Challenge the status quo.* Question established norms and encourage objective dissention. Ask penetrating questions to 'think the unthinkable', even to the extent of challenging the very fundamentals of the business. Practise Ricardo Semler's (1999) 'Three Whys': only after asking the question three times are you likely to have achieved the depth of understanding necessary to determine the true value of any accepted practice. It may also be necessary to address those within the organization who are happy within their 'comfort zones', with no intention of facing up to the reality of the future.

3 *Create a learning organization.* The organization should be imbued with a culture of development: searching for new avenues of learning. Strategic leaders should lead by example by addressing failure, their own and others, in an open and constructive way as a means of identifying hidden contributing factors: viewing mistakes as opportunities for learning. At the same time, success should be celebrated as an incentive for others to aspire to join the party.

4 *Take decisions.* Strategic leadership calls for decisions to be made, based upon a disciplined process that is rigorous, but not interminable; flexible, but not indecisive; objective, but not dismissing

the personal values and opinions of the leader who is charged to take responsibility for the decisions. The leader should, however, be continually vigilant for any biases that may influence the validity of decisions made.

5 *Seek stakeholder buy-in.* For strategic planning to have the best chance of success, all those with a stake in the organization should be aligned with the plans. Success depends on continual communications, the building of mutual trust and frequent engagement. Stakeholders include external customers and funders, as well as management and staff at all levels. Those at the helm of the organization should recognize the need for a supportive senior management team, as well as middle managers who are committed to the future vision. Strategic leaders are well advised to recognize people's innate resistance to change, especially if its necessity is questioned, and be prepared to share information regarding it, where confidentiality permits.

Chapter summary

In the current environment of varied and complex challenges and opportunities, where the future of national and international trade and commerce is uncertain, there has never been a greater need for effective strategic thinking and planning. Effective strategic leaders balance the need for short-term stability with a sustainable and prosperous future: articulating a compelling vision that all stakeholders are inspired to buy in to.

This chapter explored both the strategic thinking and planning processes necessary to ensure a viable future for an organization. It starts with a comprehensive assessment of current operations and competitors before assessing what the future holds. Penetrating questions should be asked and current assumptions challenged as a means of clarifying the foundation upon which progress can be planned. The analytical and human dimensions of strategic leadership were discussed, as were the four design criteria for crafting a realistic vision of enhanced organizational performance; along with associated theories concerning strategic planning.

The final section of the chapter considered the psychological aspects of decision-making: how cognitive functioning, biases, and other experiential and behavioural influences can affect the decisions-making process. It concluded with a set of five essential skills required of strategic leaders if they are to plot a positive future for their organizations.

Extreme
leadership
– leading when
life is threatened

08

So far in this book we have explored leadership and, in particular, its psychological foundations: how leaders can benefit from an understanding of how their, and notably their followers', minds influence behaviour and, ultimately, the fulfilment of their vision. However, the context within which these leaders operate has been relatively stable – certainly not life-threatening. The decisions that the leaders take may affect their followers' general well-being, their jobs even – but not their life or death. In this chapter I consider leadership in extreme conditions: where the leaders' role is to give purpose, motivation and direction to their people in situations where there is a real – and often imminent – physical, material or psychological risk. Here, the leader's actions will impact on others' physical well-being or even their eventual survival. He or she may be operating in a military or extreme survival environment, facing direct human or natural threats; or in a political or public service context, reacting to national or local emergencies. We will examine the approaches that these leaders take to ensure the safety of those they are responsible for, as well as considering whether experiences gained by leading in extreme conditions can be translated into lessons beneficial for those occupying positions of authority within organizations and businesses.

Much has been written about 'crisis management', but my focus here is on a different set of circumstances. Wikipedia defines crisis management as: 'the process by which an organization deals with a major event that threatens to harm the organization, its stakeholders, or the general public'. Hence, whilst the crisis poses a threat, was not predicted, and requires a degree of urgent action, the concept is much more about a planned process of change at the organizational level. The event may pose far-reaching, unwanted implications, but the threat is of a different magnitude in terms of safety and the threat to life.

'We have just finished developing a new learning module for our leaders, entitled 'Leading in a Crisis', because we can operate in some quite extreme times. If you run a hotel and the area is hit by a tsunami it is different from running a factory where you just have to get your people home. The hotel actually becomes a port of safety for a lot of the community and for your people. Part of our Corporate Social Responsibility policy is called 'Shelter in the Storm', which allows our hotels to open for the community without worrying about the financial implications. You need a very different type of leadership in such times. It is about connecting with your values and having the freedom to do the right thing.'

Gregor Thain
VP Global Leadership Development
InterContinental Hotels

Hannah *et al* (2009) define the context in which extreme leadership is required as 'an environment where one or more extreme events are occurring, or are likely to occur, that may exceed the organization's capacity to prevent, and (may) result in an extensive and intolerable magnitude of physical, psychological, or material consequences to – or in close physical or psychosocial proximity to – organization members'. So far as this chapter is concerned, the 'organization' involved could be a military patrol operating in a combat zone; a polar expedition; a threat to national security; or a fast-response team reacting to a fire, or other emergency situation. How do the leaders of those 'organizations', large or small, apply their skills to mitigate the threat to those whose safety, or even continued existence, they are responsible for?

Threats calling for extreme leadership are determined by a number of factors, which are, in turn, made more or less extreme by certain modulators. Figure 8.1 offers a diagrammatic representation of their relationships.

Let us consider the four factors that define the extreme event:

1 *Immediacy.* Perhaps one's initial concept of a threat facing leaders would involve a relatively speedy change from a stable environment to one that poses the potential of physical or psychological injury: the appearance of an armed enemy, or an industrial explosion, for example. Effective leadership then ensures the disposal of the enemy

FIGURE 8.1   Threat factors and modulators

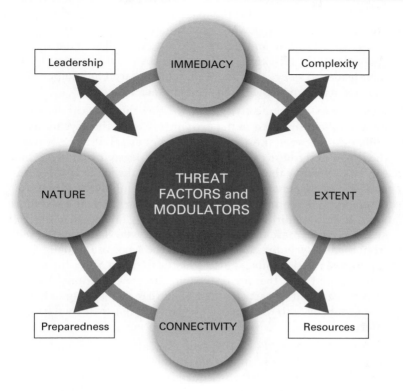

or the extinguishing of the fire resulting from the explosion. The drama mirrors a parabolic curve, with a quick transition from its base to a peak of activity, which subsequently tails off back to a situation of relative stability. Yet, alternatively, the event may require leadership input over an extended period, for example the Bhopal gas leak in December 1984 resulted in an immediate death toll of over 2,250, with estimates of a further 8,000 dying over subsequent weeks. The Chernobyl nuclear disaster in 1986 will continue to claim the lives of those subjected to the fallout – for many years to come. The success of the leadership reaction to such events, especially one with a high immediacy factor, will be modulated to a large extent by the extent of preparedness, especially planning and training, undertaken beforehand.

2   *Extent.* Extreme events can vary in terms of their scale: from a mountaineering accident, to Hurricane Katrina devastating New Orleans in August 2005. The magnitude and resulting consequences of the former example are less than the widespread effect of the latter. The extent of the extreme event will affect those involved in a

number of ways, including psychological responses such as stress and fear, which in turn can cause the person to become ineffective or paralysed into inaction. As the magnitude of the event increases, so does the call for leaders who can navigate their people through the crisis towards a safe and secure outcome. We will see later in the chapter that, in such circumstances, the trust that followers have in their leader to safeguard their well-being is based more upon the leader's task competence than their character.

3 *Connectivity.* By connectivity I mean either the physical distance between those involved in the extreme event, or the psychological affiliations between those involved. The physical distance between the leader and followers will influence the degree of influence that can be exerted by the leader as well as how the leader's style and behaviours are perceived and interpreted by followers. A platoon commander operating alongside his men, sharing their discomfort and extreme conditions, will be seen as being 'in touch' with them and, therefore, more trustworthy than one who distances himself from them. Psychological closeness, in the sense of mutually supportive relationships, is also a factor that can affect the levels of cohesion and trust that are critical in extreme conditions. A collective identity can lead to participants feeling that they belong to a close-knit group, even to the extent that they will put their own personal safety at risk in the service of other group members.

4 *Nature.* Hannah *et al*'s (2009) definition, above, of the context in which extreme leadership is required referred to physical, psychological or material consequences. The nature of the threat will therefore influence the responses of those involved. The risk of physical injury or death may result in high levels of fear for those facing the threat, whilst material consequences are more likely to engender responses based upon self-worth or an uncertain future. Followers' reactions will also be dependent upon the nature of the threat, with those facing physical consequences more likely to be energized towards immediate counter-attack. The form of threat may also be, of course, multilayered – householders defending their properties against fire, for example – thus requiring an adaptive leadership style from those charged with co-ordinating the response.

Taken in isolation, these four threat factors – immediacy, extent, connectivity and nature – only paint half a picture, as their influence on the extreme event will be modulated by four variables: complexity, resources, preparedness and, last but not least, leadership. These variables can, and will, intensify or reduce the strength or effect of the four primary factors.

Complexity

The threat factors relate to extreme events, the complexity of which can be dramatically influenced by variables enfolding in unexpected ways. When this happens, insignificant happenings can interact to generate unpredictable, dramatic end results. The complexity of the event can be affected by the interaction of a multitude of factors, for example on the battlefield; or a relative few, as in a domestic fire. Moreover, the variables can be occasioned either by factors outside the leader's sphere of influence, or from those he or she has a degree of control over, for example the leader–follower relationships.

Communication flow during extreme events, within the organization or between it and outside agencies, can create a degree of complexity due to a cocktail of information and misinformation. One is reminded of the First World War fable of this message sent from the trenches, 'Send reinforcements, we are going to advance', which after transmission through various third parties, was received by HQ as 'Send three and fourpence, we are going to a dance'. The efficacy of technical communications, even in our modern 'communication age', can add to the complexity of a crisis event, for example the unreliable battlefield radios used by British troops during the early stages of the Iraq war. Hence, both the content of the communication and method of delivery can, and will, contribute to the degree of complexity.

Clear, concise communication in advance of any extreme intervention can also clarify its complexity. The US Marine Corps, for example, uses a specific mission combat order – the strict format of which every marine must learn and adhere to – known as the 'Five-Paragraph Order':

1 Situation – explains what's happening on the ground.
2 Mission – contains the task and purpose for the action.
3 Execution – describes how the leader intends to accomplish the mission.
4 Administration and logistics – identifies the information necessary for the operation to be successful.
5 Command and signal – details the plan for command and control of the operation.

This combat order is designed to clarify all the essential elements of the operation in the hope that, by doing so, the number and extent of unexpected ensuing variables will be reduced. Hence, it addresses the *complexity* modulator, as well as the *preparedness* modulator (discussed below).

Resources
The extent and availability of organizational and psychological resources will also modulate the impact of the threats associated with an extreme event. The former can be classified in terms of technical, financial, logistical or human resources. The number of rifles, and soldiers trained to use them effectively, will obviously affect the outcomes of a military campaign, as will the number of sandbags available to combat the effects of flooding. At the macro level, the degree of financial support allocated to the event will have a profound influence on its overall threat level.

There is also a connection between the level of physical and human resources allocated to those charged with reacting to an extreme event, and their psychological resources available to cope with it. The operators' belief in the extent to which the resources are fit for purpose, hence contributing to a reduced threat to their personal well-being, can have a significant impact on their motivation, morale and, hence, performance. The extent of trepidation, even fear, is increased when the assessment of the threat exceeds that of the resources available to counter it. Jervis (1976) states that: 'predisposition to perceive a threat varies with the person's belief about his ability to take effective counteraction'. Conversely, when those facing an extreme event have confidence in the support they are receiving to counter it, their performance can be enhanced proportionally. Speedy, earnest and public political support for those facing the aftermath of natural disasters can induce resilience and hopefulness in them. It is incumbent, therefore, on national leaders to be visible following such disasters in order to offer psychological, as well as practical, support. Compare President George W Bush's reaction after Hurricane Katrina to that of New York Mayor Rudy Giuliani in the aftermath to 9/11. President Bush took three days to respond appropriately, whilst Mayor Giuliani was highly visible from the onset of the attack, assuring city residents that 'we will come through the tragedy together'. Even political rivals praised Giuliani for the 'right emotional tone'.

Preparedness

It is the strategic leader's responsibility to provide foresight, planning and training to combat the effects of extreme situations. The leader must counter the natural tendencies to think 'it will never happen to us' in order to determine an appropriate level of preparedness, even for relatively rare events. The country may be enjoying an extended period of reduced threat, or the neighbourhood is classified as low on crime, yet Murphy's Eighth Law – 'if everything is going according to plan, then it is a sure sign that something is about to go wrong' – may well arise to surprise the unprepared leader. Many will cite global warming as encouragement to prepare for natural disasters – such as the unprecedented flooding in the south of England during January and February of 2014, during which the government's Environment Agency was heavily criticized for not allocating sufficient resources to flood defences and river dredging in previous years.

Training is crucial if the worst effects of life-threatening events are to be minimized. On 14 December 2012 a former student walked into the Sandy Hook Elementary School in Newtown, Connecticut and within five minutes had killed six adults and 20 children. When the initial shots were heard, the school principal, Dawn Hochsprung, ran out of her office to confront the gunman. It is thought that, whilst doing so, she turned on the school intercom to alert others to the fact that it was a real emergency, not a planned practice. After she was shot and killed, the other school teachers and staff put into action the crisis response training they had received, which included actions to be taken when faced with bomb threats and armed intruders.

They hid students; barricaded classrooms, bathrooms and storage rooms; and isolated the section of the school where the armed person was located. In doing so, it is thought that they saved the lives of numerous children and adults.

Preparation for life-threatening situations not only involves the provision of training and resources, but also involves the concept of being psychologically prepared. Be they soldiers training for combat, medical response units treating mass casualties, or those planning for natural disasters – being emotionally prepared for an extreme event can help participants feel more confident, more in control and better able to perform during the crisis. It can also help to reduce the psychological distress and long-term mental health problems resulting from post-event trauma. When people are not prepared for extreme stress they may not be able to think as clearly as usual, thus affecting decision-making and overall performance. However, when those involved have a better understanding of their own likely responses to being faced with the threat of serious injury, loss of life or property, they are better placed to control their responses. Psychologists call the process of preparing people for extreme situations 'stress inoculation': working through likely psychological reactions and learning coping strategies.

The Australian Psychological Society proposes a three-step approach to prepare oneself emotionally for extreme conditions, including natural disasters:

1 Anticipate that you will be feeling worried or anxious and remember that these are normal, although not always helpful, responses to a possible life-threatening situation.

2 Identify what the specific physical feelings associated with anxiety are and whether you are having any frightening thoughts that are adding to the fear.

3 Manage your responses using controlled breathing and self-talk so that you stay as calm as possible and can focus on the practical tasks that need attention.

Leadership

The fourth and final modulator that can increase or reduce the threat factors associated with extreme events is leadership – which we will consider at some length in terms of its application in survival, political, emergency response and combat scenarios. The chapter will conclude with consideration of how the lessons learnt from extreme leadership can translate to more moderate business and organizational situations.

Survival leadership

I started this chapter explaining that its purpose is to consider leadership in extreme conditions: where the leaders' role is to give purpose, motivation and direction to their people in situations where there is a real – and often imminent – physical, material or psychological risk. In terms of the natural world there can be few places more extreme than the highest peaks on the planet, or the polar regions at its northern or southern-most points. It is here that the very next step taken by the expedition leader or his group members may result in injury or death. History records the feats of mountaineers such as George Mallory and Sir Edmund Hillary – who, along with Sherpa Tenzing, was the first person to climb to the summit of Mount Everest. Notable polar explorers include Robert Falcon Scott and Roald Amundsen, yet it is perhaps Sir Ernest Shackleton's *Endurance* expedition from which we can learn the most salient lessons in extreme leadership.

In August 1914, Shackleton set sail with his team of mariners and scientists with the objective of crossing the unexplored Antarctic continent. Problems began on 19 January the following year when the Weddell Sea ice closed around the SS *Endurance*, trapping it 60 miles from Antarctica. In the period up to their eventual rescue on 30 August 1916, Shackleton and his crew experienced the ship being crushed by the pack ice; being stranded on the floes of the frozen Weddell Sea; two perilous journeys in open boats across the Southern Ocean; and being marooned on the desolate Elephant Island. It is testament to Shackleton's exceptional leadership qualities that every one of the 28 crew members survived the extreme ordeal.

Parmenter (2010) suggests that Shackleton's example offers us 10 lessons in extreme leadership:

1 *Manage the immediate crisis* by, for example, respecting and
   fully utilizing senior team members; being flexible in decision-
   making; and maintaining a sense of humour even in the most
   dire situations.

BEST leadership quote

'No matter how much you know, when you are making decisions that will affect the future of the business you need to have a fantastic team around you. What you learn is that no one person will have the skills for everything. So the mix of skills and the dynamics of the team is very important. You have got to have good people around you – people who are going to challenge you and your thinking.'

Carmen Watson
Chief Executive
Pertemps

2 *Recruit your team with care* by identifying character, competence and multi-skills that can create leaders with the team.

3 *Show an abundance of positive energy* by, in Shackleton's case, working the hardest, sleeping the least, leading from the front and never admitting defeat.

4 *Communicate effectively and positively* by continually engaging in informal, personal consultations and discussions. By doing so, bad news is never unexpected and group dissention is avoided.

BEST leadership quote

'In a leadership and cultural framework, how do we create positive energy? It's about communication and trust: removing any distortion between what I say and what you hear. If you trust me you will hear what I have to say with clarity. If you don't, there will be something between us that will cause it to be misinterpreted.'

Phil Loach
Chief Fire Officer
West Midlands Fire Service

---

5 *See and own the future* by visualizing ahead and planning accordingly. Shackleton was bold in planning but careful in execution, thus minimizing potential risk.

6 *Develop, engage and demonstrate trust* by removing barriers associated with rank and assigning tasks according to a person's qualities and skills. In Shackleton's team, menial tasks were undertaken by all members, with no exceptions afforded to rank or seniority.

7 *Reinvent yourself and constantly innovate* by learning from past experience and mistakes.

8 *Embody personal values*, which in Shackleton's case included mutual respect, humility and shared hardship, as well as an expectation of similar standards from crew members.

9 *Be a servant leader* by serving others rather than expecting to be the one who is served. Shackleton would be the first to nurse an ailing crew member or make a cup of tea for him – viewing such service as a leadership strength, rather than a weakness (servant leadership is explored in Chapter 9).

10 *Understand the principles of psychology* and use them when dealing with individual team members. Shackleton would flatter those who responded to it, whilst managing his personal anger and frustration when faced with those whose commitment was failing. He personally engaged dissidents and avoided needless power struggles – all examples of the application of emotional intelligence.

As defined in Chapter 1, situational leadership requires leaders to adapt their style according to the situation they face – and facing the extremes of polar regions is certainly a unique situational environment. It is therefore interesting and relevant to consider Ian Lovegrove's 'Leaders in Antarctica: characteristics of an Antarctic station manager', contained in Giannantonio and Hurley-Hanson (2013). An Antarctic permanent scientific station forms an extreme environment where the necessary confinement produces social isolation and relative inactivity for many months – shared with the enforced company with colleagues not of one's choosing. The leader is the station manager, who is responsible for both the completion of the mission and the welfare of those charged to achieve it.

Lovegrove, drawing on research from a study of 26 station managers and followers, defines the necessary emotions and self-attitude characteristics of a station manager as:

- *Self-awareness, stability and self-control.* Leaders who have high levels of emotional intelligence are able to monitor and control their own mood, as well as those of their followers, and can engage in effective self-management strategies (Goleman, Boyatzis and McKee, 2001). The research identified that station managers possess significantly higher levels of self-awareness than leaders operating in less extreme environments. Numerous supporting studies have also identified emotional stability and resilience as key characteristics of leaders, scientists and support staff of various nationalities employed in Antarctic stations. In respect of the station leaders themselves, emotional stability provides a foundation from which status-levelling can be tolerated more easily, without loss of personal respect. The emotional trait of self-control links with emotional stability, which is characterized by high levels of conscientiousness, self-discipline and orderliness, although there is a risk that followers can perceive their leader as somewhat clinical and lacking in passion.

- *Low anxiety and neuroticism.* Station personnel questioned in the research voiced a preference for station leaders who are calm, relaxed, quietly confident and optimistic: qualities that were, indeed, identified in the leaders. They were found to be extremely relaxed and lower in neuroticism than non-extreme leaders: providing a stable platform for routine decision-making, as well as displaying a confident composure during crisis events. A calm, balanced personality is seen as being a key leadership quality within the close confines of an Antarctic station, especially during the dark winter months.

- *Optimism and humour.* Followers cite the leader's optimism, related to being low on the scale for apprehension, as being a salient characteristic in confined environments. Humour can also play an important part in releasing tension. As Shackleton said: 'The man with a cheerful disposition and ready laugh is a bright sun to his companions.'

- *Integrity.* To operate effectively within the social and physical confines of an Antarctic station, the values demonstrated by the station manager are of critical importance. High on the list of values required by station staff is integrity – a specific characteristic of authentic leadership (discussed in Chapter 9). Staff look for their leader to act as a role model: leading by example, especially in terms of being tolerant, fair and just in his or her dealings with all station personnel. Within the flat hierarchy of a station, fair play, consideration and social justice must also apply to the manager him- or herself. In displaying an honest and transparent personality the leader seeks to develop a high level of psychological well-being amongst all station residents. With no opportunity to escape the scrutiny of followers, the leader's authenticity is a key factor in the creation of a social environment that will endure the long periods of intercommunity.

Leadership *BEST* practice

In 2005, Mark Wood was leading an expedition in the Arctic when, 2 kilometres from base camp, they ran into a Force 8 gale. One of their tents was blown away, which meant that all 13 of the expedition members had to occupy, in wet clothing, one very small tent. Mark's main priority over that period was to ensure they were fed; to keep them informed of the situation; and, most importantly, to maintain morale.

After three days they received clearance to return to base camp. The storm was still blowing and he began to make preparations to commence the journey. Tasks and responsibilities were allocated to team members, with Mark standing back to keep an overview of progress, when one member ran out of the tent crying 'Fire'. Luckily, one of the team was a firefighter so she quickly extinguished the blaze. However, the team were shocked and looked to Mark for reassurance and guidance.

He got them all to drop to their knees and link together like a rugby scrum whilst he assessed the situation. Speaking to them with a lightness of tone, he said, 'That was a bit of a shocker, but we are all still here.' His calm and authoritative presence helped in gaining agreement for his proposed course of action, but he noticed that one of the team had been more affected than the others and was still visibly shaken. Rather than publicly acknowledging the fact, Mark took the individual aside and told him that he needed someone to work alongside him in a specific capacity. They then commenced their way back to the safety of base camp. Mark recalls those three days as one of the sternest tests of his leadership skills.

Political leadership

Political leadership in scenarios where followers' lives are at risk inevitably suggests conflict situations at a national level. The Second World War is perhaps the most notable international conflict where individual political leaders are recognized as portraying the dominant presence on each side of the divide. Hitler and Churchill both epitomize leaders whose strength of character mobilized their countries in aggressive or defensive action respectively. As it was England and its allies who were facing the greater military might of the Axis powers, in the early stages of the conflict at least, I propose to primarily consider the leadership of Winston Churchill in this section of the chapter.

One of Churchill's most significant leadership qualities was his ability to inspire people, regardless of the apparently hopeless situation facing them. He did this largely by the demonstration of his own character – in particular determination and optimism – on the public stage, at least. He would not entertain any notion of defeat, as was noted by his official biographer, Sir Martin Gilbert: 'It was Churchill's own opposition to all forms of defeatism that marked out the first six months of his war premiership and established the nature and pattern of his war leadership.' He was also able, crucially, to infect the British people with his own determination and, thus, strengthen their resolve and fortitude. His determination is perhaps best exemplified by his speech of June 1940 that, famously, included:

> We shall go on to the end. We shall fight in France; we shall fight on the seas and oceans; we shall fight with growing confidence and growing strength in the air; we shall defend our island, whatever the costs may be. We shall fight on beaches; we shall fight on the landing grounds; we shall fight in the fields and in the streets; we shall fight in the hills – we shall never surrender.

One can hear the passion in his voice by reading that excerpt from his speech. As Anita Roddick, founder of the Body Shop retail chain in the UK, once said, 'We communicate with passion, and passion persuades.' Churchill's communication skills were exemplary: he would honestly explain the current realities, then create an inspirational vision for the future. Who could contest the passion contained in his words: 'Never give in, never give in, never, never, never – in nothing, great or small, large or petty. Never give in, except to convictions of honour and good sense.'

His vision for the future was not only founded upon optimism and determination, but also on highly tuned strategic foresight. For example, he had early misgivings about Russia's intentions, proposing in a speech he made in New York in 1931 that the struggle for the future would be between English-speaking countries and communism: correctly forecasting the Cold War that followed the Second World War.

Churchill's personality was characterized not only by his aforementioned optimism and determination, but also by charm, wit and humour, often bitingly delivered; as well as a surprising degree of humility: 'The nation had the lion's heart. I had the luck to give the roar.' He used his unique charm and personality to inspire others – individually or collectively.

Both he and Hitler were, in my estimation, transformational leaders, defined by Bass (1985) as those 'who stimulate and inspire followers to achieve extraordinary outcomes'. But were they both charismatic leaders? Do transformational leaders have to be charismatic? Are all charismatic leaders transformational?

It is said that when a charismatic person enters a room they attract the attention of all its occupants. They exude a magnetism that draws others towards them: people want to be associated with them, to be part of their coterie. A charismatic person is surrounded by an aura of self-confidence and positivity. Charismatic leaders have a firm belief that they can lead by the power of their personal charm: either face-to-face, or by any indirect means, they seek to make those they meet feel like the most important person on the planet. They instinctively assess the concerns of each individual and can even extend that ability when addressing large audiences, adopting their words and actions to maximum effect in both scenarios. They are masters of body language – both using it personally and assessing it in others. Exceptional communication skills are, however, perhaps the most essential attribute of a charismatic leader – the ability to communicate at a very powerful, emotional level.

We can certainly picture Churchill, dressed in his bow tie and tall hat, smoking his large cigar and raising his two fingers in a victory salute, to be exerting his personal charm and communicating at a powerful and emotional level. His charisma was a powerful adjunct to the transformational necessity of defending a nation against an enemy of superior magnitude.

However, we can also picture Hitler, dressed in immaculate uniform, raising his arm in salute to the adoring, frenzied crowd at the Nuremberg Rally, and at the other rallies that followed.

It seems to me that if a leader is to transform the hearts, minds and actions of a nation facing extreme conditions, charisma is a most powerful and effective personal quality. Recall, however, from Chapter 1 that Burns (1978) defined transforming leadership as occurring: 'when one or more persons engage with others in such a way that leaders and followers raise one another to higher levels of motivation and morality'. Note the reference to morality. The values that charismatic leaders promote often define them: if they are well-intentioned and benevolent they can be transformational over long periods of extreme hardship and danger. If, however, they are self-serving or Machiavellian, history has proved that they can create powerful and destructive cults. As Patricia Sellers wrote in an article in *Fortune* magazine in 1996:

> Charisma is a tricky thing. Jack Kennedy oozed it – but so did Hitler and Charles Manson. Con artists, charlatans and megalomaniacs can make it their instrument as effectively as the best CEOs, entertainers and Presidents. Used wisely, it's a blessing; indulged, it can be a curse. Charismatic visionaries lead people ahead, and sometimes astray.

So we are left with two powerful political leaders operating in extreme conditions, Churchill and Hitler, both charismatic and transformational in their own way – but with very different agendas. As Hitler wrote in *Mein Kampf* (translated as 'my struggle'): 'The broad mass of nation... will more easily fall victim to a big lie than to a small one.' Churchill, however, understood the transient nature of such an approach, saying: 'Dictators ride to and fro upon tigers which they dare not dismount – and the tigers are getting hungry.'

Churchill's appeal was to the aspirations and emotions of the nation facing an extreme threat – offering hope and salvation: 'Do not let us speak of darker days; let us rather speak of sterner days. These are not dark days; these are great days – the greatest our country has ever lived.'

Emergency response leadership

This section will explore the styles and required competencies of leaders who are reacting to emergency situations that are life-threatening and allow a limited time in which to respond. While such events may have been anticipated in concept, planned for, and the responders trained, the extreme threat they pose, along with the associated uncertainty of outcome, call for a unique set of leadership skills.

The skills and qualities required of emergency response leaders differ somewhat from the charismatic and transformational styles considered in the previous section. Whilst charismatic competencies – such as self-confidence, intelligence and social skills – overlap, the requirement of emergency response leaders to use analytic skills and flexibility in order to address fast-emerging problems differ. Similarly, the qualities required of a transformational leader, including inspirational motivation, role-modelling and trustworthiness, relate to leaders responding to emergencies – although their prime focus is not the change of attitudes and beliefs. Transformational leadership's objective is performance improvement, through shared values, over the long term, whilst emergency response leadership has a much more immediate focus on results based upon decisive decision-making. The former seek organizational change through collaboration and consultation, whilst the latter must be willing to assume immediate responsibility for unfolding events.

BEST leadership quote

'In the Fire and Rescue Service you have to apply a very literal situational leadership approach. The transformational model is correct for 96 per cent of the time, either in headquarters or in fire stations. However, in extreme conditions, that approach has to be flipped. I believe this is the USP [unique selling point] of people in roles like mine.'

Phil Loach
Chief Fire Officer
West Midlands Fire Service

Compared to the wealth of research associated with other leadership situations, there is a relative paucity relating to the extreme environments we are considering in this section of the chapter. It appears to be a specific example of situation leadership that has not widely engaged the attention of researchers and writers. One exception, however, is a project undertaken by Van Wart and Kapucu (2011), in which emergency management officials across the United States were questioned regarding the competences required of those facing extreme events such as Hurricane Katrina and the 9/11 terrorist attacks in New York. Each participant was asked to choose 5 to 10 leadership competences, from a total of 37, which most related to immediate extreme events, as opposed to routine emergencies where the system operated largely as expected. They were also asked to offer comments, which provided a substantial qualitative base. Comments included:

'When there is a catastrophic event, the successful leaders are the ones who have the willingness to accept responsibilities outside their experience and training.'

'A leader must be able to formulate a message and communicate that message, not only to first-responders, but also to the general public. A successful disaster response occurs as much in the crisis communication action as in other steps taken.'

'In catastrophic events, events unfold too quickly for indecisiveness. Leaders must be decisive, and willing to take risks, in order to be successful. Timid leadership in a (routine) emergency can still achieve results; timid leadership in a catastrophic event will always lead to failure.'

'Catastrophic events require greater ability to work under stress.'

The main hypothesis of the research was that emergency managers would identify significant distinctions in competency requirements in the crisis response phase as opposed to other leadership roles, including routine emergencies, change management and transformational leadership situations. Table 8.1 shows the list of generic leadership competencies offered to the respondents; those they selected as especially necessary for emergency response leaders are shown in brackets.

This quantitative data supports the research hypothesis, reinforced by the qualitative comments, in that 'willingness to assume responsibility' was both the most widely selected category and the most commented upon. The unique requirements of emergency response leadership was also substantiated by the fact that over one-third of the generic leadership competencies were seldom chosen by the respondents. Scores for 'flexibility', however, were supported by comments such as: 'Emergency managers cannot be too rigid in (the) decision process, since during a catastrophic-type disaster things may change rapidly, which could require a change of direction' – as was the score for 'communication', as managers need to be sure that: 'An order/guidance is understood and, critically, not misunderstood.'

The highest-scored task-oriented leadership behaviour, 'delegation', also featured significantly in research undertaken by Klein *et al* (2006) with extreme action medical teams in emergency trauma centres in the United States. Here, victims of shootings, stabbings, car crashes or other traumatic injury are transported to the centre by ambulance or helicopter to be treated with the utmost urgency by a medical team. Errors or delay in the process can result in the death of the patient, whilst quick and appropriate treatment is likely to save his or her life. Although operating in a different environment,

TABLE 8.1 Leadership competences required of emergency response leaders (from Van Wart and Kapucu, 2011)

Leadership Characteristics		Leadership Behaviours		
Traits	Skills	Task-oriented	People-oriented	Organizational
Willingness to assume responsibility (13)	Communication (9)	Delegate (8)	Manage teams and team-building (8)	Network and partner (7)
Flexibility (12)	Analytic skills (9)	Operations planning (6)	Motivate (6)	Decision-making (6)
Decisiveness (11)	Social skills (6)	Problem-solving (4)	Develop staff (4)	Articulate the mission and vision (6)
Self-confidence (8)	Influencing and negotiating (5)	Inform (4)	Manage personal conflict (2)	Strategic planning (4)
Resilience (7)	Technical skills (2)	Monitor and assess work (4)	Manage personnel change (0)	Scan for environment (3)
Energy (5)	Continual learning (2)	Clarify roles (3)	Plan and organize personnel (0)	Manage organizational change (1)
Emotional maturity (5)		Manage innovation and creativity (2)		Perform general management functions (0)
Personal integrity (3)				
Service motivation (3)				
Need for achievement (2)				

the leaders of these medical teams face similar imperatives as those we have previously considered, in terms of the extreme threat, degree of urgency and uncertainty of outcome.

What the researchers termed 'dynamic delegation' of the active leadership role was found to foster learning and reliability within the teams. When the senior leaders delegate the active leadership role, junior leaders learn by doing. Yet when the need to prevent or manage errors arose, the senior leaders were seen to retain or reclaim the active role. In such circumstances, leadership took the form of a baton, whose possession is controlled by the most senior medical professionals but can be passed to those lower in the hierarchy, with the senior leaders staying at arm's length to ensure a satisfactory outcome.

BEST leadership quote

'Across the firm, we try not to go to meetings on our own: we take a junior member of staff so they gain exposure to different issues and they learn from that experience.'

Will Schofield
Partner
PwC

Kolditz (2007), a retired US Army colonel, details three studies he has undertaken to compare the leadership competences required of those actively engaged in dangerous activity, with leaders who do not operate in extreme circumstances. The first study involved leaders of the US Military Academy (USMA) sports parachute team, compared against the team and individual athletes from other USMA sports teams. Hence, he was comparing high-risk and low-risk sports teams. Leaders from both groups were asked to rank-order nine leadership competencies (endorsed by the US Army) in alphabetical order:

1 *Assessing* – the leader uses assessment and evaluation tools to facilitate consistent improvement.
2 *Building* – the leader spends time and resources improving teams, groups and units, and fosters an ethical climate.
3 *Communicating* – the leader displays good oral, written and listening skills for individuals and groups.
4 *Decision-making* – the leader employs sound judgement and logical reasoning, and uses resources wisely.
5 *Developing* – the leader invests adequate time and effort to develop individual followers as leaders.

6 *Executing* – the leader shows proficiency, meets standards, and takes care of people and resources.

7 *Learning* – the leader seeks self-improvement and organizational growth, and envisions, adapts to, and leads change.

8 *Motivating* – the leader inspires, motivates and guides others towards goals and objectives.

9 *Planning* – the leader develops detailed, executable plans that are feasible, acceptable and suitable.

The second study, undertaken in April 2003, saw Kolditz and colleagues accompany US soldiers as they fought their way towards Baghdad in Iraq. Here, they sought followers' perspectives of what competences they principally sought from their leaders. They asked the question of 54 US soldiers and marines, as well as 36 Iraqi military prisoners.

The third research project involved interviews with 24 leaders who fulfilled two criteria: i) they were currently leading teams in dangerous environments, such as FBI SWAT team leaders; and ii) they had each, in the past, had someone they were responsible for die during an extreme event.

The common factor, therefore, across all three studies was that those involved in the event – leaders and followers – were putting their personal well-being at risk. The findings common to all three projects were as follows:

1 *Competence is critical in high-risk environments*, especially in developing trust in the leader. It is not legitimate or legal authority that will command respect in a life-threatening environment: it is a belief that the leader has the ability to see the activity through to an uneventful conclusion. The average soldier is likely to find a court-martial a more attractive option than having to follow an incompetent leader into action. The troops may not actually like their leader, but will follow him if they have confidence in his ability. As Kolditz summed it up: 'Only competence commands respect, and respect is the coin of the realm in extremist settings.'

BEST leadership quote

'When people go out on the ice with me they know I am an experienced explorer so they feel confident in my abilities. However, that confidence will be enhanced if I show my other leadership qualities, such as leading by example and team development.'

Mark Wood
Explorer

2 *Motivational skills are of less importance for extreme leaders.* For the routine USMA sports team athletes, motivation was by far the most important competence required of their leaders. Indeed, one would expect it to feature highly in the needs of most followers operating outside extreme conditions. Yet this is not the case for followers when their life is at risk. For the USMA sports parachutists 'motivating' was ranked second to the bottom of the nine leadership competences. The researchers concluded that extreme situations are inherently motivating: the element of danger energizes those facing it. Inherent motivation was seen as different to intrinsic motivation (which is caused by internal drivers) as it occurs due to the most compelling reason – the threat of death or serious injury. Followers facing such threats do not want a cheerleader: they want a quiet, calm professional, as most extreme leaders were found to be. Indeed, unlike the Hollywood image of the larger-than-life leader wildly encouraging his people during a crisis, in reality the more critical events get, the quieter a true-life extreme leader becomes.

3 *Extreme leaders embrace continuous learning.* 'Learning' was ranked the number one leadership competence by the parachutists and was also recognized as crucial by other respondents. Extreme situations demand an outward, learning focus, which is heightened by the level of the threat. Extreme leaders need to continually take stock of their operational environment in order to make sense of it and to identify aspects of it that may be wrong and, hence, pose a threat. Learning through continual vigilance is found to be the key to successful outcomes in life-threatening environments.

4 *Extreme leaders share risk with their followers.* This characteristic sets extreme leaders apart from others and constitutes a defining difference: it is leading from the front. The interviews confirmed that sharing risk with followers was not merely a form of leadership hubris or show-boating – it is an instinctive aspect of the leader's style. Moreover, it has a profound effect on followers, who recognize it as representing their leader's values and character. Leaders who stand side-to-side with their people inspire trust, whilst those who lead from a distance are not trusted. Compare the words of a US soldier fighting in Iraq – 'The officers here, they showed leadership and they got out there and did the same things that me and him were doing' – with a captive Iraqi soldier who reported: 'The leader, a lieutenant colonel, was a simple person, but the instruction came from the command in Baghdad, like "do this", but he doesn't do that, and he ran away. He told us "if you see the American or British forces, do not resist".'

5 *Extreme leaders share a common lifestyle with their followers.* Both parties often operate in miserable conditions: poor quality and/or inadequate food, cold temperatures and lack of basic amenities. Leaders who share the misery, with no suggestion of

elitism, create environments where mutual trust and respect flourish. In life-threatening contexts, the value attached to the continuation of life is morally superior to material values. Kolditz suggests that extreme situations 'are the perfect incubator for transformational leadership. Due largely to the irrelevance of symbolic value, transactional leadership is almost completely ineffective in extremist settings.' The immediacy of threat to life nullifies any incentives relating to future rewards or punishments – all that is important is a safe passage. Leaders who share the conditions of their followers, however meagre or unpleasant, offer an example of transformational values that do not go unnoticed by their people.

BEST leadership quote

'People know that our chief executive is prepared to do things himself. He doesn't just tell other people what to do and then stand back – he will get involved himself. People see that, and respect him for it, so when he has to be a bit more forceful he has enough respect in the bank for people to go along with him.'

Antony Smith
Culture and Development Manager
Bourne Leisure

Combat leadership

Whilst some of the examples of emergency response leadership in the previous sections were set in a military context, let us now focus entirely on leadership in conflict situations. Leading armed forces within a war zone calls for men and women of exceptional abilities as the extreme circumstances they are likely to face call for leadership qualities unlike those experienced elsewhere – as we will see later in this section in the case study concerning Captain Simon Cupples CGC.

The military trains its officers to assume exceptional levels of responsibility at a relatively young age: Lieutenant Cupples (as he was ranked at the time) was only 25 years of age, and his second-in-command Second Lieutenant Rupert Bowers was a mere 20 years old, when they faced a Taliban attack. The fact that they performed their duties professionally and fearlessly is due largely to the progressive series of carefully planned selection, training, educational and experiential events they had undertaken – far more extensive and expensive than any equivalent training in civilian organizations (I remember well the similar selection and training process I undertook to become a commissioned officer in the Royal Air Force in 1973). Another crucial factor is that military leadership is underpinned by a deep sense of duty, service and self-sacrifice. Officers should view their responsibility to, and for, their men and women as a duty – defining their leadership as placing their own needs below those of their troops, which also encompasses the troops' families, especially during deployment.

This ethos is well exemplified by the following 'Ten Rules of Command' of a certain commanding officer of a front-line unit in the UK:

1 I am here to serve you as your commander, mentor, companion and brother-in-arms.

2 When we are facing the enemy I will be in front of you. When the enemy is behind us, I will be watching your backs.

3 I will remind you that each of you is responsible to, and for, one another. You must ensure that I remember that I am responsible to, and for, you all.

4 I will give you loyalty, integrity and trust for free; I must earn yours.

5 Professionalism knows no shortcuts. There are no runners-up in our business.

6 Your job is to soldier; my job is to empower you to do your job to the best of your ability.

7 When I ask you to do something, know that I do so because you are the best person I know to do it.

8 Success is your crown; wear it with modesty and humility. Failure is my burden, for it will be I who has failed you.

9 You are our most valuable asset; yours are your families. When you are away, your family becomes my family.

10 Your job is a profession; my job is a privilege that I must re-earn every day.

These powerful, self-effacing words may come as a surprise to those who consider that military leadership is based upon autocratic, authoritarian principles, delivered by officers steeped in their own self-importance and superiority. Discipline is without question the bedrock of service within the armed forces, but the 10 undertakings listed above demonstrate that service extends in both directions through the ranks. For me, these 10 undertakings exemplify the very essence of servant leadership (to be considered in Chapter 9). In the heat of battle, soldiers are not serving their queen, country, or even the army – they are serving their brothers-in-arms.

Leadership, within the military or outside, calls for a set of qualities – many of which are common across all occupations, the difference very often being merely one of emphasis. Maxwell D Taylor (1977), a distinguished

American general and close advisor to two presidents, classified the requirements of military leadership in four categories:

1 *Professional competence:* as confirmed by the research undertaken by
   Kolditz (2007) in the previous section of this chapter.

2 *A disciplined and orderly mind:* having intellectual interests as broad
   as the scope of the national interests for which his profession
   undertakes to provide security, as well as clarity in oral and written
   expression.

3 *Inspirational qualities:* that can encourage men to unusual acts of
   valour. A spark is required, Taylor suggests, to stir a pulse, raise a
   cheer or release the enthusiasm in quite ordinary men to move them
   towards the enemy.

4 *Strength of character:* based upon traits such as reliability, dedication
   to mission, determination, self-discipline and courage.

Courage, indeed, was the only common leadership quality listed by
Adair (2006) as being taught to officer cadets from the US Marine Corp,
British Royal Naval College, RAF College, and RMC Canada. Moral
courage involves having the strength to be true to one's own values, whilst
facing up to one's shortcomings – which becomes easier the more you apply
it. Failure to take the difficult decisions of conscience, however, create
situations that are difficult to address in the future. Failure as a junior officer,
for example, to impose authority over perhaps more experienced junior
ranks will make it more difficult to apply moral integrity when more
demanding circumstances occur.

Wise but inexperienced military leaders encourage and rely upon the
advice of their senior non-commissioned officers. Field Marshal Sir Peter
Inge, writing in *Leaders on Leadership* (1996) tells the story of a lesson in
moral courage taught to him early in his career by his regimental sergeant
major (RSM). Even as an officer, the young Sir Peter would avoid the RSM
whenever he could, but one evening he had to sit next to him in the
sergeants' mess when he was orderly officer. The RSM mentioned that he
had noticed that a soldier had failed to salute Lieutenant Inge earlier that
day and had not been spoken to for his misdemeanour. What mattered much
more than the soldier's lack of salute, the RSM explained, was that the
lieutenant had noticed it but failed to do anything about it. If he did not
enforce discipline in the barracks, how could he expect to do so on operations?
Reflecting on the matter years later, Sir Peter saw it as a salutary lesson that
if you ignore apparently trivial matters you will need even more courage to
take moral decisions in more extreme circumstances.

Sir Peter had also learnt that the human side of leadership in the armed
forces must contain a strong element of ethos – the spirit that motivates
service personnel to the extent that they will risk their lives in combat.
He describes it as a mixture of comradeship, team spirit, integrity and service,
as well as pride in their regiment or whatever other group they belong to.
He quotes Field Marshal Montgomery, addressing his officers in Africa in

1942, as saying, 'I believe one of the first duties of a commander is to create what I call "atmosphere"; and in that atmosphere, his staff, subordinate commanders and troops will live and work and fight.'

This sense of ethos that creates a depth of inherent motivation within service personnel is found in armed forces across the world. Qiao Taiyang (2010), retired major-general of the People's Liberation Army Air Force, speaking from over 40 years' service as an ordinary soldier and as a commander, proposes four motivational incentives within the Chinese Army:

1 *The flag – defining goals.* The army flag is the badge of the army, as well as the symbol of the honour, bravery and goal of the soldier. Throughout progressive military training, the flag reinforces the concept of task priority, responsibility for the people, and the desire to achieve honour for the army. The red flag flying engages and motivates the troops in extreme conditions.

2 *Role model – defining correct direction.* Chinese role models and heroic groups are used extensively to encourage bravery and devotion to duty. Role models can be created contemporaneously or belong to history, such as in the Chinese song 'Learn from Lei Feng, who is a good example'. When Qiao Taiyang inspected his troops he would often notice them displaying their heroes' photographs.

3 *Award – promoting incentive.* Transactional incentives, such as awards and honorary titles, are used extensively in the Chinese Army. Personnel or teams who perform exceptional service can be allowed to keep a red flag until their next weekly appraisal is completed. However, Taiyang suggests that an officer's highest spiritual award is the respect and trust afforded him by his subordinates.

4 *Culture – creating good atmosphere.* The Chinese Army places great importance on culture, which although invisible and intangible is the 'tradition and soul of each troop'. Culture is, Taiyang asserts, 'the most important of the four motivational incentives as it exerts the greatest influence on troops'.

Leadership *BEST* practice

Leadership and stress in combat

In February 2014, I was privileged to have been afforded permission by the commandant of the British Army's Royal Military Academy Sandhurst to attend a presentation to officer cadets by Captain Simon Cupples CGC, which forms part of the training programme for regular army officers, at a stage just over half-way through their 48-week commissioning course.

He told the story of when, over the night of 7 September 2007, he led his platoon in Operation Palk Pechtaw, Afghanistan, with orders to clear several major Taliban objectives in order to secure the southern flank of the company's attack. At just before 1 am in the morning the platoon was engaged simultaneously by very intense and accurate fire from three to four Taliban, which included medium machine guns at a range of only 25 metres. They sustained several casualties, three of them very serious, from the enemy attack – the intensity of which was unlike anything experienced in more than 300 contacts in the previous five months. The enemy action did not abate for over five hours, during which time Lieutenant Cupples, according to the citation for his Conspicuous Gallantry Cross:

> *With exceptional courage, purpose and determination led [his men] forward into the killing area under concentrated and withering enemy fire, and with complete disregard for his own safety, in order to extract the casualties. At one stage, he crawled to within 15 metres of the main enemy defensive position, placing himself between the wounded men and the enemy. Cupples and his platoon had been in contact for over three hours and, in spite of the pressure, he remained utterly calm and focused on the task in hand. The leadership that he demonstrated throughout the night was truly inspirational.*

In the event, two soldiers died and seven were injured, three very seriously. It was an intensive fire-fight that tested to the limit the physical and moral courage of all those involved, including the 25-year-old Lieutenant Cupples. It is in extreme situations like those he experienced that new lessons are learnt, and existing knowledge is reinforced. During the presentation, Captain Cupples encouraged the officer cadets to consider and embrace the following leadership lessons:

- *Put your soldiers before yourself.* Absolutely key to creating effective working relationships within a military team is for the commanders to put the welfare of their followers before themselves. This is appropriate back in camp, but especially so in a combat zone.

- *Listen to your SNCOs.* Whilst you have the ultimate authority to make decisions, never ignore the advice of your platoon sergeant. You do not always have to take it, but you must always consider it.

- *Never lose your self-discipline.* When you leave Sandhurst you are in command: there will be no Directing Staff to rely upon. You must then apply your training to ensure you fulfil every aspect of your officer responsibilities.

- *Communications are critical.* Effective communications are one of the most critical aspects of operating in extreme conditions. You may be the best commander in the army but if you cannot communicate your plans to your subordinates, or your reports to your superiors, you cannot lead anyone. Moreover, whenever possible, apply that communication face-to-face.

- *Clarify your priorities.* To demonstrate this point, Captain Cupples used the example of having to take the difficult decision to leave the action within the killing zone to withdraw in order to retake command of the overall situation.

- *Manage risk.* In order to gain the upper hand in conflict situations it is sometimes necessary to take calculated risks. Look at risk as an opportunity; mitigate the potential dangers as much as possible, then seize the opportunity. Effective commanders cannot be risk-adverse.

- *Lead by example.* Take every opportunity to demonstrate by your own actions that you are prepared to do what you are asking your people to do. That is why they will follow you.

- *Learn to adapt to changing situations.* In battle, the picture is continually changing. Events unfold at a frightening pace, hence the effective leader must be prepared to change with it. Flexibility and adaptability are key leadership qualities.

- *Trust those by your side.* Your soldiers and SNCOs have also received extensive training. If you do not trust them to put that training into effect you will never be an effective unit.

- *Maintain distance.* Captain Cupples stressed this as a particularly important aspect of military leadership. Whilst during operations you will share hardships with your soldiers, hence live more closely with them, you are their commander – not their friend. The army is not a democracy. You will maintain respect by keeping the command structure in place, especially when returned to base.

- *Cope with the aftermath of battle*, especially if it has resulted in fatalities. Captain Cupples offered four pieces of advice from his personal, painful experience:
  - Take time in the immediate aftermath to release your personal emotions. It is no sign of weakness to cry. Three months after the battle, one of Cupples's men, Platoon Sergeant Lockett, explained:

'When we got back to base we felt like shit. Everyone was crying for six to eight hours solid. I had to sit back in a Viking (armoured vehicle) and get it out of me.'

– Realize that, if you are feeling like that, so will your men – they will need your support.

– Recognize that everyone is different and will, hence, react to the trauma of battle differently. Know your subordinates and support them as individuals.

– Discuss the events of the conflict with your men. You will have had much more incoming information during the battle so explain to them what happened and the reasons why. Also invite them to describe what they saw, thought and experienced.

After the lecture I had the opportunity to ask Captain Simon Cupples some supplementary questions, which I detail below, along with his answers:

AC: How would you describe a military leader's role away from the combat zone?

SC: The key responsibility is to maintain operational readiness to deploy at a moment's notice. Everything is geared towards operational effectiveness, such as team-building and career development for the soldiers, as well as role responsibilities and training.

AC: How does that role change during periods of conflict?

SC: Fundamentally, as a leader, the principal role is to plan for and achieve your given mission. A very close second is the welfare of your soldiers, with your own well-being some way behind that.

AC: What skills, qualities and competencies do soldiers look for in their commanders?

SC: This is difficult because what they look for may not necessarily be what they need. During operations they want you to be an example. They also want to be led – to know what they need to do next. However, back in the barracks some soldiers may seek to become overfamiliar with their officers, which if allowed will cause future problems. Good officers will be able to maintain an appropriate distance according to the situation in which they are operating: in extreme conditions they become so embedded with their troops that a degree of familiarity can have a positive effect but, back at base rank, boundaries must be enforced.

AC: What factors affect morale and motivation on active service?

SC: *The following are of primary importance:*

- *Shared hardship*, whereby everyone is treated as equally as possible, especially as demonstrated by officers: either in the allocation of duties to individuals or sections; or by personal example. [Simon cited the case of him taking his turn in burning the contents of latrine buckets that the soldiers had used – not a pleasant thing to do, he remembers!]
- *Contact with family and friends back home*, especially if the telecommunications can be pre-booked.
- *Food*, in particular fresh food as an alternative to composite rations. [Interestingly, from a personal recollection, when I was serving in the Falkland Islands shortly after the war in the mid-1980s, the only thing that was seen as more important than food by the troops out there were 'blueys' – airmail letters from home (there was no internet back then!).]
- *Shared understanding between officers and their troops*. This involves the officers appreciating the implications of what they are asking their soldiers to do; and the soldiers understanding why they are being asked to do it, hence a glimpse of the bigger picture. Whilst it is not a required responsibility of officers, if the reasons behind the orders can be explained and understood it can act as a powerful motivator.

AC: *What leadership lessons are transferable from military to civilian life?*

SC: *There are several 'takeaways', including:*

- *The primacy of the mission:* focusing firmly on given objectives, including business objectives.
- *Discipline:* both self-discipline and the appropriate use of rewards and punishment (in other words transactional leadership).
- *Work ethic:* servicemen and women are willingly prepared to work long hours if the task requires it, as well as being adept at finding innovative solutions when resources are scarce – a 'can-do' attitude.
- *Communications:* using a wide range of communication methods to get the message across effectively.
- *An ethos of service:* Sandhurst's motto is 'Serve to Lead', and officer cadets undergoing training there are continually taught to appreciate how much they will rely on their troops, especially in combat conditions.
- *Leadership development:* the army places great store in selecting and developing leaders throughout the rank structure.

Leadership theories

Certainly one of the most striking aspects of extreme leadership is the need to react and adapt to individual, unique situations as they are initially presented and subsequently unfold. Hence, the principles of situational, also termed contingency, leadership are obviously most relevant for extreme leaders. However, surely there are few other examples of leadership where those directing operations rely so heavily on their followers – who are prepared to follow their leader into situations where life may be at risk. Be they soldiers, emergency responders, explorers, or members of the public coping with the horrors of war – before assuming that role, voluntarily or imposed upon them, they existed in a much safer environment. Their lives were transformed from relative security to personal threat. The physical and psychological demands associated with the extreme conditions they then faced can only be endured if they possess exceptionally high levels of determination and motivation – and it takes a transformational leader to achieve those emotional heights. Such a leader taps into his or her followers' higher needs and values; inspires them with new possibilities that have strong appeal; and raises their levels of confidence, conviction and desire to achieve a common, moral purpose.

BEST leadership quote

'The credibility I gain as a leader is through that 96 per cent of the time I spend talking, listening, considering options and making decisions. That translates through to the command and control environment, where the baseline is a high level of trust that ensures people will respond to my instructions. The transformational style feeds into the transactional approach and makes it work. However, if the transformational approach does not persuade people that the leader is effective, they will not trust him in an incident command scenario.'

Phil Loach
Chief Fire Officer
West Midlands Fire Service

Hence, in my view the two leadership theories, developed in Chapter 1, that relate most appropriately to leading in extreme environments are situational and transformation. However, there is more to understanding extreme leadership than merely the adoption of a recognized style. The bonds that tie leaders and followers together whilst sharing the threat to life are so intensely personal and interdependent that they create not only psychological connections, but are also founded upon philosophical principles of service, values, morality, ethics, conviction and authenticity. Moreover, I have sought to prove in this chapter that the skills, qualities and behaviours of extreme leaders translate to those required by business and other organizational leaders. Hence, in the next and final chapter, I propose two approaches to leadership of a psychological nature, and three from a more philosophical perspective, which I believe are crucial to leaders facing the unchartered waters of the 21st century.

Chapter summary and leadership lessons

Let us look back through this chapter and elicit how extreme leaders perform in the face of imminent danger, and draw any parallels with the responsibilities of leaders from business and other organizations, thus summarizing the lessons learnt throughout the chapter. It is interesting, in the first instance, to apply the threat factors and their modulators in Figure 8.1 to non-extreme events. Doing so, confirms that the threat factors can as easily be applied to problems faced by business leaders, although obviously without the life-threatening consequences of their ineffective outcomes. The immediacy of the problem could be a factor, although the requirement for leadership action may not be as extreme as within a combat or catastrophic event, as would the extent or scale of the problem. The degree of connectivity between leader and followers is certainly an increasing contemporary factor with the growth of virtual- and home-working. The final factor, the nature of the event, may not involve serious physical harm but it could result in job losses. These factors will also be modulated in non-extreme situations by their complexity, or unpredictability; the extent and availability of human and physical resources; and the degree of preparedness resulting from, for example, strategic planning and training.

It is, however, the fourth modulator, *leadership*, that offers the most illuminating comparisons between extreme and non-extreme events. There follows my assessment of the ways in which business leaders can learn from the experiences of those faced with leadership when life is threatened:

- *Demonstrate professional competence.* Both Kolditz (2007) and Taylor (1977) stressed the prime requirement of followers to be that leaders have the necessary competences to lead them through adversity. This requires leaders to accept the responsibilities of their roles – the most important leadership trait for emergency response officials as identified by Van Wart and Kapucu (2011). Calculated risk-taking was also cited in that study, and was also advocated by Captain Cupples. Both sources also stated the need for flexible and adaptable decision-making, as was exemplified by Shackleton during his two-year perilous journey back to England.

- *Create supportive teams based upon mutual trust and respect.*
  Perkins (2000) and, indeed, other Shackleton chroniclers, including
  Shackleton (1999) himself and the captain of his ship SS *Endurance*,
  Frank Worsley (2011), described how he carefully selected his crew,
  based upon physical and emotional qualities, and both Captain
  Cupples and Sir Peter Inge stressed the importance of listening to,
  and using, the knowledge of more experienced team members.
  Klein *et al* (2006) explained how the leaders of medical teams in
  emergency trauma centres used 'dynamic delegation' as a means of
  team development.

  Leadership by example was cited throughout the chapter as
  a powerful method of creating a culture of trust within a team.
  Sharing hardship during extreme situations was encouraged by
  Kolditz (2007) and Captain Cupples and was practised by
  Shackleton, who endured the extreme conditions of the Antarctic
  as well as taking his share of the most menial of tasks along with
  every other crew member, irrespective of seniority. Looking up to
  a role model of good example was cited as a powerful motivator
  for soldiers of the Chinese Army.

- *Display the highest personal qualities.* Whether it was the calmness,
  confidence and integrity required of leaders within the social and
  physical confines of an Antarctic station, or the passionate conviction
  demonstrated by Churchill, followers look to their leaders to
  demonstrate exemplary values. Self-discipline and moral courage was
  stressed by several sources, notably Captain Cupples, Sir Peter Inge,
  Adair (2006), Taylor (1977) and Kolditz (2007).

  Although not included previously in this chapter, a working paper
  produced by the American National Bureau of Economic Research
  (NBER, 2014) identified three predominant traits of CEOs who have
  previously served in the military as: they are more conservative with
  their financial and investment policies; they are less likely to be
  involved in corporate fraud; and they outperform their peers in
  stressful times.

- *Understand the power of communications.* Van Wart and Kapucu
  (2011) identified effective communications as the most important
  leadership competence amongst emergency managers. Captain
  Cupples stated that commanders will never realize their potential
  unless they can communicate their plans *down* to their subordinates
  and their reports *up* to their superiors. In extremis, Shackleton
  continually engaged with his crew, especially in sharing with them
  the reality of the situation they faced.

- *Understand the emotional needs of yourself and your followers.*
  Antarctic station managers were found to be applying emotional
  intelligence to monitor and control their moods and those of the
  station personnel. Captain Cupples recognized the need to release

his own emotional tension after battle – which was confirmed by his platoon sergeant's own words. Churchill was a master at directing his message towards the hopes and fears of the nation, especially in creating a positive vision for the future, as did Mayor Giuliani to the residents of New York in the aftermath of 9/11.

- *Create a positive organizational culture.* Within this chapter, the importance of creating a positive working culture was highlighted by several leaders and leadership research. Field Marshal Sir Peter Inge, drawing on the words of the 'Desert Rat', Field Marshal Montgomery, wrote about an ethos founded upon a spirit of comradeship, team spirit, integrity and service, whilst within the Chinese Army it was the 'tradition and soul of each troop'. Ernest Shackleton, on the other hand, used many devices to maintain morale in the face of extreme polar conditions.

- *'Serve to Lead'.* The motto of the British Army's Royal Military Academy Sandhurst refers to the concept of service leadership that was alluded to throughout this chapter, and in the one that follows is advocated as being particularly appropriate for leaders as the 21st century unfolds.

Future leadership
– the way forward

09

In Chapter 2 I proposed the challenges facing leaders as the 21st century unfolds to be:

- innovation;
- talent management;
- communications, especially social media;
- globalization.

These challenges call for new ways of thinking: ones that recognize that the world is changing and that the expectations of all parties involved in leader/follower relationships and interactions will not be fully met by the application of previous leadership theories. Successful leaders will increasingly be aware of the psychological and philosophical factors underpinning their role of influencing the behaviour of their people. Leaders at all levels within an organization will have to develop and enhance their understanding of how to engage with their people.

BEST leadership quote

'If you look at the predominant management cultures they are still bureaucratic, autocratic and hierarchical – and that is true in the UK, it's true in the United States – yet these kinds of cultures result in less well-being, less engagement, less productivity and less growth. Management cultures need to become more diverse, more inclusive, more ethical, more rounded in how they are rewarding their top executives: ones that will help their people become better managers and leaders.'

Ann Francke
Chief Executive
Chartered Management Institute

In this chapter I suggest five approaches to leadership that I believe will add to the necessary skill sets of future leaders. Two are based upon an understanding of the psychological connections between leaders and followers:

- engaging leadership;
- the integrated psychological approach.

A further three are more philosophical in nature, involving consideration of a leader's responsibility from a human viewpoint, namely:

- servant leadership;
- authentic leadership;
- ethical leadership.

Engaging leadership

On 29 March 2011, British Prime Minister David Cameron gave his backing to a new independent employee engagement movement entitled 'Engage for Success', which is committed to the concept that there is a better way to work: a better way to enable personal growth, organizational growth and, ultimately, national growth by releasing more of the capability and potential of people at work (see Figure 9.1). It is founded on three principal beliefs:

- Everyone should have the opportunity to work to their full potential.
- Employee engagement derives measurable improvement in performance, creativity and innovation.
- The next generation of successful organizations will be those that free the potential of people within them.

BEST leadership quote

'As a company, PwC is passionate about its people and we want to give them the best opportunities, the best work, and the best challenge – but also having a good time whilst doing their work. I think that is exactly what the government is trying to do with Engage for Success.'

Will Schofield
Partner
PwC

FIGURE 9.1 The bigger picture (from www.engageforsuccess.org)

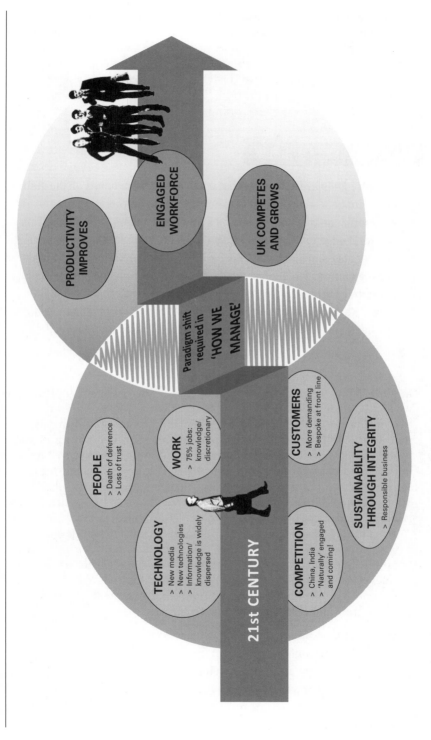

TECHNOLOGY
> New media
> New technologies
> Information/ knowledge is widely dispersed

PEOPLE
> Death of deference
> Loss of trust

WORK
> 75% jobs: knowledge/ discretionary

21st CENTURY

COMPETITION
> China, India
> 'Naturally engaged and coming!'

CUSTOMERS
> More demanding
> Bespoke at front line

SUSTAINABILITY THROUGH INTEGRITY
> Responsible business

Paradigm shift required in 'HOW WE MANAGE'

PRODUCTIVITY IMPROVES

ENGAGED WORKFORCE

UK COMPETES AND GROWS

Employee engagement is designed to ensure that employees are committed to their organization's goals and values; are motivated to contribute to organizational success; and are able, at the same time, to enhance their own sense of well-being. It is a two-way process: leaders at all levels must work to engage their people who, in turn, have a choice about the level of engagement they offer their organization.

Leadership *BEST* practice

It is a tradition at TGI Friday's that when a new store opens all the staff and managers, including chief executive Karen Forrester, celebrate, eat spaghetti together, and tell stories about the company's traditions. This results in what they call the Magic Circle: the staff believe in the company and become engaged; when they are engaged they want to deliver a great guest experience; the guest feels it because it is real; the guest comes back; they tell others, who come and experience it; and the company grows. Karen told me that they have had 16 quarters of continuous growth and have advanced ahead of the market by 30 percentage points.

In 2011, Mind Gym released its white paper, 'The Engaged Employee', which was based on a review of over 30 independent academic studies, in addition to consultation with a number of public and private organizations. It found that how employees feel about their organization is a strong predictor of future financial performance (Harter *et al*, 2009). Yet, despite well-intentioned initiatives undertaken by some companies, employee engagement is deteriorating: in 2010 the number of highly engaged employees in the UK fell by 10 per cent to 32 per cent (CBI and Harvey Nash, 2010), whilst it was even lower in the United States at 28 per cent (Rath and Harter, 2010).

Even more critically, high-performing staff's engagement levels have fallen to a greater extent – with 12 per cent seriously considering leaving their organizations and another 17 per cent uncertain about staying. Yet the business case for employee engagement is clear (Harter *et al*, 2009): business units scoring in the top quartile of employee engagement, compared to those in the bottom quartile, enjoyed an average:

- 12 per cent higher customer satisfaction;
- 16 per cent higher profitability;
- 18 per cent greater productivity;
- 37 per cent lower absenteeism;
- 49 per cent lower staff turnover;
- 49 per cent fewer safety incidents;
- 60 per cent fewer quality defects.

Unfortunately, however, even in the face of such stark statistics, relatively few business leaders are reaping the rewards of employee engagement, despite the growth in related initiatives within organizations over recent years. Mind Gym's white paper found that leaders were frequently failing in one, or more, of five ways:

- *The survey takes over.* Whilst effort is expended in gathering data and disseminating results, insufficient action is taken to address the issues raised. As one HR manager commented, 'You don't fatten a pig by weighing it!'
- *The debate is parent–child.* Leaders are quick to admit mistakes and accede to employees' requests, which can result in a culture of dependence and ever-increasing expectations (and disappointment).
- *Reliance on a few grand gestures.* Leaders offer new headline benefits, rather than addressing the fundamental issues that affect satisfaction levels at work.
- *Easily distracted leaders.* Leaders who were initially enthusiastic about changing working practices but then lose interest when more urgent or glamorous opportunities arise.
- *Delegated to HR.* The 'people' department is charged with fixing the engagement 'problem' without support from the senior leadership.

Company-wide, broad-brush employee engagement initiatives will not have the most lasting, positive effects. The enduring solution is for leaders to understand individual employees in terms of what they want and expect from their working life and how they can achieve those objectives – their psychological contract. To achieve a situation where employees throughout the organization are committed, motivated and enjoy a sense of well-being, contributions are required from four parties: the individuals themselves, their line managers, the senior leaders and the individuals' colleagues.

The individual

Two people can have the same experience in different environments, yet have very different reactions to it. The facts of a situation can have little bearing on how one individual feels about it, compared with another. Research by psychologists Avey, Wernsing and Luthans (2008) identified the five most critical mindsets for individuals to feel engaged in any type of work. They are basic human needs. However, how we adopt them, and how relevant they are, will vary according to the country, culture, organization, occupation or team we belong to. They are:

- *Optimism.* Psychologist Mihaly Csikozentmihalyi found that employees are more likely to be happy and optimistic at work when they have a balance of challenge and skill. Hence, the 21st-century leader must understand how applying basic psychology in terms of encouraging individuals to take a more positive outlook at work can result in them enjoying their work more. Encouraging them to actively choose how they view their employment, and to make small changes that will mean they enjoy it more, can have a very positive impact on staff engagement.

- *Purposefulness.* A study by Wrzesniewski, McCauley and Rozin (1997) found that, whatever the occupation, there was an even split between employees who regarded their work as a job (done purely for the money), a career (achievement measured by financial reward and advancement), and a calling (involving a passionate commitment to work, which is regarded as contributing to the greater good). The standing of the job did not affect the sense of it being a calling, with a hospital janitor being just as likely as a surgeon to see his job as a calling. It was not the job that mattered, rather what the post-holder felt about it. Moreover, those who saw their job as a calling enjoyed significantly greater satisfaction at work and in life generally. People who believe they are contributing to their organization feel engaged, and the most powerful contributors to that belief is that their commitment is valued (Rolfe, 2010). Their philosophy is: 'What I am doing matters to me, and also to someone or something other than me.'

- *Autonomy.* Self-determination theory (Deci, Connell and Ryan, 1989) states that in order to have high levels of psychological well-being, three intrinsic needs are required to be met: autonomy, competence and connectedness. Yet the degree of autonomy does not depend on the job itself, but how we perceive it. Understanding the extent of self-control one has at work, rather than focusing on controls from other sources, helps to engender a feeling of autonomy. Employees who recognize they have a degree of autonomy and have control over their destiny take a more positive and proactive approach to their work and career.

BEST leadership quote

'One of the things that is unique about us is that we delegate more responsibility and authority to our managers than other companies in our sector. What you get is an absolute passion for the business, a real engagement, because people put their hand on the tiller of the boat and push it – and you know what, the boat moves in a different direction!'

William Rogers
Chief Executive
UKRD

- *Competence.* Peter Drucker (2005) wrote that to flourish at work, people must understand how they can apply their strengths and values to contribute to their job and organization. More important than the person's actual competence is the belief in what can be achieved. If our manager, for instance, makes us feel incompetent we begin to believe it. As a consequence, our performance drops as our self-confidence declines and we become less engaged. Our actual competence has now altered – we are not any less able to do our job, we just *feel* that we are. It is, therefore, the leader's responsibility to find ways to reinforce people's belief in their competence, as a means of boosting their level of engagement.
- *Resilience.* This is the ability to react positively and constructively when faced with adversity. Margolis and Stoltz (2010) suggest that, rather than looking back and analysing contributing circumstances, people are more likely to bounce back from setbacks if they seek solutions, especially in collaboration with colleagues.

The line manager

Whilst individual employees contribute greatly to their own levels of engagement via the five mindsets detailed above, their line manager also has a part to play. Of the 50 most effective levels of employee engagement identified by an international research project conducted by the Corporate Leadership Council in 2004, 36 were concerned with the behaviours of line managers, the two having the greatest impact being: i) having energizing, dynamic performance conversations; ii) building and sustaining trust.

Similar results were obtained by Robinson and Hayday (2009) for the Institute for Employment Studies, who interviewed 25 managers and their teams who had been nominated by their organization as scoring highly in their attitude survey. Interestingly, although the managers displayed some shared characteristics, personality was not one of them, as they displayed a range of personality types, including being quiet (even shy) by nature. The behaviours they adopted towards their teams were, however, very consistent.

Dynamic performance conversations involve five factors:

- Giving challenging goals and providing regular feedback on progress.
- Treating people as individuals and applying consistent differentiation according to their strengths and weaknesses.
- Holding forward-looking discussions to address an individual's problems and agree constructive solutions.
- Adapting roles and career paths to suit the individual's skills and experience, rather than trying to change the individual to meet generic job roles.
- Selling the benefits of great performance in terms of personal and job enhancements and encouraging individuals to take personal responsibility for them.

'A very, very senior person in a global organization told me that he was bringing together his top 150 leaders to discuss "how to have an honest conversation". So here are these paragons of corporate stewardship and they do not know how to have an honest conversation with their people!'

Ann Francke
Chief Executive
Chartered Management Institute

The building of trust between leaders and followers is seen as crucial to creating an engaging culture. Trust is the confidence people have that others will act in their best interests and not knowingly take actions that will disadvantage them. It has a biochemical component in that when you experience trust you benefit from increased levels of dopamine, serotonin and oxytocin – all combining to create a positive influence on interpersonal relationships. Paul Zak, pioneer in the field of neuroeconomics, calls the hormone oxytocin 'the trust molecule' in that it makes people more trustworthy. It is produced in the brain, especially when connecting with other people, and is inhibited during periods of stress. David Maister and co-authors in their book *The Trusted Advisor* (2001) suggest that the extent to which people trust others is determined by their assessment of four values: credibility; reliability; intimacy; and whether we are seen as self-oriented or other-oriented. I, personally, would also add the requirement for leaders to:

- set clear objectives;
- delegate and empower;
- share information openly;
- recognize and praise good work;
- encourage innovation;
- support and defend their staff.

So the line manager is a crucial player in generating high levels of staff engagement – not least in that many employees regard their immediate manager as their actual employer. Far-looking companies recognize and reward those managers who lead highly engaged teams – and take remedial action to address those that don't.

The senior leader

One thing is certain: organizations will not benefit from highly engaged individuals, working in high-performing teams, if their senior leaders are not totally committed to the concept of staff engagement – and act as visible champions of it.

Charles Snyder, professor of clinical psychology at University of Kansas, proposed that building belief in the future of an organization is created when the senior leader tells a compelling corporate story that includes:

- why the company does what it does and how society benefits as a result;
- where the company is heading and why that is the right destination;
- what the journey looks like – how the company will get there;
- what the destination will be like when the company gets there;
- persuasive reasons to believe it can be achieved.

Moreover, the story must be delivered by a senior leader who is seen as authentic and true to him/herself. Slick presentations are no compensation for a leader who does not speak from the heart. People will look through the superficial media-speak to the inner person and be inspired, or not, by what they see there. Trust is the key. Yet a YouGov poll of 1,918 adults on 27–28 March 2013 found that only 22 per cent of those polled trusted 'bosses of large companies' to tell the truth – only 1 per cent more than for trusting 'senior Tory politicians'!

One story that some senior business leaders are expounding to internal and external stakeholders regards the company's societal purpose. Corporate statements of purpose identify the reasons that the company exists and will include its mission and/or vision and/or philosophy, depending on the nature of its operation and market. A societal purpose aims to define an organization's products and services (through which it makes a profit) in terms of the positive contribution it makes to wider society through, perhaps, enhancing quality of life. Examples of stated societal purpose include:

- Alliance Boots – 'To deliver products that help people look and feel their best.'
- GlaxoSmithKline – 'To improve the quality of human life by enabling people to do more, feel better and live longer.'
- Vale – 'To transform mineral resources into prosperity and sustainable development.'

Leadership *BEST* practice

Pertemps recognize that the success of the company is due, to a large extent, to the clients and the candidates from within their local communities. Hence, each branch can choose their own charity to sponsor. In 2012 the company as a whole contributed to around 250 charities, including children's charities, local football teams, and cake-baking for a local hospice.

A report in January 2012 by the Economist Intelligent Unit, sponsored by Deloitte, and entitled 'Societal Purpose: A Journey in its Early Stages', explored the reason why some companies defined the purpose of their core business in terms of benefits to society. It sought the views of 390 executives of internal companies across the world and found that there were regional differences in views: in Asia Pacific respondents viewed societal purpose as reflecting business maturity and strong corporate leadership, whilst European and North American leaders were more ambivalent. It was in Latin America and the Middle East where respondents felt most strongly about the link between societal purpose and business success.

The motivation for companies to define their business in terms of the benefits it accrues to the greater community is principally one of profitability, although measuring company performance against societal purpose is not straightforward. People have different perspectives on it, including those customers who hold companies accountable for how their actions impact on society and the environment – and will base their purchasing decisions on that assessment.

Yet there is an increasing number of potential customers with a clearly defined social conscience, especially those from Generations X and Y, hence the report concludes that tomorrow's business leaders will have to forge a positive connection between their organization's purpose and action taken to resolve society's major challenges at local, national and international levels. However, the report found that, whilst many company leaders are making progress in telling the story internally, much work is still required to promote and explain their community impact targets on a wider stage.

Ken Blanchard, quoted in *Training Journal* in January 2011, makes an interesting point in relation to the relative roles of line managers (operational leaders) and senior (strategic) leaders. He said that, whilst operational and strategic leadership are different, they have to work 'end to end' because 80 to 85 per cent of the impact on employee engagement comes from operation leadership: 'The major role for strategic leaders is to establish an organization's culture so operational leaders can keep it going. People will kill for you if they think you're on their side – and that's what the great companies are able to do.'

Colleagues

Rath and Harter (2010), for Gallop, analysed the responses of 15 million people and found that employees who have a friend at work are seven times more likely to be engaged. Also, staff turnover, work quality, safe working and customer service levels are boosted by positive social relationships at work. Positive psychologist Barbara Frederickson (1998) found that when people operate within a positive, supportive environment they adopt more creative actions and are more resilient, tolerant and receptive to new ideas.

Hence, all work colleagues have a role to play in creating levels of staff engagement. They can choose whether or not to be friendly and welcoming, especially to new starters. They can be involved in creating close relationships with other staff, or elect to work in isolation or disruptive cliques. The leader's role is to create a culture where people are encouraged to make connections and build social networks: it is then up to the followers to play their part in contributing to an enjoyable workplace.

To summarize the findings of Mind Gym's white paper, creating engaged employees requires commitment and effort from four parties to ensure that:

- *individual employees* think positively about their organization and their role within it;
- *line managers* seek to build trust and have energizing, dynamic performance conversations;
- *senior leaders* tell a compelling corporate story about a positive, achievable future;
- *colleagues* contribute to making their workplace an enjoyable environment.

The 'Engaging for Success' report, produced in 2009 for the UK's Department of Business, Innovation and Skills, by David MacLeod and Nita Clarke, was the catalyst for the movement endorsed by the prime minister two years later. The report proposed that, whilst there is no magic bullet for the creation of employee engagement, there are four enablers that provide a powerful platform to achieve it:

- *a strong strategic narrative* from visible, empowering senior leaders about where the organization has come from and where it is going;
- *engaging managers* who treat their people as individuals and offer coaching to achieve challenging objectives;
- *an employee voice* existing at all levels within the organization, and outside it, for both reinforcing and challenging existing views;

- *organization integrity* that connects stated values with the reality of daily behaviours and engenders high levels of trust.

The integrated psychological approach

Many of the factors influencing staff engagement – personal effectiveness, trust, an individual's well-being – are explored in James Scouller's 2011 book *The Three Levels of Leadership: How to Develop Your Leadership, Presence, Knowhow and Skill*. In it, Scouller seeks to link the more traditional leadership theories with modern psychological and philosophical approaches. He has termed this approach 'integrated psychological' in nature, in that it combines the strengths of earlier theories with leadership philosophies more relevant to the 21st century, such as servant leadership, authentic leadership and values-based leadership (to be expanded on later in this chapter). In relation to previous leadership thinking, Scouller observes: 'These older leadership models have strengths and weaknesses. They capture part of the trust about effective leadership, but in largely ignoring "leadership presence" and the leader's psychology, they don't offer a complete guide to becoming a better leader.'

Scouller suggests that leadership is a process with four dimensions:

1 Setting a purpose and vision that inspires people to combine and work together willingly (similar in many ways to Charles Handy's definition cited in Chapter 1).

2 Paying attention to the means, pace and quality of progress towards the vision.

3 Maintaining group unity and team spirit.

4 Attending to individual selection, motivation and effectiveness.

Note the parallel with John Adair's Action-Centred Leadership model, explained in Chapter 1, which requires a leader to meet the needs of the task, team and individual.

Scouller describes leadership as a process – 'a series of choices and actions around defining and achieving a goal' – which therefore helps us to differentiate between 'leadership' and the 'leader'. Scouller recognizes that leadership of a group can be shared according to the circumstances that the group faces, although all groups do require a recognized overall leader to define, for example, its vision. As he explains:

> The purpose of the leader is to make sure there is leadership – to ensure that all four dimensions are being addressed. This means that the leader does not always have to lead from the front: he or she can delegate, or share part of their responsibility for leadership. However, the buck still stops with the leader.

BEST leadership quote

'For a contemporary leader, it is about making the transition from the traditional understanding of a leader as someone who stands on "the mount", giving instructions to someone below. What we need for success in the 21st century is a relearning of coaching, nurturing, and leading from behind (as opposed to the front). It all comes down to personal accountability.'

Phil Loach
Chief Fire Officer
West Midlands Fire Service

Adair (2009) describes how different situations determine who emerges as the leader and what style of leadership he or she has to adopt. He uses the example of survivors of a shipwreck who are having to exist on a desert island. One can imagine the artillery officer taking control of their defence against attacking savages; the ship's cook being responsible for gathering and preparing the food; and the ship's carpenter leading the effort to build the necessary shelter. However, if the survivors' continued well-being is to be assured, the ship's captain must co-ordinate and control all the efforts directed towards that objective.

Scouller's Three Levels of Leadership model (sometimes termed the 3P model in recognition of its personal, private and public levels) aims to help leaders understand their role, equipping them to perform effectively whilst also staying true to their character – being authentic to themselves.

Scouller proposes that for leaders to be effective in all four dimensions (see above) they must operate on three levels simultaneously: public – dimension 1, 2 and 3; private – dimensions 2 and 4; and personal – all four dimensions. The first two levels (public and private leadership) are behavioural levels in that they explain how leaders should act to influence two or more people simultaneously (public) or individuals on a one-to-one basis (private). The personal level concerns a leader's presence, knowhow, skills, beliefs, emotions and unconscious habits, or, as Scouller describes it: 'the leader's self-awareness, progress towards self-mastery and technical competence, and his sense of connection with those around him. It's the inner core, the source of a leader's outer leadership effectiveness.'

In more detail, the three levels are as follows:

- *Public leadership* involves leaders operating in a group setting, where they are seeking to influence a number of people or the organization as a whole. It includes setting and communicating the vision; creating a unity of endeavour towards high standards of purpose; engendering an atmosphere of trust and team spirit; and driving action towards successful outcomes. To be successful in all these, the leader must allocate appropriate time and resources to all aspects. According to the model, the key to developing the necessary public leadership behaviours is through attention to the personal leadership level.

- *Private leadership* is the leader's handling of group individuals on a one-to-one basis. Scouller recognizes that team spirit is crucial to completing the task because individuals within the team vary in their confidence, experience and psychological make-up. The leader must, therefore, display behaviours that will realize the potential of each individual to contribute to team and task objectives. Some of the required behaviours, such as holding performance appraisals, can be seen as intimate and uncomfortable and, hence, result in underperformance, or even avoidance, by leaders. Scouller suggests that such negative responses to the more difficult aspects of private leadership may be caused by the leaders' negative self-image – which is why the personal leadership level is so important in improving their one-to-one encounters and reducing their interpersonal fears and inadequacies.

- *Personal leadership* adds a different dimension to previous leadership thinking in that it centres on a leader's psychological, moral and technical development, which, Scouller asserts, has a powerful effect on his or her presence, behaviours and skills – hence, followers' response to the leader. Personal leadership has three parts:

  - *Technical:* not only in terms of specialist knowledge in the field that the leader operates in, but also in public and private leadership application. It is incumbent upon every leader to identify technical weakness and continually update his or her necessary knowledge and skills.

  - *Attitude towards other people:* appreciating that others are as important as you, rather than viewing and using colleagues to be exploited for one's personal gain. This introduces a moral dimension to leadership: moving from good leadership to leadership for good. A leader's attitude, benevolent or malevolent, will determine the extent to which followers develop degrees of trust with him or her. Leaders should see their role as serving the best interests of all those associated with their role – not only customers/clients, but also all those within their organization, below and above the leader's position within it (the concept of the servant leader will be explored later in this chapter).

  - *Self-mastery:* defined as 'being aware of, understanding, taking command of, integrating and transforming the limiting parts of your psychology to overcome inner divisions and become whole, to grow and to express your highest potential'. Scouller expands the concept of 'self' and the psyche required to progress towards self-mastery, which enables leaders to:

- dissolve limiting beliefs, shift self-image and raise self-esteem;
- focus and direct their energies better, enabling them to achieve more in less time;
- handle pressure more effectively so as to enjoy their leadership role better;
- sense and express their unique presence.

The concept of 'presence' is fundamental to the third level of leadership – personal leadership – as it inspires people to become followers. The root of presence is inner wholeness: an alignment of self-identity, purpose and feelings that lead to freedom from fear. Revealing itself as a magnetic, radiating effect that a leader has on others, it could be seen as similar to charisma. However, Scouller suggests that a leader with presence may or may not be charismatic, whilst a charismatic leader will not always have presence. He considers presence to be an inner psycho-spiritual state with an outer reflection, whereas charisma can be merely an outer image without a deeper spiritual core. Charismatic leaders may influence others by an aura based upon high social status or reputation, or by finely tuned presentational skills. Presence, however, is not an act: it emanates from being comfortable in one's own skin and letting one's own natural character flow outwards from an inner sense of wholeness. Presence is therefore more deep, powerful and durable than charisma.

For Scouller, his inner sense of wholeness, and the external presence it engenders, is achieved through the mastery of seven qualities:

1 *Personal power*: accepting responsibility for, and exercising your will over, the direction of your life – resulting in power over one's actions and purpose.

2 *High self-esteem*: feeling good about yourself and your relations with others.

3 *A drive to do better*: by understanding and addressing often-hidden limiting beliefs and mindsets.

4 *Balance*: a strong sense of personal purpose balanced with concern and respect for others' needs.

5 *Intuition*: a creative insight in complex situations.

6 *In the here-and-now*: not limited by negative past memories, beliefs or feelings, or doubts for the future.

7 *Inner peace of mind*: freedom from fear and perceived inadequacy, coupled with a sense of fulfilment and joy.

It can be seen that Scouller's 'integrated psychological' approach to leadership takes into consideration past leadership thinking, but adds a cerebral component, more relevant to relationships and expectations between leaders and followers in the 21st century. Table 9.1 considers and compares this against some of the theories expounded in Chapter 1.

TABLE 9.1 Comparison of integrated psychological approach with traditional leadership theories

Leadership Theory	Weaknesses	Integrated Psychological Approach
Trait theory	Impossible to identify a definitive list of traits or qualities required by every leader	Leadership presence cannot be defined by a common list of traits. Leaders should express their own personal qualities through their individual personality
Behavioural theory	A specific set of behaviours will not suit all circumstances. Leaders' behaviours may be restricted by limiting beliefs and poor self-image	Provides a mechanism for leaders to develop their psychological well-being as a means of overcoming obstacles that could limit them displaying appropriate behaviours
Situational leadership	Although this theory seeks to match leaders' behaviour to specific situations, it assumes that they can change their behaviour as the need arises. Yet, as above, they may be restricted in doing so by negative psychological influences	Shows how leaders can address negative beliefs and attitudes by practising self-mastery, hence remaining authentic to themselves
Functional leadership	Although functional leadership theory is based upon what leaders must do to achieve their objectives, it places insufficient importance on the role of a leader to create a 'brightness of future' for followers	Self-mastery is used to develop their leadership presence, which will inspire followers

Prior to the 21st century, recognized leadership models were largely about what leaders should do to achieve their objectives through their followers. Scouller's integrated psychological approach introduces another dimension – one that explores how a leader's behaviour is influenced by his or her beliefs, values and attitudes. He asserts that 'true leadership presence is synonymous with authenticity, expressing one's highest values and attitude of service'. This leads us towards consideration of leadership philosophy – a way of thinking and behaving according to values and beliefs: a subtle but powerful moral compass or behavioural code.

Leadership philosophies involve deeper consideration of human behaviour, politics and civilization than leadership models. They are less like a toolkit or model to be applied; rather an underpinning consideration of the implication of a leader's responsibilities from a wider human viewpoint. Examples of leadership philosophies are:

- servant leadership;
- authentic leadership;
- ethical leadership.

Servant leadership

The concept of servant leadership focuses on the leader's duty to serve his or her followers, rather than to emphasize the requirement to lead. Whilst transformational leaders have a vision and inspire others to realize it, servant leaders put the needs of others as the highest priority and use the authority vested in their position to ensure that their people have the resources they need to achieve their personal and organizational objectives.

The concept was first proposed by Robert Greenleaf (1977) who went on to found the Center for Servant Leadership. He describes the process as beginning: 'with the natural feeling that one wants to serve, to serve first. Then conscious choice brings one to aspire to lead. Servant leadership encourages collaboration, trust, foresight, listening, and the ethical use of power and empowerment.'

Spears (2004) identified 10 main characteristics of servant leaders from Greenleaf's work, namely:

- *Listening:* they should listen to others.
- *Empathy:* they should accept and recognize fellow workers.
- *Healing:* they should recognize the emotions of others.
- *Awareness:* they should be aware of issues, including ethics and values.
- *Persuasion:* they should convince rather than coerce others.
- *Conceptualization:* they should be able to have a vision of the future whilst maintaining day-to-day activities.

- *Foresight:* they should appreciate the likely consequences of their future decisions.
- *Stewardship:* they should motivate people to maintain trust for the betterment of society.
- *Commitment to the growth of people:* they should be committed to individuals within an organization as well as the organization itself.
- *Building community:* they should lead the way by demonstrating their unlimited liability for a community-related association.

BEST leadership quote

'By leading from the back you allow people to utilize their own personal skills, which makes them feel good because they have free range. It allows them to be a little bit more experimental in what they do; push out more ideas; feed off other people; and have the confidence to come back to the leader. All the leader is doing is keeping his eye on the final objective and seeing how the team is developing forward with that – which completely parallels a polar or mountain expedition.'

Mark Wood
Explorer

Examples of servant leaders on the world stage include Mahatma Gandhi, Nelson Mandela, Martin Luther King and Aung San Suu Kyi, who are recognized and revered not for leading their people for reasons of status, wealth, popularity or lust for power – rather a fervent desire to make a difference to the lives and well-being of their followers. They adopt their roles knowingly, willingly and often at great personal cost: acting as servants of their cause and those who follow it. As Muhammad said, 'On a journey, the Lord of a people is their servant.'

The concept of serving one's people is, indeed, an ancient philosophy. The teacher, philosopher and royal advisor Chanaka (circa 370–283 BC) wrote in his *Arthashastra* – a treatise on statecraft, economic policy and military strategy: 'The King shall consider as good, not what pleases himself but what pleases his subjects. The King is a paid servant and enjoys the resources of the state, together with the people.' For 'king' substitute 'leader', and for 'subjects' substitute 'followers'.

By its very nature, servant leadership is different from all other theories and models, as by 'leading from behind' leaders are relegating their own personal needs in order to meet those of their followers. Rather than adhering to more traditional top-down and/or bottom-up approaches to authority, here both directions are covered. Top-down leadership presupposes that leadership authority is determined by the relative positioning within a social hierarchy and that power flows from the highest to the lowest levels. The bottom-up direction of flow relates to the power that the lower echelons hold and can impose by rejecting a directive from above. By agreeing to, or rejecting, this directive, the follower is affirming or denying the authority of those who issued it. In successful top-down leadership models, power flows down from the highest level of authority and support flows back up to reinforce the leader's authority. When leaders enjoy the trust of their followers, the power flows up from them, although they will withdraw support from a leader whom they assess as not having their best interest at heart.

Servant leadership, on the other hand, relies on the transfer of power in multiple directions – allowing leaders to serve both their followers and successfully utilize their power to delegate authority accordingly. By adopting this middle-ground position in terms of the flow of power and support, servant leaders are in a position to achieve objectives that will be in both their and their followers' best interests. Leaders always retain the authority, and the ability to use it when necessary, but will prefer to defer its use in the best interests of those they serve. Servant leadership is not about personal status or the search for material rewards, instead it is founded on a motivation to serve the best interests of others.

From a modern business perspective, companies such as Starbucks, Federal Express and Asda have adopted servant leadership throughout their organizations as a means of focusing on all stakeholders, including employees, customers and the community in general. Putting the well-being of their employees alongside the need to make a profit engenders a high level of trust and loyalty, whilst also promoting their company as a good employer. Employees from all levels are encouraged to develop their careers within the organization and to regard themselves as having a long-term future within it.

Corporate proponents of the servant leadership philosophy believe that it helps to create a culture within their organizations where the thoughtful, exemplary treatment of their employees leads to high levels of customer service and hence, in turn, customer loyalty. The investment made in their staff produces better performance from them, which in turn results in ongoing financial benefits. It should, however, be viewed not as the latest quick-fix management fad – more a deeply held philosophy that permeates throughout the organization, from the most senior leader through every level of employment. It requires a cultural change that encompasses and influences the company's beliefs, values and attitudes.

Hardy (2010) identified 10 traits – initiative, listening, empathy, awareness, foresight, persuasion, stewardship, commitment to the growth of others, trust and visibility – as the most important and identifiable attributes that servant leaders exhibit. These traits are not too dissimilar to those of Spears

(2004) listed above, although Hardy proposed that trust, foresight, persuasion and stewardship are the most crucial when examining servant leadership. Hardy then went on to apply those traits to Winston Churchill as an examination of his credentials as a servant leader, arguing as follows:

- *Trust.* Churchill was largely successful in maintaining the confidence of the majority of the British people during the Second World War – largely by being open, truthful, visible and confident.

- *Foresight.* Greenleaf (1977) believed that 'the ability to foresee the likely outcome of a situation enables servant leaders to understand the lessons of the past, and identify the likely consequences of a decision for the future'. Churchill readily referred back to his, and other leaders', mistakes and successes in order to develop (ultimately successful) military and political strategies.

- *Persuasion.* Churchill used his range of skills, including a deep understanding of emotional intelligence (long before the term was coined), to convince the nation of the imperative and validity of his strategies through a strong sense of patriotism.

- *Stewardship.* At a time when Britain faced an uncertain and deeply troubling future, Churchill rose to guide it towards eventual victory. From the beginning, when he assumed the role of prime minister in 1940, he recognized the importance of his role as the guardian for the safety and security of his country and its people.

Authentic leadership

In essence, authentic leadership connects who you are as a human being (your beliefs and values) with how you lead your people (your thinking and behaviours). Beddoes-Jones (2012) proposed a model for authentic leadership, developed from initial work done by Novicevic *et al* (2006), which linked two psychological aspects of leadership – self-awareness and self-regulation – with two philosophical aspects – moral virtue and moral actions. Hence, it combined cognitive elements of self-awareness and the behavioural element of self-regulation, and a leader's ethical thinking (which she called moral virtue) with his or her actual behaviour (moral actions) (see Figure 9.2).

Bill George is an early proponent of authentic leadership. In his 2004 book *Authentic Leadership: Rediscovering the Secrets of Creating Lasting Value* he stated:

> We do not need executives running corporations into the ground for personal gain. We do not need celebrities to lead our companies. We do not need new laws. We need new leadership. We need authentic leaders: people of the highest integrity, committed to building enduring organizations. We need leaders who have a deep sense of purpose and are true to their core values. We need leaders who have the courage to build their companies to meet the needs of all their stakeholders and who recognize the importance of service to society.

FIGURE 9.2   Beddoes-Jones's authentic leadership model

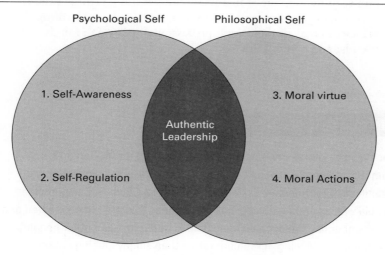

Adapted from Novicevic *et al* (2006)

We can distil from George's explanation that authentic leaders differ from the conception of more traditional business leaders in three respects:

1 They conceive the purpose of their companies to be meeting the needs of all stakeholders, not just the shareholders who seek maximum financial gain. Authentic leaders will also consider employees, customers, partners and the broader needs of society and the environment. That is not to say that both priorities are unconnected: shareholder value will be heavily influenced by the performance of the staff; the reliability of suppliers; and the opinions and purchasing behaviours of customers. It is a matter of priorities: a traditional leader will not flinch from sacking staff to move the business overseas if labour rates are cheaper, or driving suppliers mercilessly to reduce their prices. An authentic leader, on the other hand, sees a greater benefit in building long-term, mutually beneficial relationships with both those sets of stakeholders.

2 Thus, authentic leaders tend to think long term, with the intention of building sustainable business, rather than making quick financial returns. They are also conscious of their responsibilities in terms of the sustainable future of the planet. They face the threat of global warming full on, for example, whilst traditional leaders are more likely to be swayed by the negative PR implications of decisions that may affect the environment – modifying their decisions and behaviours accordingly.

3 Authentic leaders aspire to a more equitable work–life balance by seeking fulfilment in personal relationships outside work, as well as within. Others may be prepared to forsake health, happiness and family in the pursuit of financial remuneration. George (2004) encourages business leaders to stay grounded by integrating the four principal areas of their lives: professional; personal; family and friends; and community.

Leadership *BEST* practice

For David Fairhurst, chief people officer (Europe) for McDonald's, authenticity means a focus on: sharing thoughts, ideas, and emotions; identifying opportunities; asking for opinions and then listening to other people's ideas and feedback; looking for ideas that are not connected and then connecting them; committing time to understanding other people's perspectives; winning agreement rather than simply gaining passive acceptance.

Recent research into authentic leadership by Avolio *et al* (2010) described it as being confident, hopeful, optimistic, resilient, transparent, moral or ethical, and future-oriented. They introduced the concept of 'root leadership features', based upon the leader's morality and/or values – their root or core. The style of leadership adopted, though, was a surface function: be it behavioural, situational, functional, transformational, etc. This adopted style, however effective, may or may not have a sound moral foundation – history abounds with leaders who were extremely successful, in the short–medium term at least, but could never be described as having high moral principles. It is the difference between *good leaders* and *leaders for good*.

Avolio *et al* therefore focused on what makes a leader authentic, rather than considering the effectiveness of various leadership styles. In doing so they discovered four key components to authentic leadership:

- *Relationship transparency*: this is about being true to what you are, not pretending to be something or someone you are not when relating to others. The authentic leader gains trust through honest, open disclosure of personal thoughts and emotions, especially those likely to enhance mutually beneficial, supportive relationships. They are aware of their personal strengths and weaknesses and the impact they will have on others.

BEST leadership quote

'The more information you share with people, the more responsible and reasonable they will be in terms of their own assessment of what is possible and what is not. It is like treating people in your business like mature adults, rather than children that you just need to tell.'

William Rogers
Chief Executive
UKRD

- *Internal morality:* this ensures that authentic leaders have a deep sense of what is right and what is wrong – a finely tuned moral compass. They are able to fall back onto their moral code, and apply it, even during difficult economic and business periods.

BEST leadership quote

'You are the soldiers' moral compass.'

Captain Simon Cupples
British Army

- *Adaptive self-reflection:* thoughtful consideration about one's own attitudes, values and resulting behaviours, as a means of understanding more about oneself. It requires open and honest self-assessment allied to a desire for self-improvement. The purpose of the reflection is to learn, rather than apportion blame; to prepare for the future, rather than to dwell in the past; to enhance one's capabilities to react appropriately to new challenges. It is often occasioned by exposure to new circumstances such as changing job, embarking on new projects, or working with new people or within different cultures.

- *Balanced processing:* this involves handling and evaluating information honestly and without bias, denial or exaggeration. The authentic leader can objectively analyse available evidence before coming to a balanced decision. The judgement will balance the needs of all stakeholders involved and effected by the outcome, as well as the needs of the task to be completed.

CASE STUDY   Innocent

An example of a company founded on, and adhering to, the principles of authentic leadership is Innocent, which produces fruit juices and smoothies. Owned by Coca-Cola since 2013, the company was originally founded in the UK in 1999 by three university friends, entrepreneurial Generational X-ers, and has enjoyed remarkable growth and brand recognition since then, whilst maintaining their initial core values, examples of which include:

- Business ethics – they state that they want to leave things a little better than they found them: doing business in a more enlightened way and taking responsibility for its impact on society and the environment. They profess: 'We sure aren't perfect but we are trying to do the right thing.'

- Sustainability – they seek to lower the impacts associated with making their products, for example buying from suppliers who look after both their workers and their environment.

- Relationships with suppliers – in 2007 they commenced a programme of supplier visits by Innocent team members, as well as independent auditors and global sustainability organizations.

- The Innocent Foundation – 10 per cent of company profits go to the foundation, which supports charitable projects, especially development initiatives in countries they source their raw ingredients from.

- 'Innocent Inspires' evenings – the company founders hold regular innovative evenings for staff, designed to reinforce and bring to life their values.

- Retailers – enjoy an open invitation to call or visit the company headquarters to discuss any queries regarding their products.

- Staff – the staff are offered a range of personal and professional development opportunities, including three £1,000 scholarships every quarter to help people do something they have always wanted to do.

- Values – they aspire to live the values that 'are closest to our hearts', which are: be natural; be entrepreneurial; be responsible; be commercial; be generous.

Innocent is an example of authentic leadership in action, but not all people holding leadership positions share its principles. Clinical psychologist Oliver James, in his book *The Selfish Capitalist: Origins of Affluenza*, stated that the most prevalent personality traits displayed by today's leaders are:

- anti-social personality disorder – that encourages a focus on task completion to the detriment of developing successful personal relationships;
- obsessive compulsive personality disorder – where the leaders are rule-driven and gain pleasure from working excessively hard;
- narcissistic personality disorder – that encourages grandiose ideas and a sense of entitlement, albeit often apparently outwardly charming.

Patently, these three personality traits are likely to result in behaviour rather different than those displayed by authentic leaders. They will engender a task-obsessed, intolerant culture that is directed towards, and may indeed achieve, short-term results. For these role-holders, the thirst for personal power and position will negate any consideration of other stakeholders within the company.

BEST leadership quote

'Contemporary leaders need to remember that they are hugely important to the people they manage. They need to remember that they cannot hit their targets without the people they manage, and they need to remember to leave their egos at the door.'

Henry Engelhardt
Chief Executive
Admiral Group

China's interpretation of authentic leadership

Having proposed in Chapter 2 that one of the main challenges facing 21st-century leaders is that of globalization and the growth of international trade, it is interesting to consider the philosophy of authentic leadership as it applies to the greatest emerging international market, China. Is the existing Western approach valid in a non-Western context?

Confucianism is the dominant philosophy in China and plays a pivotal role in Chinese management thinking and behaviour. Confucians believe that morality and leadership are inseparable in that there is always a connection between the ethical stance of leaders and their behaviours. Immoral behaviours are regarded as inauthentic in Chinese contemporary society, despite negative reports of corruption amongst some public and private leaders. In Confucianism, self-awareness, associated with an ability to empathize with others' business, forms the foundation of a leader's positive psychological states and moral behaviours. Practically, it requires a daily review of one's actions against moral principles: recognizing and correcting mistakes in behaviours. Positive recognition of their own strengths and weaknesses assists in reinforcing leaders' belief in their original values and goals. Indeed, in Confucian culture, self-regulation is a recognized precondition to enter society, as people are educated to behave according to *ren* (humaneness), *yi* (appropriateness) and *li* (ritual) in relation to a given context.

Zhang *et al* (2012) examined the Western authentic leadership model to gain insight into its application in the Chinese cultural setting. They propose that, whilst self-authenticity is a predominant aspect of authentic leadership within Western literature, relational authenticity is an additional major factor in the Chinese context. Real authenticity is achieved in a dynamic process when both forms integrate (see Figure 9.3).

FIGURE 9.3 Zhang's refined model of authentic leadership

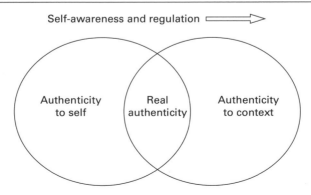

Self-awareness and regulation ⟹

Authenticity to self | Real authenticity | Authenticity to context

Preconditions: positive psychological capital and moral perspective

The Chinese perspective on authenticity, therefore, requires leaders to transcend their own values and moral code, aligning more readily with the given context. They must draw upon their psychological and moral resources – such as self-confidence, optimism and integrity – to become fully authentic in changing circumstances.

Zhang *et al* suggest that Western leaders hoping to work within a Chinese environment and culture should be aware of that country's understanding of authenticity. Based upon the philosophy of Confucianism, authentic leaders give dual emphasis to both the need to be authentic to oneself and to the relational context they are operating in. Chinese authentic leaders achieve their self-authenticity by being true to themselves and creating harmony within social interactions. The Western assumptions of autonomy as best practice are rejected in the Chinese culture, which encourages both self-awareness and self-regulation, encompassing virtues and moral principles.

Zhang *et al* conclude:

> In the continuous transformation, two factors act as polar attractors – the reflexive social self and the spontaneously-arising creative individual self – bringing harmony as the purpose and meaning for human life in Chinese society.

Ethical leadership

Also sometimes termed values-based leadership, ethical leadership is defined in general terms by the Center for Ethical Leadership as 'knowing your core values and having the courage to live them in all parts of your life in service of the common good'. In a business context it involves leaders considering the implications of their decisions against measures of honesty, integrity, fairness and relevant rules and laws; as well as how the decisions reflect and reinforce their own personal values. In the global environment, where decisions have implications in different cultures and countries, other ethical standpoints are brought into focus. For example, trading in countries where bartering and financial inducements are the norm places additional pressures on ethical decision-making. Hence, ethical leadership could be described as the application of authentic leadership within a moral context.

Brown, Trevino and Harrison (2005) proposed three key building blocks of ethical leadership to be: being an ethical example; treating people fairly; and actively managing morality. The third component, managing morality, requires leaders to encourage ethical behaviour within their teams by adopting transactional measures such as rewarding ethical behaviour and punishing actions that are deemed to be unethical.

The first of Brown *et al*'s building blocks involve ethical leaders displaying traits such as:

- *Respecting the dignity of others:* an ethical leader should not view his or her followers as a resource to achieve personal goals, rather treating them in a manner that recognizes and supports their values, beliefs and dignity.

- *Serving others:* placing followers' interests ahead of one's own and using one's authority to support and develop them.
- *Equality of treatment:* all followers should be treated fairly and without personal bias. When circumstances require differential treatment, it should be fair, open and based on a moral foundation.
- *Community building:* decisions are always taken with the needs of the community (team, organization, external stakeholders) in mind. Wherever possible, the goals of the leader and followers are allied to those of the broader community.
- *Honesty:* honesty and integrity are essential traits of an ethical leader as they form the foundations of mutual respect between leader and followers. Ethical leaders openly disclose the reasoning behind decisions, no matter how critical or unpopular they may be.

Leadership *BEST* practice

New Charter Housing has a set of clearly defined and communicated values, upon which all staff are recruited and subsequently measured. They are: genuineness, respect for self and others, excellence, achievement and togetherness. Forming an easy-to-remember acronym, GREAT, it is reinforced by the organization's core mission: Great homes, Great neighbourhoods, Great people.

The Institute of Business Ethics proposes three tests that leaders should match their decisions against:

- *Transparency:* do I mind others knowing what I have decided?
- *Effect:* who does my decision affect or hurt?
- *Fairness:* would my decision be considered fair by those affected?

Alan Chapman, creator of the Businessballs website (**www.businessballs.com**), introduced the P4 model (not to be confused with the Four Ps of Marketing) as a maxim for 21st-century management philosophy that defines the character of a sound ethical organization. The aim of a modern organization should reconcile its *purpose* (be it shareholder benefit or cost-effective service delivery in the public sector) with the needs of *people* (staff, customers and local communities) whilst giving due consideration to the *planet* (in terms of sustainability, the environment, natural resources, our heritage, and 'fair trade' with other cultures and societies) and at all times acting with *probity* (or *principles*) – thus enabling the other, potentially conflicting, aims to be harmonized in a sustainable, ethical and successful mix.

The Institute for Ethical Leadership has attempted to identify the qualities that constitute ethical behaviour and leadership across cultures. It has created a set of competencies, designed to facilitate business transactions and maintain sound human relationships, which can be used by leaders to measure the psychological basis upon which they make decisions. Entitled 'The Ethical Leadership Scales', they are used for teaching and research purposes and consist of three scales:

- the ethical competence scale;
- the ethical leadership scale;
- the ethical organization scale.

Full details can be found at **www.ethicalleadership.com**, whilst selected examples of the Ethical Leadership Scale are shown in Table 9.2.

TABLE 9.2 Ethical Leadership Scale

Characteristic	Explanation
Relationship to Self 1. Acts with integrity	*Personal qualities of the ethical leader* • Keeps promises and commitments and expects others to keep theirs • Maintains loyalty to those not present • Apologizes sincerely • Acts with honest • Takes responsibility and clears up mistakes
Relationship to Others 26. Compassionate	*Qualities that allow the ethical leader to connect with and empower others* • Caring and empathetic • Is sympathetic to the needs of others • Does not turn away from helping others • Acts from a good heart • Treats people with genuine affection
Relationship to the Whole 38. Tolerates contradiction and anxiety	*Qualities that reveal the ethical leader's sense of connection with a grand design and a higher purpose* • Is able to live with contradiction • Is prepared to wait for closure • Is able to tolerate large amounts of anxiety • Understands that contradiction and anxiety can be the accompaniments to creative growth

It is true that some situations that leaders face do pose ethical dilemmas such as: purchasing; international trade negotiations; and aspects of personnel management such as recruiting, promoting, dismissal and setting bonuses. Yet the scale and frequency of scandals involving unethical behaviour by senior leaders during the first decade of the 21st century has been breathtaking. Whether in the financial sector – where corporate greed has resulted in the near-demise of some countries' entire monetary structure, or in politics – with senior representatives acting without any semblance of morality in order to avoid taking responsibility for their actions, or sports personalities – who are prepared to lie on oath in order to escape the truth emerging of their cheating: those years will forever be remembered for striking examples of unethical behaviour.

Quoted in *Training Journal* in January 2011, leadership guru Ken Blanchard stated:

> We've seen the ramifications of self-serving leaders. They think leadership is all about them. They couldn't care less about their people or their customers. That's why we have had this economic downturn – a lot of self-serving leadership by people concerned about themselves, not about making smart decisions. Whenever you look at some kind of epic failure there's always a leader in the middle of it. Over the last 10 years, there have been so many failures.
>
> A soft measure of companies' success that's become very important is the correlation between social responsibility and performance. There's tremendous social pressure for companies to show they are good companies that are doing good in the world.

BEST leadership quote

'Organizations that are very clear about their purpose, and are clear about where they are heading, tend to have what Jim Collins described as "Level 5 Leaders" – they focus on the organization's performance and sustainability beyond their own tenure. "Level 4 Leaders", on the other hand, tend to be more concerned with their own performance than that of the organization they lead.'

Jonathan Austin
Managing Director
Best Companies

Excluding decisions taken by individuals to avoid the truth of their misdemeanours coming to light, we should consider why leaders make unethical decisions, including those on a relatively minor scale. Ethical transgressions can be the result of leaders facing a number of ethical dilemmas or personal biases, including:

- Confirmation bias can cause leaders to select information that justifies the decisions they have made, or are considering making. They may, for example, only consider selective arguments or data when judging ethical issues.
- Self-promotion bias may result in leaders considering their own needs, as opposed to those of others, when making decisions. They may be more influenced by their own ambition at the expense of the well-being of their people.
- Subjective views can cloud judgement, resulting in inappropriate decisions. The leader may let personal assessments, rather than objective reasoning, override ethical considerations.
- Situational pressures or deadlines can result in bias that persuade leaders to forego their own values and sense of morality.

Moreover, people often overpredict how ethically they will react to a given situation. When people are faced with an ethical dilemma they generally behave less fairly than they would have estimated beforehand. It is suggested that this bias is because people predict future behaviour on their perceived values rather than examples of their past behaviour. Indeed, history tends to indicate that people's future decisions are based more on previous experience than on personal values.

It is incumbent on leaders to consider very deeply the ethical implication of their decision-making, especially in terms of the effect it will have on their followers. This is particularly important in terms of their status as role model – positive or negative. At all levels within an organization, leaders will influence the behaviours of those they lead. The power they hold to deal out both rewards and punishments will strengthen the extent to which followers seek to emulate their behaviour. Hence, if ethical leaders reward the ethical behaviour of others, and condemn unethical behaviour, they hold the power to influence the moral standing of the organization as a whole.

The ethical leader's influence also extends to interpersonal relations within groups. By experiencing the attitude and actions of an ethical leader, followers become more prepared to allow colleagues to express their own views and have more consideration for their needs. Group members, by role-modelling the ethical behaviours of their leader, are more likely to contribute to reducing the risk of tension resulting from interpersonal relationships.

Schaubroeck *et al* (2012) studied connections between ethical leadership and ethical culture, both across and within organizational levels, and how both factors related to the behaviours of lower-level followers. They found that:

- Ethical leaders embed their expectations into the ethical culture, which is shared and understood by their people. They therefore indirectly influence their immediate followers' cognitions (for example, moral efficacy) and behaviours through group ethical culture.

- Ethical culture cascades across hierarchical levels to a substantial extent, thus enabling a new and previous unstudied pathway for leadership influence to transmit across levels.
- Leaders who exhibit a high level of ethical leadership may facilitate the influence of subordinate leaders' ethical leadership on their followers.

The research concluded that more attention should be paid to the role of shared understandings about ethical conduct and culture at each hierarchical level of an organization. This imperative is shared by the UK's Chartered Management Institute, whose research has identified that: 'Too many businesses – and public sector organizations – have visibly failed to ensure that ethical standards are maintained, at huge cost to them, their reputations and their customers.'

CASE STUDY   Procter & Gamble

Although Bob McDonald is not one of the leaders interviewed for this book, he is a very good example of someone who applies the principles of ethical leadership within his role as Procter & Gamble's president and CEO. Over the period 2008–09, he visited several US universities to present his views as a values-based leader, and the impact that this leadership philosophy has had during his 28 years with the company. He commenced his presentation by stating: 'I start with the premise that it's better to have a goal in life, and to lead your life by a set of principles, values or morals.'

His main piece of advice to the students in the audience was that they should 'develop a values system that keeps you grounded in this ever-changing world'. Great companies change everything but their values, and those entering them as leaders have to be prepared to change everything except their ethical values, because if they do not they will not grow personally, nor will they be able to contribute to the growth of their company. McDonald explained that when he joined Procter & Gamble in 1980 it was good enough to be an effective leader in one's own culture but that today, in the global economy, you have to be an effective leader in cultures outside one's own – you have to learn.

To demonstrate his point he referred to the company's purpose statement:

We will provide branded products and services of superior quality and value that improve the lives of the world's consumers, now and for generations to come. As a result, consumers will reward us with sales, profit and value creation; allowing our people, our shareholders, and the communities in which we live and work to prosper.

He explained that the company's values and his own are as one, and are condensed to:

- *Leadership and ownership.* Every employee is expected to be a leader and to act like an owner of the company. Indeed, more than 10 per cent of the stock is owned by employees, which inspires them to run the company as if the dollars they spend and the decisions they make are their own.

- *Integrity.* The company does not lie, cheat or steal and it doesn't tolerate people who do.

- *Passion for winning.* The goal on the job every day is to win with consumers and to beat the competition.

- *Trust.* The fact that Procter & Gamble has a built-from-within culture, and that employees trust each other, makes it a much more efficient company.

McDonald went on to explain that to sustain the company it has to deliver outstanding business results, as well as taking care of the environment and the people and communities where it operates now and in the future. Its stated growth strategy is: 'Touching and improving more consumers' lives in more parts of the world... more completely.'

In terms of the company's impact on the environment, its sustainability vision is:

- powering our plants with 100 per cent renewable energy;

- using 100 per cent renewable materials or recyclate for all our products and packaging;

- having zero consumer or manufacturing waste going to landfills;

- designing products that delight consumers, whilst maximizing the conservation of resources.

On a more personal note, McDonald shared his principal beliefs with his student audience, encouraging them to identify and get in touch with their own values system. For him, his number one belief is that: 'Living a life driven by purpose is more meaningful and rewarding than meandering through life without direction.' He believes that his life's purpose is to improve lives on many levels: those of the 6.5 million people in the world using Procter & Gamble brands; as well as having a positive impact on the life of everyone he meets.

To support his contention that values-based, ethical leadership is not merely a soft option, but that it creates real value within a company, he revealed how Procter & Gamble has grown during his 28 years of involvement with it, as shown in Table 9.3.

TABLE 9.3   Procter & Gamble growth figures 1980–2008

	1980	2008
Annual sales	$10 billion	$83 billion
Sales outside US	32%	63%
Billion-dollar brands	0	24
Employees	62,200	129,000
Split-adjusted stock price	$2.32	$61.00

Chapter summary

In this final chapter I suggested five approaches to leadership that will allow leaders to face better the challenges of the 21st century: two based upon the psychological relationships between them and their followers; and three that are more philosophical in nature.

Engaged staff have been proven time and time again to be more committed and effective in their work roles, and I have detailed the approach and guidance of the UK's 'Engage for Success' initiative, as well as research supporting the benefits of employee engagement, including a white paper produced by Mind Gym. The contributions of individual staff, line managers, senior leaders and peers towards an engaged workplace was considered. The second leadership model discussed was Scouller's integrated psychological approach, which connects more traditional leadership theories with modern psychological concepts and applications.

The second group of theories cover a leader's responsibility from a human standpoint. Servant leaders willingly relegate their own needs for those of their followers, and use the authority vested in their position to enable and empower them. Authentic leaders, on the other hand, readily connect their beliefs and values with their leadership behaviours. The company Innocent was used as a corporate example of ethical leadership; and the Chinese interpretation of authenticity, based upon Confucianism, was also explored. The fifth, and final, leadership approach best suited to meet future challenges was ethical leadership, also known as values-based leadership. The competences and traits of ethical leaders were examined, including those from the Institute for Ethical Leadership. The chapter ended with a case study involving Bob McDonald from Procter & Gamble.

A final thought...

If you have read this book from cover to cover, or merely browsed and selected the bits that interested you most, you will have, hopefully, understood that it is based upon the premise that, to be an inspirational leader, you must understand your people: how they think; what they expect; and what they need in order to contribute to your vision. Leadership is all about recognizing the mutual dependency that exists between leader and follower. The relationship is symbiotic, with both parties requiring the support of the other if they are to grow and develop – even in some cases, as has been explored, to sustain life in extreme conditions. The fact is, however, that as the 21st century is unfolding, the needs and expectations of followers are changing: gone are the days when a junior member of staff would automatically show, let alone have, respect for his or her manager. Those holding positions of authority have to earn the respect of their people – and that is going to be increasingly the case as Generation Y becomes more prevalent and influential within the workplace. The times when autocratic, command and control management cultures were effective are behind us. The organizations that will face future challenges most successfully will be headed by leaders who have the energy and ability to develop an emotional buy-in with all stakeholders, rather than merely relying on the authority vested in their role. They will be like the *BEST* leaders I have quoted extensively throughout this book.

Interestingly, *The Sunday Times*' 2012 'Best Companies to Work For' report began: 'Difficult times require strong leaders and the evidence of this year's report shows a resurgence amongst businesses with the most dynamic and forceful personalities leading them.' Certainly, it was a privilege to experience the energy and commitment from the leaders I interviewed for this book. Without exception, they fully appreciated the critical importance of having engaged staff who associate their future with that of their organization. Unfortunately, however, not all leaders are so enlightened: the Chartered Management Institute (CMI), with a membership community of over 100,000 managers, states: 'Employee engagement remains an aspiration, not a reality, in too many organizations.'

A central theme in modern business is the primacy of the customer, yet not all organizations have recognized that the true value of customer satisfaction is created largely at the interface between customers and those who serve them: both external customers, and those who require support from colleagues within the organization. That being the case, by prioritizing the engagement levels of employees, even ahead of customers, companies focus their energies and resources on customer service, either directly or indirectly, through those who deliver it. This requires a change of emphasis for many strategic leaders, both within the UK and elsewhere. The 2013 CMI report, entitled, 'The CEO Challenge: The UK Challenge' identifies UK CEOs as being unique in placing customers so high up their challenge lists. By contrast, the report concludes that business leaders across the world are more focused on innovation and developing their workforces. Business leaders globally see their human resource as the top strategic challenge, yet it is ranked third in the UK, with only US respondents ranking it lower.

The problem is, I fear, that many organizations, especially during difficult trading periods, are not persuaded of the value of committed, loyal, engaged staff: staff development is often seen as an easy target for cost reduction. Yet many of the leaders who have created trusting, collaborative cultures have more than weathered the recessional storm of recent years. Take TGI Friday's, one of the companies recognized in *The Sunday Times'* 2013 report, whose vision is: 'Our people are family; our guests become friends; our competitors envy us; our people come first'. Since Karen Forrester took over as chief executive in 2008 the company has enjoyed a 27 per cent annual increase in sales, with staff turnover reduced from 157 per cent to 38 per cent. Her total belief in her people, and the value they can contribute to the business, shone bright when I met her. Yet TGI Friday's is not a lone example of the business benefits of inspirational leadership. The companies that have consistently featured in *The Sunday Times'* survey over the five years from 2007 to 2012 enjoyed an average 50 per cent increase in turnover, with 152 per cent increase in profit. Figure C.1 highlights the combined share performance of all quoted companies featured in the 2013 survey in comparison to the performance of the Financial Times Stock Exchange (FTSE100).

Recall from the book's Introduction that psychology is about 'understanding the mind and how it affects behaviour' – which is what the leaders of these *BEST* companies appreciate and consistently apply. The ones I have had the pleasure to interview were a representative selection from those leading large multinationals, to not-for-profit organizations, yet they all demonstrated the same determination to create positive cultures that result in the *BEST* places to work. The challenge for other leaders, in other organizations, across other countries is to learn by their example. I truly hope that this book will assist in that learning process and inspire you also to be the *BEST* leader you are capable of becoming.

FIGURE C.1 Five-year returns comparison FTSE – Best Companies

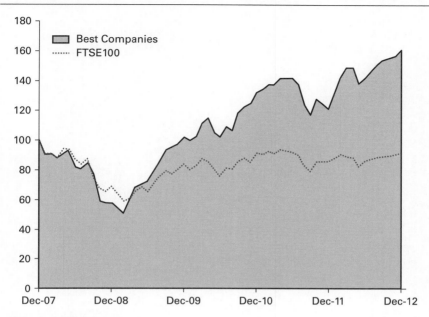

© Copyright Best Companies 2013

REFERENCES

Adair, J (1973) *Action-Centred Leadership*, McGraw Hill, New York

Adair, J (1989) *Great Leaders*, Talbot Press, Surrey

Adair, J (1996) *Effective Motivation*, Pan Books, London

Adair, J (2006) *Leadership Development Trainer's Manual*, Adair Leadership Foundation, Godalming, Surrey

Adair, J (2009) *Effective Leadership*, Pan Macmillan, London

Aldehayyat, J S and Anchor, J R (2010) [accessed 14 January 2014] Strategic planning implementation and creation of value in the firm, *Strategic Change*, **19**, pp 163–76 [Online] interscience@wiley.com

Arvey, R *et al* (2006) The determinants of leadership role occupancy: genetic and personality factors, *The Leadership Quarterly*, **17** (1), pp 1–20

Avey, B, Wernsing, T and Luthans, F (2008) Can positive employees help positive organisational change? Impact of psychological capital and emotions on relevant attitudes and behaviours, *Journal of Applied Behavioural Science*, **44** (1), pp 48–70

Avolio, B *et al* (2010) What is authentic leadership development? in *Oxford Handbook of Positive Psychology and Work*, eds P Linley, A S Harrington and N Garcea, Oxford University Press, Oxford

Bal, P M, De Lange, A H, Jansen, P G W and Van Der Velde, M E G (2008) Psychological contract breach and job attitudes: a meta-analysis of age as a moderator, *Journal of Vocational Behaviour*, **72**, pp 143–58

Bar-On, R (2006) *EQ-i Leadership Users Guide*, Multi-Health Systems, Toronto

Bass, B M (1985) *Leadership and Performance Beyond Expectations*, Free Press, New York

Bass, B M and Avolio, B J (1994) *Improving Organizational Effectiveness Through Transformational Leadership*, Sage Publications, Thousand Oaks, CA

Bassett-Jones, N and Lloyd, G C (2005) Does Herzberg's motivation theory have staying power?, *Journal of Management Development*, **24** (10), pp 929–43

Beddoes-Jones, F (2012) Authentic leadership: the key to building trust, *People Management*, August, pp 44–47

Bellou, V (2009) Profiling the desirable psychological contract for different groups of employees: evidence from Greece, *International Journal of Human Resource Management*, **20** (4), pp 810–30

Bennis, W G (1998) *On Becoming a Leader*, 2nd edn, Basic Books, New York

Bennis, W G (2009) *On Becoming a Leader*, 4th edn, Basic Books, New York

Bersin, J (2013) Millennials will soon rule the world: but how will they lead?, *Forbes Leadership*, 9 December

Blake, R and Mouton, J (1964) *The Managerial Grid: The Key to Leadership Excellence*, Gulf Publishing, Houston, TX

Boal, K B and Hooijberg, R (2001) Strategic leadership research: moving on, *Leadership Quarterly*, **11** (4), pp 515–49

Bonn, I (2005) Improving strategic thinking: a multi-level approach, *Leadership and Organizational Development Journal*, **26** (5), pp 336–54

Book, H and Stein, S (2001) *The EQ Edge*, Kogan Page, London

Brown, M E, Trevino, L K and Harrison, D A (2005) Ethical leadership: a social learning perspective for construct development and testing, *Organisational Behaviour and Human Decision Processes*, **97**, pp 117–34

Burns, J M (1978) *Leadership*, Harper Row, New York

Carter, L F (1953) Leadership and small group behaviour, in *Group Relations at the Crossroads*, eds M Sherif and M O Wilson, Harper, New York

CBI and Harvey Nash (2010) *Employment Trends Survey*

Chen, J Q and Lee, S M (2003) An exploratory cognitive DSS for strategic decision making, *Decision Support Systems*, **36**, pp 147–60

Collins, J (2001) *Good to Great*, Random House Business, London

Collinson, C and Hearn, J (2003) Breaking the silence: on men, masculinities and management, in *Reader in Gender, Work and Organisation*, eds R Ely, E Foldy and M Scully, pp 75–78, Blackwell, Oxford

Corporate Leadership Council (2009) Driving Performance and Retention Through Employee Engagement: A Quantitative Analysis of Effective Engagement Strategies, Corporative Executive Board

Coyle-Shapiro, J A-M and Neuman, J H (2004) The psychological contract and individual differences: the role of exchange and creditor ideologies, *Journal of Vocational Behaviour*, **64** (1), pp 150–64

Cutler, A M (2004) *One Piece Short of a Jigsaw*, Management Books 2000, Cirencester

Cutler, A M (2010) *Aspire to Inspire*, www.lulu.com

Daft, R L (1999) *Leadership: Theory and Practice*, Dryden Press, Oak Brook, IL

Day, D V (2000) Leadership development: a review in context, *Leadership Quarterly*, **11** (4), pp 581–613

Deci, E L, Connell, J P and Ryan, R M (1989) Self-determination in a work organisation, *Journal of Applied Psychology*, **74** (4), pp 580–90

Delcampo, R G, Haggerty, L A, Hanley, M J and Knippel, L A (2011) *Managing the Multi-Generational* Workforce *From the GI Generation to the Millennials*, Gower Publishing Ltd, Farnham

Drucker, P F (1992) *Managing the Non-Profit Organisation: Practices and Priciples*, Butterworth-Heinemann, Oxford

Drucker, P F (2005) Managing oneself, *Harvard Business Review*, **83** (1), pp 100–09

Eisenhardt, K M and Brown, S L (1998) Competing on the edge: strategy as structure chaos, *Long Range Planning*, **31** (5), pp 786–89

Feldman, D C and Lankau, M J (2005) Executive coaching: a review and agenda for future research, *Journal of Management*, **31**, 829

Fielder, F E (1967) *A Theory of Leadership Effectiveness*, McGraw-Hill, New York

Finkelstein, S and Hambrick, D (1996) *Strategic Leadership: Top Executives and Their Effects on Organizations*, West Publishing Company, St Pauls, MN

Fischhoff, N (1975) Hindsight and foresight: the effect of outcome knowledge on judgement under uncertainty, *Journal of Experimental Psychology: Human Perception and Performance*, **1**, pp 288–99

Ford, C M (1996) A theory of individual creative action in multiple social dimensions, *Academy of Management Review*, **21**, pp 1112–42

Forehand, Garlie A and Von Haller, G (1964) Environmental variation in studies of organisational behaviour, *Psychological Bulletin*, **62** (6), pp 362

Frederickson, B (1998) What are positive emotions?, *Review of General Psychology*, **2**, pp 300–19

Freedman, J (2012) Women's Leadership Edge: Global Research on Emotional Intelligence, Gender, and Job Level [online] http://www.6seconds.org/2012/09/11/research-emotional-intelligence-gender-career/

Garcia-Retamero, R, Lopez-Zafra, E and Pilar Berrios Martos, M (2012) The relationship between transformational leadership and emotional intelligence from a gendered approach, *The Psychological Record*, **62**, pp 97–114

Gavetti, G (2011) The new psychology of strategic leadership, *Harvard Business Review*, **89** (7–8), pp 118–25

George, B (2004) *Authentic Leadership: Rediscovering the Secrets to Creating Lasting Value*, Jossey-Bass, San Francisco, CA

Giannantonio, C M and Hurley-Hanson, A E (2013) *Extreme Leadership Leaders, Teams and Situations Outside the Norm*, Edward Elgar, Cheltenham UK and Northampton, MA

Goldberg, L R (1990) An alternative description of personality: the big five factor structure, *Journal of Personality and Social Psychology*, **59**, pp 1216–29

Goldsmith, M, Lyons, L and Freas, A (eds) (2000) *Coaching for Leadership*, Jossey-Bass, San Francisco, CA

Goleman, D (2005) *Emotional Intelligence: Why It Can Matter More Than IQ*, 10th edn, Bantam Books, New York

Goleman, D (2011) Are women more emotionally intelligent than men?, *Psychology Today* blog, 29 April

Goleman, D, Boyatzis, R and McKee, A (2001) Primal leadership: the hidden driver to great performance, *Harvard Business Review*, December, pp 43–53

Goleman, D, Boyatzis, R and McKee, A (2002) *Primal Leadership*, Harvard Business School Press, Boston, MA

Greenleaf, R K (1977) *Servant Leadership: A Journey into the Nature of Legitimate Power and Greatness*, Paulist Press, New York

Guest, D E and Conway, N (2002) *Pressure at Work and the Psychological Contract*, CIPD, London

Hambrick, D C and Finkelstein, S (1987) Managerial discretion: a bridge between polar views of organizations, *Research in organizational behavior*, **9**, pp 396–406

Hambrick, D C and Mason, P A (1984) Upper echelons: the organization as a reflection of its top managers, *Academy of Management Review*, **9** (2), pp 193–206

Handy, C (1992) *The Language and Leadership in Frontiers of Leadership*, eds M Syrett and C Hogg, Blackwell, Oxford

Hannah, S T, Uhl-Bien, M, Avolio, B J and Cavarretta, F L (2009) A framework for examining leadership in extreme context, *The Leadership Quarterly*, **20**, pp 879–919

Hardy, B (2010) Servant Leadership and Sir Winston Churchill, Honors College Capstone Experience/Thesis Project Paper 280

Harter, J, Schmidt, F, Killham, E and Agrawal, S (2009) *The Relationship Between Engagement at Work and Organizational Outcomes*, Gallup Press, Washington, DC

Haslam, S A, Reicher, S D and Platow, M J (2011) *The New Psychology of Leadership: Identity, Influence and Power*, Psychology Press, Hove and New York

Heide, M, Gronhaug, K and Johannessen, S (2002) Exploring barriers to the successful implementation of formulated strategy, *Scandinavian Journal of Management*, **18** (2), pp 217–31

Hersey, P And Blanchard, K H (1977) *Management of Organizational Behaviour: Utilizing Human Resources*, 3rd edn, Prentice Hall, Englewood Cliffs, NJ

Herzberg, F (1959) *The Motivation to Work*, John Wiley and Sons, New York

Herzberg, F (1968) One more time: how do you motivate employees?, *Harvard Business Review*, **46** (1), pp 53–62

Hodgkinson, G P and Sparrow, P R (2002) *The Competent Organization: A Psychological Analysis of the Strategic Management Process*, Open University Press, Buckingham

Hooper, A and Potter, J (1997) *The Business of Leadership: Adding Lasting Value to Your Organisation*, Ashgate, Aldershot

House, R J (1977) A 1976 theory of charismatic leadership, in *Leadership: The Cutting Edge*, eds J G Hunt and L L Larson, pp 189–207, Southern Illinois University Press, Carbondale IL

House, R J (1997) Path–goal theory of leadership: lessons, legacy and reformulated theory, *Leadership Quarterly*, **7** (3), pp 323–53

House, R J et al (2004) *Culture, Leadership and Organisations: The GLOBE Study of 62 Societies*, Sage, London

House, R J and Aditya, R (1997) The social scientific study of leadership: Quo Vadis?, *Journal of Management*, **23**, pp 409–74

James, O (2008) *The Selfish Capitalist: Origins of Affluenza*, Vermillion, London

Jarrett, M (2008) The new change equation, *Business Strategy Review*, Winter

Jervis, R (1976) *Perception and Misperception in International Politics*, Princeton University Press, Princeton NJ

Jones, J R and George, G M (2004) *Contemporary Management*, p 405, Irwin/McGraw Hill, Boston, MA

Judge, T A, Bono, J E, Ilies, R and Gerhardt, M W (2002) Personality and leadership: a qualitative and quantitative review, *Journal of Applied Psychology*, **87**, pp 765–80

Jung, C G (1971) *Psychological Types: Collected Works of C. G Jung*, Vol 6, Princeton University Press, NJ

Kaplan, R S and Norton, D P (2000) Having trouble with your strategy? Then map it, *Harvard Business Review*, Sept/Oct, pp 167–76

Kaufmann, R (1991) *Strategic Planning Plus: An Organizational Guide*, Scott Foresman, Glenview, IL

Kegan, R and Lahey, L L (2009) *Immunity to Change*, Harvard Business Press

Kets de Vries, M (2004) *Global Executive Leadership Inventory: Participant Workbook*, p 5, Jossey-Bass, San Francisco, CA

Kets de Vries, M, Guillen, L, Korotov, K and Florent-Treacy, E (2010) *The Coaching Kaleidoscope: Insights from the Inside*, Palgrave MacMillan, Basingstoke

Kets de Vries, M, Hellwig, T, Guillen, L, Florent-Treacy, E and Korotov, K (2008) Long Term Effectiveness of a Transitional Leadership Development Program: An Exploratory Study, INSEAD Working Paper 2008/24/EFE

Kets de Vries, M, Vrignaud, P and Florent-Treacy, E (2004) The global leadership life inventory: development and psychometric properties of a 360-degree feedback instrument, *International Journal of Human Resource Management*, **15** (3), pp 475–92

Kets de Vries, M, Vrignaud, P, Korotov, K, Engellau, E and Florent-Treacy, E (2006) The development of the Personality Audit: a psychodynamic multiple feedback assessment audit, *International Journal of Human Resource Management*, **17** (5), pp 898–917

Kiewitz, C, Restubog, S L, Zagenczyk, T and Hochwarter, W (2009) The interactive effects of psychological contract breach and organizational politics on perceived organizational support: evidence from two longitudinal studies, *Journal of Management Studies*, **46** (5), 806–34

Kirkpatrick, S A and Locke, E A (1991) Leadership: do traits matter?, *Academy of Management Executive*, **5** (2), pp 48–60

Klein, K J, Ziegert, J C, Knight, A P and Xiao, Y (2006) Dynamic delegation: shared, hierarchical and deindividualized leadership in extreme action teams, *Administrative Science Quarterly*, **51**, pp 590–621

Kolditz, T A (2007) *In Extremis Leadership: Leading as if Your Life Depended on It*, Jossey-Bass, San Francisco, CA

Kouzes, J and Posner, B (2001) *Leadership Practices Inventory (LPI) Participant's workbook*, 2nd edn, Jossey-Bass, San Francisco, CA

Kouzes, J and Posner, B (2008) *The Leadership Challenge*, 4th edn, Jossey-Bass, San Francisco, CA

Leaders on Leadership (1996) ed S Crainer, The Chartered Institute of Management, Corby

Leavy, B (2012) Collaborative innovation as the new imperative, *Strategy and Leadership*, **40** (2)

Lewin, K, Lippit, R and White, R K (1939) Patterns of aggressive behaviour in experimentally created social climates, *Journal of Social Psychology*, **10**, pp 271–301

Lewis, D (2002) The place of organizational politics in strategic change, *Strategic Change*, **11**, 25–34

Lewis, S (2011) *Positive Psychology at Work*, John Wiley and Sons, Chichester

Liden, R C, Sparrowe, R T and Wayne, S J (2006) Leader-member exchange theory: the past and potential for the future, *Research in Personnel and Human Resources Management*, **15**, pp 47–119

Linley, A (2008) *Average to A+: Realising Strengths in Yourself and Others*, CAPP Press, Warwick

Loftus, E F and Palmer, J C (1974) Reconstruction of automobile destruction: an example of the interaction between language and memory, *Journal of Verbal Learning and Verbal Behaviour*, **13** (5), pp 585–89

Lord, R G, De-Vader, L and Alliger, G M (1986) A meta-analysis of the relation between personality traits and leadership perceptions: an application of validity generalization procedures, *Journal of Applied Psychology*, **71**, pp 402–10

Louis, M R and Sutton, R I (1991) Switching cognitive gears: from habits of mind to active thinking, *Human Relations*, **44**, pp 55–76

McDermott, A M, Conway, E, Rousseau, D M and Flood, P C (2013) Promoting effective psychological contacts through leadership: the missing link between HR strategy and performance, *Human Resource Management*, **52** (2), pp 289–310

McGregor, D (1960) *The Human Side of Enterprise*, McGraw-Hill, New York

McInnis, K J, Meyer, J P and Feldman, S (2009) Psychological contracts and their implications for commitment: a feature-based approach, *Journal of Vocational Behaviour*, **74**, pp 165–80

Maister, D H, Gleen, C H and Galford, R M (2001) *The Trusted Advisor*, Simon and Schuster, London

Margolis, J and Stoltz, P (2010) How to bounce back from adversity, *Harvard Business Review*, **88** (1), pp 86–92

Maslow, A (1954) *Motivation and Personality*, Harper, New York

Maslow, A (1971) *The Farther Reaches of Human Nature*, The Viking Press, New York

Meyerson, D and Fletcher, D (2000) A modest manifesto for shattering the glass ceiling, *Harvard Business Review*, **78** (1), pp 126–37

Michaels, E, Handfield-Jones, H and Axelrod, B (2001) *The War for Talent*, Harvard Business Press

Miettinen, R (2000) The concept of experiential learning and John Dewey's theory of reflective thought and action, *International Journal of Lifelong Education*, **19** (1), pp 54–72

Miller, G (1975) *The Philosophy of Communication*, Harper and Row, New York

Millet, S M (2006) Futuring and visioning: complementary approaches to strategic decision making, *Strategy and Leadership*, **34** (3), p 50

Mind Gym Ltd (2011) 'The Engaged Employee: How to Keep Your People Flourishing Whatever the Weather', 2nd edn, September

Mintzberg, H, Ahlstrand, B W and Lampel, J (1998) *Strategy Safari: A Guided Tour Through the Wilds of Strategic Management*, Free Press, New York

Momeni, N (2009) The relationship between managers' emotional intelligence and the organizational climate they create, *Public Personnel Management*, **38** (2), pp 35–48

Morrison, J L (1992) Environmental Scanning, in *A Primer for New Institutional Researchers*, eds M A Whitely, J D Porter, and R H Fenske, pp 86–99, Florida Association for Institutional Research (FAIR)

Nadin, S J and Williams, C C (2012) Psychological contract violation beyond an employees' perspective, *Employee Relations*, **34** (2), pp 110–25

Nair, L (2013) The changing face of the leader, *Management Today*, June, pp 53–55

NBER Working Paper, (Military CEOs) No 19782, January 2014

Noe, R A and Schmitt, N (1986) The influence of trainee attitudes on training effectiveness: test of a model, *Personnel Psychology*, **39**, pp 497–523

Notter, J and Grant, M (2012) *The Social Media Survey*, Greenlight, London

Novicevic, M M *et al* (2006) Authentic leadership: a historical perspective, *Journal of Leadership and Organisational Studies*, **13**, pp 64–76

Nutt, P C and Backoff, R W (1997) Crafting vision, *Journal of Management Enquiry*, **6**, pp 308–28

Orme, G and Langhorn, S (2002) Emotional intelligence lessons learnt from implementing EI programmes – the cutting edge of EI interventions, *The Journal of Performance through People*, **10** (2), pp 32–39

Parmenter, D (2010) Crisis Leadership: Ten Lessons from Sir Shackleton, *Leadership Excellence*, June, pp 6–7

Parnell, J A and Lester, D L (2003) Towards a philosophy of strategy: reassessing five critical dilemmas in strategy formulation and change, *Strategic Change*, **12** (6), pp 291–303

Paul, J P, Niehoff, B P and Turnley, W H (2000) Empowerment, expectations, and the psychological contract – managing the dilemmas and gaining the advantages, *Journal of Socio-Economics*, **29**, pp 471–85

Peltier, B (2001) *The Psychology of Executive Coaching: Theory and Application*, Sheridan Books, Ann Arbor, MI

Perkins, D N T (2000) *Leading at the Edge*, American Management Association

Peterson, C and Seligman, M E P (2004) *Character Strengths and Virtues: A Handbook and Classification*, Oxford University Press, American Psychological Association, Washington, DC

Raja, U, Johns, G and Ntalianis, F (2004) The impact of personality on psychological contracts, *Academy of Management Journal*, **47** (3), pp 350–67

Rath, T and Harter, J (2010) *The Economies of Wellbeing*, Gallup Press, Washington, DC

Richard, O C, McMillan-Capehart, A, Bhuian, S N and Taylor, E C (2009) Antecedents and consequences of psychological contracts: does organizational culture really matter?, *Journal of Business Research*, **62**, pp 818–25

Robinson, D and Hayday, S (2009) *The Engaging Manager*, Institute of Employment Studies

Rolfe, J (2010) 'What does it mean to flourish at work?', MSc Applied Positive Psychology Dissertation, University of East London

Rousseau, D M (2005) *I-Deals: Idiosyncratic Deals Employees Bargain for Themselves*, M E Sharpe, New York

Rowe, G and Nejad, M H (2009) Strategic leadership: short-term stability and long-term viability, *Ivy Business Journal*, Sept/Oct

Salovey, P and Mayer, J D (1989) Emotional intelligence, *Imagination, Cognition and Personality*, **9** (3), pp 185–211

Schaubroeck, J M *et al* (2012) Embedding ethical leadership within and across organisation levels, *Academy of Management Journal*, **55** (5), pp 1053–78

Schein, E (2004) *Organizational Culture and Leadership*, 3rd edn, Jossey-Bass, San Francisco

Scouller, J (2011) *The Three Levels of Leadership: How to Develop Your Leadership Presence, Knowhow and Skills*, Management Books 2000, Cirencester

Seligman, M (2002) *Authentic Happiness: Using the New Positive Psychology to Realise Your Potential for Lasting Fulfilment*, Nicholas Brealey Publishing, London

Seligman, M (2006) *Learned Optimism: How to Change Your Mind and Your Life*, Vintage, New York

Semler, R (1999) *Maverick*, Random House, London

Shackleton, E (1999) *South: The Endurance Expedition*, Signet, Penguin Group, New York

Slaski, M and Cartwright, S (2002) Health, performance and emotional intelligence: an exploratory study of retail managers, *Stress and Health*, **18**, pp 63–68

Spears, L C (2004) Practicing servant-leadership, *Leader to Leader*, **34**, pp 7–11

Specht, L and Sandlin, P (1991) The differential effects of experiential learning activities and traditional lecture classes in accounting, *Simulations and Gaming*, **22** (2), pp 196–210

Spielberger, C (2004) *Encyclopedia of Applied Psychology*, Academic Press, San Diego, CA

Srikanth Iyengar (2013) The changing face of the leader, *Management Today*, June, pp 53–55

Stanley, T J (2001) *The Millionaire Mind*, Andrews McMeel Publishing, Riverside, NJ

Startle, C L (1956) *Executive Performance and Leadership*, Prentice-Hall, New York

Stein, S J, Papadogiannis, P, Yip, J A and Sitarenios, G (2009) Emotional intelligence: a profile of top executives, *Leadership and Organizational Development Journal*, **30** (1), pp 87–101

Stogdill, R M (1974) *Handbook of Leadership: A Survey of Theory and Research*, Macmillan, London

Stogdill, R M (1975) The evolution of leadership theory, *Academy of Management Proceedings* (00650668), p 4

Taiyang, Q (2010) Military motivation the Chinese way, *Harvard Business Blog*, **23**, November

Tannenbaum, R and Schmidt, W (1958) How to choose a leadership pattern, *Harvard Business Review*, Mar/Apr

Taylor, M D (1977) Military leadership: what is it? Can it be taught? *Distinguished Lecture Series National Defence University*, Washington, Spring, pp 84–93

Thomas, R *et al* (2012) Global leadership teams: diagnosing three essential qualities, *Strategy and Leadership*, **40** (3), 25–29

Vaccaro, I G *et al* (2012) Management innovation and leadership: the moderating role of organisational size, *Journal of Management Studies*, **49** (1), January, pp 28–51

Van Wart, M and Kapucu, N (2011) Crisis management competencies: the case of emergency managers in the USA, *Public Management Review*, **13** (4), pp 489–511

Welte, B (2004) 'What's holding women back? Barriers to women's advancement as perceived by top executives', Paper presented at the 19th Annual Conference of the Society for Industrial and Organisational Psychology in Chicago, IL

Wessel, J R (1993) The strategic human resource management process in practice, *Planning Review*, **21** (5), pp 37–39

Worsley, F A (2011) *Endurance*, W W Norton & Co, London

Wrzesniewski, A, McCauley, C and Rozin, P (1997) Jobs, careers and callings: people's relations to their work, *Journal of Research in Personality*, **31** (1), pp 21–33

Zaccaro, S J, Kemp, C and Bader, P (2004) Leader traits and attributes, in *The Nature of Leadership*, eds J Antonakis, A Cianciolo and R J Sternberg, pp 101–24, Sage, Thousand Oaks, CA

Zagenczyk, T J, Gibney, R, Kiewitz, C and Restubog, S L D (2009) Mentors, supervisors and role models: do they reduce the effect of psychological contract breach?, *Human Resource Management Journal*, **19** (3), pp 237–59

Zhang, H, Everett, A M, Elkin, G and Cone, M H (2012) Authentic leadership theory development: theorizing Chinese philosophy, *Asia Pacific Business Review*, **18** (4), pp 587–605

INDEX

NB: page numbers in *italics* indicate figures or tables